1972

COURTSHIP IN SHAKESPEARE

COURTSHIP IN SHAKESPEARE

Its Relation to the Tradition of
Courtly Love

By WILLIAM G. MEADER

1971

OCTAGON BOOKS
New York

Reprinted 1971
by special arrangement with William G. Meader

OCTAGON BOOKS
A DIVISION OF FARRAR, STRAUS & GIROUX, INC.
19 Union Square West
New York, N. Y. 10003

LIBRARY OF CONGRESS CATALOG CARD NUMBER: 78-120649

ISBN-0-374-95553-0

Printed in U.S.A. by
NOBLE OFFSET PRINTERS, INC.
NEW YORK 3, N. Y.

ACKNOWLEDGMENTS

MANY PEOPLE, primarily those who supervised my graduate Shakespearean study, helped me with this dissertation. The late Walter Morris Hart and John Strong Perry Tatlock, of the University of California at Berkeley, suggested the idea and were of great aid in the primary delineation and criticism. Oscar James Campbell, Alfred Harbage and Roger Sherman Loomis, all then of Columbia University, and Edwin Maurice Moseley, now of Skidmore College, helped me to carry the idea through to completion. Without their continuing encouragement I could never have completed the work.

I have intended to give credit in the bibliography, but I wish here also to express my gratitude to the following publishers for permission to quote from works referred to in this study: Cambridge University Press, for John W. Cunliffe's edition of the works of George Cascoigne; Columbia University Press, for John Jay Parry's translation of Andreas Capellanus's *The Art of Courtly Love*, for Chilton Latham Powell's *English Domestic Relations, 1487-1653*, and for Charles T. Prouty's *George Gascoigne, Elizabethan Courtier, Soldier, and Poet*; E. P. Dutton and Company for Baldassare Castiglione's *Book of the Courtier* (translated by Sir Thomas Hoby), for Chrétien de Troyes's *Arthurian Romance* (translated by W. W. Comfort), and for Sir Thomas Elyot's *The Governour*, all Everyman editions; Ginn and Company for George Lyman Kittredge's edition of *The Complete Works of Shakespeare*; Houghton Mifflin Company for F. N. Robinson's edition of *The Complete Works of Chaucer*; Iowa University

Press for Ruth L. Anderson's *Elizabethan Psychology and Shakespeare's Plays;* The Macmillan Company for Edvard Westermarck's *A Short History of Marriage;* Oxford University Press for *Shakespeare's England* (edited by Sir Walter Raleigh), for *The Shakespeare Apocrypha* (edited by C. F. Tucker Brooke), and for Lane Cooper's translation of Plato's *Phaedrus;* Tudor Publishing Company for Robert Burton's *Anatomy of Melancholy;* and the University of Illinois Press for Ruth Kelso's *The Doctrine of the English Gentleman of the Sixteenth Century.*

In addition, the Folger Library furnished me a microfilm copy of Fenton's *Monophylo* and granted me permission to quote extensively from that work.

Most importantly, after the passage of so many years since the earlier edition, I am indebted to Henry Schlanger, editor-in-chief of Octagon Books, for his having encouraged and undertaken republication of this work. It is a heartening sign that interest in Shakespeare continues even in this troubled world.

WILLIAM G. MEADER

New York
September, 1970

CONTENTS

COURTSHIP IN SHAKESPEARE

Chapter I

FINE AMOR

To SAY that courtly love or *fine amor* had its beginnings in the twelfth century and died out, under ridicule, to be replaced by the romanticism of the sixteenth, is to avoid recognizing the permanent aspects of both manifestations. Courtly and romantic love have a common basis in fact in that they reflect actual relationships between living men and women. The courtly love formalized at the Poitevin court of Eleanor of Aquitaine, and definitively codified by Andreas, was not and could not be one which sprang full-blown through the invention of any single group. " 'Courtly love' aided in the growth of romantic love, which has always existed but did not become articulate before the midst of the Middle Ages, and then became intensely so."[1]

It is the primary function of this book, without considering ritual before the time of Eleanor, and without determining sources, to show the process of courtship as conceived by Shakespeare in his plays. This will be preceded by an amplificatory investigation of *fine amor* of the twelfth to the sixteenth centuries to determine the debt of Shakespeare to courtly and non-courtly traditions, and to show Shakespeare's dependence upon or independence of the concepts of his contemporaries. The proof will utilize reference to his works, filling it in and corroborating it with materials of contemporaries and with records of the sixteenth century.

Courtly love, originally contrary to Christian monogamy in its philosophy, soon added a type of Platonic idealism which tended to ally it with the concepts of the Church. It presented a formalization of the external courtship ritual of romantic love, suggesting that a rigid following of these rules would lead to the eventual capitulation of the woman being courted. It became a game, and the rules were merely a codified statement of the interactions expected of the participants.

In Andreas Capellanus' *The Art of Courtly Love,* written between 1184 and 1186,[2] are incorporated many of the concepts of the courts of love, which apparently were established by Eleanor of Aquitaine and her followers in France in the latter half of the twelfth century. These courts seem to have been used as pastimes which pretended to rules and regulations, or laws, and tribunals of women which handed down decisions on love to supplicants. Andreas's work, addressed to a young Walter who would learn the processes of formalized love, is a careful study of the prevailing rules. Because of its detail, and because of Andreas's probable connection with the courts, the work has been accepted as authoritative of the feelings of the recherché twelfth century in cultured Europe.

The love which Andreas discusses he defines as " 'an inordinate desire to receive passionately a furtive and hidden embrace.' " The embrace, however, seems not to be the culmination of the love of which he is speaking, for he says that "a woman who gives any man other than her lover a kiss or an embrace is acting shamefully, since these are always considered signs of love and are given to men as an indication that love is to follow." Since, too, one of Andreas's woman speakers says unchallenged that " 'whatever lovers do has as its only object the obtaining of the solaces of the lower part [of the body], for there is fulfilled the whole effect of love, at which all lovers chiefly aim and without

which they think they have nothing more than certain prel-
udes to love," his definition would have to be somewhat
extended, so that "embrace" has a stronger sense, before it
could be definitive.[3]

Further, Andreas defines two types of love: pure and
mixed. The first kind " 'goes as far as the kiss and the embrace and the modest contact with the nude lover, omitting
the final solace,' " and the latter permits "the final solace."
He declares that "all men ought to choose a pure love rather
than a mixed or common one" but adds that if either lover
wishes the mixed love the other should accede to his wishes.
"For all lovers are bound, when practicing love's solaces, to
be mutually obedient to each other's desires."[4]

Andreas considers love to be a clandestine permanent monogamous lust informing mental and spiritual ennoblement.
His definition of it as " 'an inordinate desire to receive passionately a furtive and hidden embrace' " neither takes into
account the spiritual aspects nor the physical culmination he
elsewhere mentions as almost inevitable. He declares, too,
" 'that marital affection and the true love of lovers are wholly
different and arise from entirely different sources.' " Such
distinction emphasizes that the love must be exercised without church or highly moral social sanction, and that if such
sanction is granted the love of necessity changes to mere
marital monotony, principally because it is no longer furtive.[5]

Courtly love and *fine amor* are used synonymously in this
paper to refer to the ritualistic courtship by which a man and
woman proceed to achieve their desire to satisfy a clandestine
permanent monogamous lust informing mental and spiritual
ennoblement.

By the end of the twelfth century *fine amor* had become
so formalized that it had rules and regulations and examples

to cover almost any contingency of courtship. And at the same time literary romances based on these concepts had become so much alike in plot and temper that they impress a modern reader as stereotypes, expressing no intellectual conviction. The origins of *fine amor* are by no means lost in the past: earlier European cultures seem to have had some concepts of romance, presenting established rituals of conduct which later developed into the conventions of courtly love.

The distinction which the Poitevin culture of Eleanor of Aquitaine brought to the systems of love was principally that the position of the woman and the man in courtship was reversed. Whereas previously the man had been superior in all affairs of love before and after marriage, under the influence of Marie de Champagne and her mother the woman in pre- and extramarital affairs was exalted to a position of eminence similar to that of a goddess.

The stages of courtship, as exemplified in the medieval romances, were five:[6] (1) the Inception, (2) the Development, (3) the Betrothal, (4) the Ordeal, and (5) the Union. Andreas, not using such terminology but in a similar order, deals with most of these stages. I propose to define the topics listed here through Andreas' references to them, and later to reexamine them in determining their applicability to succeeding ages.

The Inception, or first recognition of love, is possible only after the two lovers have fulfilled certain requirements as to age, rank, and attitude. Andreas declares that "a girl under the age of twelve and a boy before the fourteenth year do not serve in love's army. However, I say and insist that before his eighteenth year a man cannot be a true lover. . . ." He feels that an older lover is preferable to a younger and even requires adulthood in one of his thirty-one concluding rules:

"VI. Boys do not love until they arrive at the age of maturity."[7]

To Andreas the lovers must be of rank high enough to give them leisure for all the intricacies of courtship. The two people need not necessarily be of the same rank, but both must be above the working classes. He is very specific in mentioning the difficulties and benefits of love with a peasant girl. That, he feels, is not love but lust, and Walter is advised, if such a situation should occur to him, to rape the peasant at the earliest practicable moment. A peasant man, of course, is not capable of finer instincts since he has so little leisure time, and therefore he is incapable of love.[8]

Among the idle rich, however, love is a complete leveler of rank, and a knight may fall in love with and court a princess, and a king a mere lady. Rank, says Andreas, is after all determined by character rather than birth, and, although the two should be of equal rank if possible, rank is not alone a cause of love, and all differences of rank disappear when the two are in love.[9]

The only restriction to love insofar as rank is concerned, then, is expressed in his rule "XI. It is not proper to love any woman whom one would be ashamed to marry."[10] This obviously denies love to a peasant.

Physically, the lovers should be beautiful, for beauty is a cause of love. However, beauty can be empty if unaccompanied by good character, and such beauty alone is not sufficient cause for love. Good character alone, without physical attractiveness, can cause love, and beauty may be merely in the eyes of the prospective lover, for even the ugly can seem beautiful to a lover. Andreas inveighs against the over-perfumed man and recognizes a tradition of worn-out clothes in a lover, for he " 'should devote only a moderate amount of care to the adornment of his person.' " His conclusion is that "character alone, then, is worthy of the crown of love."[11]

Since the lover must be a knight or higher, he seems to be quite limited in profession. Battles were the chief function of the upper classes, and the lover is therefore expected to be a military man. Further, if he should become deformed in any way in the course of his military activities, he is not to lose his beloved for that reason alone. She is to retain him as her lover even though he may be missing an arm.[12]

Andreas insists that the lover must be courageous and adds that lack of courage can cause the decrease and termination of love. He must accomplish good deeds, even though he cannot do this until he is in love because good deeds are impossible without love.[13]

Neither person may be avaricious, for love cannot coexist with avarice, and as a matter of fact it is a deterrent to, or cause of decrease of, love; both lovers should avoid blasphemy; they must be chaste except with each other; they are not permitted heresy, which causes a termination of love; the impotence of either is sufficient cause for the cessation of love, and by implication for the avoidance of love; incest is forbidden, and, if two who are actively in love discover they are related more closely than allowed by the laws of consanguinity, they must immediately terminate the affair; "an excess of passion is a bar to love"; although in his retraction Andreas claims that poverty is caused by love, earlier he declares it to be a deterrent to love; pride and quarrelsomeness are to be avoided; and slander is forbidden.[14]

If both lovers could fulfill all of these qualifications, they were ready for the Inception of their affair. Andreas does not discuss how the lovers would meet, but they seem often in the romances to have been previously acquainted before they recognize the state of affairs can lead to love. The Duke in *The Book of the Duke of True Lovers,* for instance, has known his beloved for some time before the inception of the affair. The ideal of love at first sight, which is presented so often in Elizabethan works, was not all-important during the twelfth century.

In the Development of his love the lover usually suffers from lovesickness and seeks to bear his torture in solitude. At the same time he is ennobled and achieves even greater deeds than he has previously.

In the late twelfth century love was considered both an illness and a perfecter of character: the lover showed symptoms of a disease which could lead to death and he became, according to convention, at the same time an exemplar of the chivalric attributes which had been fostered by church and feudal lords since the age of Charles Martel.[15]

The illness was called *"hereos,"* as Professor John Livingston Lowes has shown.[16] Its symptoms were catalogued in medical works still accepted as standard in the twelfth century. The rules of Andreas Capellanus recognize some of these symptoms which attack a man sincerely in love:

XV. Every lover regularly turns pale in the presence of his beloved,

XVI. When a lover suddenly catches sight of his beloved his heart palpitates.

XX. A man in love is always apprehensive.

XXIII. He whom the thought of love vexes eats and sleeps very little.[17]

Andreas does not amplify the specific physical failings to any great extent,[18] and he introduces few other such traits,[19] but it is evident that he considers them important since they make up a fairly large proportion of his rules at the conclusion of

the work. Chrétien, contemporary with Andreas, incorporates many of them into his romances. In his *Cligés,* when
Fenice has first seen Cligés,

. . . Love has made her give her heart to the fairest, most courteous, and valiant man that could anywhere be found . . . she . . .
must waste herself in thought and vigils. She becomes so affected
. . . that she loses her colour and it becomes plain to all that
her loss of colour betokens an unfulfilled desire. She plays less
now than she used to do, and laughs less and loses her gaiety.[20]

Chrétien declares in an aside to the reader:

Ye who are interested in the art of Love . . . tell me if there is
anything that pleases because of Love without causing us to
tremble and grow pale . . . whoever does not tremble and grow
pale, whoever does not lose his senses and memory, is trying to filch
and get by stealth what does not by right belong to him.[21]

The secrecy which Andreas declares to be required in
courtly love[22] is not completely *à deux,* for

love may be revealed to three people besides the lovers themselves,
for the lover is allowed to find a suitable confidant from whom he
may get secret comfort in his love affair and who will offer him
sympathy if things turn out badly; the woman may choose a
similar confidante. Besides these they may have one faithful intermediary, chosen by common consent, through whom the affair
may always be managed in secret and in the proper fashion.[23]

A couple, then, might have three people besides themselves
fully cognizant of the affair. The having of such a large
group of intimates might possibly lead to discovery, and
Andreas cites an example from a court of love in which a
lover was exonerated from blame for not having communi-
cated with his beloved when he was overseas, on the ground
that his refraining " 'may be considered great prudence on

his part, since he may not reveal this secret to any third party.' "[24] The censure of a go-between who broke faith with the lover and took the lady for himself is the subject of another example.[25] It would be difficult, Andreas implies, for the lovers to find completely trustworthy go-betweens or confidants. Thus he does not emphasize the necessity of others' knowing of the affair, merely apparently the convenience of a sympathetic and loyal audience.

The third stage, Betrothal, is the acceptance of the lover by the lady, and his consequent cure of the love-sickness, or *hereos*. In this stage the differentiation between a pure and mixed love becomes important.

Andreas lists no form of the Betrothal, and it would be reading too much into his inconclusive dialogues to find there hints that the rather formal betrothals which are to be found in the romances prevailed in the twelfth century. I think he considered the declaration of love and the subsequent trial of the lover as the Betrothal, and the acceptance of the lover in physical union as the Union, although he does not develop his work to a description of this fifth stage.

Andreas apparently feels of himself that the receiving of gifts by the beloved is not praiseworthy. He mentions this specifically in the passage in which he is concerned with avarice, or the getting of love with money.

For a woman who is really in love always rejects and hates gifts from her lover, and devotes her efforts to increasing his wealth so that he may always have something he can give away and thereby increase his good name; she does not expect anything from him except the sweet solaces of the flesh and that her fame may increase among all men because he praises her.[26]

But when the Countess of Champagne was asked what a

beloved should accept from her lover, she apparently disagreed with Andreas's above conclusion and specifically listed,
among other objects, a handkerchief, a purse, sleeves, gloves,
a ring, and a picture:

"and, to speak in general terms, a woman may accept from her
lover any little gift which may be useful for the care of the person
or pleasing to look at or which may call the lover to her mind, if
it is clear that in accepting the gift she is free from all avarice."[27]

Thus she seems to contradict Andreas, except that she is careful to stipulate that the woman accepting the gifts be free
from all avarice; that the presents, therefore, be accepted for
their sentimental and not their intrinsic value. Andreas perhaps overstates his case when he is discussing avarice, for
certainly he would find it necessary to agree with his patroness
for reasons of diplomacy if for no other.

The presents, however, were apparently to be given only
when the two were already in love and had been accepted by
each other as lovers. There seems to be no laudatory mention
of gifts to induce love.

The fourth stage, the Ordeal, is a probationary period for
the lovers if they are to be married, or if they are to be finally
separated it is a conclusion to the happiness of the period during which the pair are betrothed and the beginning of renewed suffering as the lover tries to recapture a lost or ap-
parently-lost love.

Andreas discusses this stage in his second book, "How
Love May Be Retained," although he does not amplify his
regulations into a plot which would necessarily lead to any
culmination beyond that achieved in the betrothal. He states
categorically that "love is always increasing or decreasing,"[28]
but he implies that there may be a constant state in the

achieved love which leads neither to a loss nor, since marriage would alter the situation and there is no possibility other
than marriage for incrementation of the situation, again. His
primary concern in this second book is with the decrease and
termination of love, and therefore he would seem to imply
that there could also be the alternative situation of a perma-
nence in love.

During the probationary period the lover attempts again
to prove his love to his beloved, much as he has done before.
He must do all things which he believes his beloved desires—
wear clothes she likes, give his services to all ladies, be polite
at all times, and be courageous in battle—and perhaps occasionally test his beloved's constancy by various stratagems.
Andreas recommends an occasional quarrel as both a test and
a strengthener of love. It is not a weakening of affection to
quarrel, he declares, "it is only clearing away the rust."[29]

Andreas apparently does not consider the Ordeal a probationary period: there is some indication that he believes the
probationary period begins after such a declaration as he
exemplifies in his dialogues. For in them the man proposes
to the woman an arrangement by which they may be made
happy in love, and they conclude either in a stalemate or with
some such indefinite promise as: " 'If you really intend to do
what you say you propose to, it can hardly be that you will not
be abundantly rewarded, either by me or by some other
woman.' "[30]

The Ordeal would normally follow upon such a statement,
the lover attempting to persuade the woman to a physical
culmination which he might make permanent by constant
effort. The beloved would have little function at this time
except to watch and judge in order to award herself as the
gesture which initiates the fifth stage.

On the other hand, if she refused him, the lover might go mad upon being deprived of his lady, and apparently madness is no more often described in the romances than it is merely because there are few lovers unsuccessful in their suits—without successful courtship there could be no romance—and few situations which could permanently separate the lovers. Yet some of the heroes do go mad. Yvain, deprived of his wife, goes temporarily insane, and so does Tristram when unjustly separated from his beloved. This seems, in the romances, to make the beloved love the hero more, perhaps as a result of her inevitable attempt to nurse him back to sanity and her arms. Andreas, however, in discussing how love may come to an end, says that "if one of the lovers becomes insane or develops a sudden timidity, love flees and becomes hateful."[31]

The last stage, Union, is often signalized by the full ritual and ceremony of marriage. If the conclusion of the affair is to be separation, at this time the lover recovers from his illness either by dying or by seeing how foolish he has been, or both. At this time, too, if not before, the beloved is revealed as faithful if marriage is to be her portion, or fickle if the hero is to be permanently separated from her.

Andreas, who has argued that marital and courtly love are entirely incompatible, arising from different causes, if he is to be consistent, cannot consider a successful marital union in his work. He is therefore limited to a consideration of separation. This is the difference between the theory of courtly love and the practice of the romances. It is impossible to have a romance strictly based on the rules of courtly love unless the author is willing to separate his lovers at the conclusion. For plot variations and for romances with happy endings, it is necessary for the romancer to deviate from the rules of courtly love and permit marriage as a development from courtship. This seems to be the discrepancy at least in part responsible for Andreas's retraction at the conclusion of his work. He could either show that marriage was bad or that *fine amor* was bad. Since he apparently was a member of the clergy, he could not in conscience show marriage as immoral. He was therefore forced by his own logic into the position of negating everything he had written concerning courtly love, of denying it on moral grounds, as a conclusion to his treatise.

There are variations on the pattern of themes in the romances, but the standard is marriage between two faithful lovers, separation if the heroine is unfaithful. The tale is always told from the point of view of the hero: there could be a romance without a heroine in that the central female character is proven to be worthless, but there could be none without a faithful hero. Whatever deviations there are tend generally to be merely slight variations of the plot of what Miss Barrow calls the medieval society romances.

Andreas's contributions to the tradition of courtly love were primarily codifications, many of them dealing with symptoms of love. Since Andreas forbids marriage and the romancers permit marriage, it is essential that Andreas's work be considered with that of Chrétien de Troyes, for only through an amalgamation of the two writers' ideas can any adequate concept of the *fine amor* of the twelfth century be ascertained.

Chrétien's *Cligés* is practically contemporary with Andreas's work, and in its plot he shows his attitudes toward love as he conceived of it. The work has the traditional form of the medieval society romance, except that there is a prefatory story of the love of Alexander and Soredamors, Cligés's

father and mother, with which I shall deal only as they aid
the understanding of the romance of *Cligés*.

The Inception of the affair between Cligés and Fenice
occurs when they first see each other. The meeting, as often,
occurs in a crowd.[32] "Blithely he looks upon the maid, but
does not note that she repays him in kind. Not flattering
him, but in sincere love, she gives him her eyes, and takes
back his."[33] Both are obviously ready for love. Fenice is
proceeding on her way to be betrothed to Alis, uncle of
Cligés, and therefore in the opinion of all is old enough for a
love affair. She is noble, for she is the daughter of the Emperor of Germany, and her beauty is beyond Chrétien's power
of description.[34] However, Cligés and Fenice do not declare
their love until later.

Cligés himself is old enough for courtship. He is fourteen.
He is the son of the rightful king of Greece, and the nephew
of the present ruler. He is also handsome and intelligent.
"Nature was so lavish with him that she gave him all she
could. . . . [He] combined good sense and beauty, generosity and strength . . . he knew more of fencing and of the
bow than did Tristan, King Mark's nephew, and more about
birds and hounds than he. In Cligés there lacked no good
thing."[35]

At the time of the first meeting, when the influence of
love begins, Cligés has an opportunity to prove his ability at
fighting. It would have been necessary for him to show his
courage to Fenice at some time, and the early opportunity is
helpful to both lovers. The nephew of the Duke of Saxony
issues a challenge which Cligés accepts. Fenice shows her
affection, for "Wherever Cligés goes, she seeks to follow
him with her eyes. And he in turn does his best for her, and
battles openly, in order that she at least may hear it said that

he is bold and very skilled: thus she will be compelled to prize him for his prowess."[36] The courage of Cligés here is rather separate from the ennoblement which occurs during the Development, and which will be discussed later.

Cligés is of course victor in the combat. And, says Chrétien, "Thus was the maiden subdued by the man."[37]

The Development begins for each as soon as they are separated. From the Inception of her love Fenice is sleepless and loses her color because she is anxious and distraught. She desires to die if Cligés dies, and she swoons when he is wounded. She is so anxious for her beloved that she "is at death's door from anxiety for his sake, although she does not know that he is . . . near." She thus is much more concerned than Andreas demands or even mentions as possible.[38]

Cligés himself is not described as suffering very greatly from *hereos*. He does turn pale upon separation from Fenice and weeps bitterly on his knees before her. He finds strength in the power of her voice, for when he is wounded by the Duke of Saxony Fenice calls " 'God help him.' Her voice restored his strength and courage."[39]

In general, however, he is too busy carrying out his father's dying wishes and trying to gain his kingdom to be so vitally concerned in the love affair as to call forth Chrétien's comments.

He is, however, completely ennobled by his love, even beyond his previous nobility, and he "feels his luck has come, when he can display his chivalry and bravery openly before her who is his very life." "Quickly drawing his keen sword from its sheath, in order to please her who awaits his love," he puts an end to another combat.[40]

There is no go-between, or courier, for Cligés until the time of the Betrothal. At that time John, a bondsman of his, assumes the function of both go-between and confidant. Fenice, as soon as she begins to suffer, turns to Thessala, her old nurse, as confidante. Cligés's parents had been married simply in a legitimate betrothal by Guenevere as soon as they had declared, or as part of their declaring, their love.

The Queen clasps them both in her arms, and presents one to the other. Then laughingly she adds: "I give over to thee, Alexander, thy sweetheart's body, and I know that thy heart does not draw back. Whoever may like it or like it not, I give each of you to the other. Do thou, Soredamors, take what is thine, and thou, Alexander, take what is thine!" Now she has her own entire, and he has his without lack. At Windsor that day . . . the marriage was celebrated.[41]

But the younger two, especially Fenice, suffer long and for many pages before there is a confession of love leading to a Betrothal.

The explanation of their love is very carefully handled. Fenice has been married to Alis, uncle to Cligés, but she has, through the services of her nurse Thessala, given Alis a potion which has kept and will perpetually keep him from physical relations with her. Thus, although she has long been married when Cligés and she declare their love for each other, she is still a virgin. She frequently and vehemently states that she will not be another Iseut, and that she will not only not have physical relations with more than one man, but also that she will not have the reputation of such a relationship, true or not. In her argument she twists the words of St. Paul into the approval of a new morality:

But fornication, and all uncleanness, or covetousness, let it not be once named among you, as becometh saints; . . . And have no fellowship with the unfruitful works of darkness, but rather re-

prove them. For it is a shame even to speak of those things which
are done of them in secret. . . . See then that ye walk circum-
spectly, not as fools, but as wise, Redeeming the time, because
the days are evil.[42]

.   .   .   .

"It is well to remember and observe the injunction of St. Paul: if
any one is unwilling to live chaste, St. Paul counsels him to act
so that he shall receive no criticism, or blame, or reproach. It is
well to stop evil mouths."[43]

She therefore gives herself to Cligés provided that she can
so arrange the assignation that to all appearances she will
die and be buried. He then can rescue her from the grave
and keep her secretly as his wife for the rest of their lives.

Fenice is, therefore, interested in maintaining a reputation for fidelity to her husband, as are most of the extramarital lovers celebrated in other romances and the works
of such writers as Andreas. "Marriage is no real excuse for
not loving," says Andreas in his first of thirty-one rules.
Even though he amplifies it by saying that "all men ought
to choose a pure love rather than a mixed or common one,"
he is forced weakly to conclude that in an extra-marital situation such as he is describing "one of the lovers may not oppose the desire of the other unless at the beginning of the
attachment they made an agreement that they would never
engage in mixed love except by the free will and the full
consent of both parties." And even then physical love may
not be refused if demanded, "For all lovers are bound,
when practicing love's solaces, to be mutually obedient to
each other's desires."[44]

Chrétien differs. His lover has always a chaste relationship
with his beloved, with the possible exception of Lancelot
and Guenevere. More important, Andreas's lovers do not

intend marriage: they desire a long courtship ending in seduction. Chrétien's lovers intend marriage: they desire exceedingly brief courtships leading to marriage. And they feel
that marriage should precede the seduction.

Fenice, however, could not marry Cligés while Alis still
lived. No church functionary could or would perform the
ceremony creating bigamy. But Fenice, having been in a peculiar situation as regards her husband, felt that her cause
was outside of the laws, and that she was justified in determining upon an extralegal solution. For, her marriage
having never been consummated, she felt she could not be
committing bigamy in marrying another.

The Ordeal here is of fear of separation. The two flee the
wrath of Alis together, and the question as to whether they
can be permanently united or not is dependent entirely upon
an external force, her husband. When he dies of jealousy or
of the disgrace of having been cuckolded, the solution of
the successful Union is obviously possible.

The Union merges with the Betrothal and the Ordeal, and
is so brief as to be almost non-existent.

The general division of the poem into its component romantic parts is as follows:

	Verses	Pages	Percent
Introduction	1-2724	91-127	41
Inception	2725-3010	127-30	3
Development	3011-5156	130-58	32
Betrothal	5157-6424	158-74	18
Ordeal	6425-6700	174-78	4
Union	6701-6784	178-79	1

Chrétien thus early brings into literature the problem romance of situations which exceed the scope of law. Fenice

becomes, through her arrangement with Cligés, his mistress. After Alis dies, she is able to marry her lover. Such a situation, Chrétien states, makes for an ideal marriage:

His mistress he has made his wife, but he still calls her his mistress and sweetheart, and she can complain of no loss of affection, for he loves her still as his mistress, and she loves him, too, as a lady ought to love her lover. And each day saw their love grow stronger.[45]

He thus advocates love in marriage and a union of love and marriage, directly opposing Christian morality to the amorality of Andreas's, and consequently Eleanor's and Marie's, theses of extramarital relationships.

The question as to whether or not this is an isolated instance in Chrétien can only be answered by an examination of his later work.

His *Yvain* is quite important. It was written after his *Cligés* and *Lancelot* and is considered a more sincere work than the latter.[46] In the poem, according to Professor Parry, "he rejects the idea of an adulterous love, which he did not like, but retains the other convention of courtly love, which apparently he did."[47] Miss Barrow uses *Yvain* as one of the romances with which she proves her thesis, and therefore she seems to consider it typical. I also have concluded that it is typical of the twelfth-century concept of courtly love.

The poem itself is not all directly concerned with the love affair of Yvain and Laudine. The first twelve hundred lines deal with circumstances which cause Yvain to be in a position to see Laudine and fall in love with her, and much of the Ordeal deals with adventures which are not directly related to the courtship. The general division of the tale is as follows:

Stage	Percent
Introduction	13
Inception	13
Development	2
Betrothal	10
Ordeal	56
Union	6

The accuracy of such figures is always open to dispute, but the general conclusion, which the above figures make clear even with a large margin allowed for error, is that the emphasis of the story is on the Ordeal. An exceedingly small portion is concerned with the Development, and there is therefore certain to be little affected *courtoisie*. From such figures as these can be determined at least trends of emphasis in the individual work.

Yvain, having killed the husband of Laudine, from a convenient place sees her following his bier, and he immediately falls in love with her.[48] Since he is in hiding, she is unable at that time to see him, and she is not even aware of his presence. She is in a public place, as are many of the central characters of the romances when they first meet. "His enemy carries off his heart, and he loves the creature who hates him most. The lady, all unaware, has well avenged her lord's death."[49] Love enters Yvain's heart through his eyes,[50] and the "wound is more enduring than any inflicted by lance or sword."[51]

Laudine falls in love with Yvain, as much as she permits herself, without having seen him, persuaded both by Lunete's recital of his qualifications and by her own need for a defender to replace her dead husband. Thus she is a medieval woman looking on marriage as a practical solution to her problems, and the fact that she gets a man she really can love is relatively unimportant to her at this point.

Yvain is in love with no one else, and he has apparently never been in love. He is a noble knight, the son of a king, Urien, and has recently proved his superiority to most men by killing a great knight, over whose grave Laudine his widow says: " '. . . never, I verily believe, did any knight ever sit in saddle who was your equal in any respect. No other knight, my fair sweet lord, ever possessed your honour or courtesy. Generosity was your friend and boldness your companion.' "[52] Yvain, therefore, is by implication superior to Laudine's husband, as Lunete tells her in so many words: " 'When two knights have met in an affray of arms and when one has beaten the other, which of the two do you think is the better? For my part I award the prize to the victor.' "[53]

Yvain loves her in secret, and Lunete acts as his go-between and confidante. He is in constant danger because he is hidden in the home of his enemy. Lunete is also confidante to Laudine, as Chrétien carefully explains.[54] Through her efforts the two lovers are brought together for a courtship.

The premarital courtship of the Development is exceedingly brief, and consists of one interview. Yvain comes into Laudine's presence terrified and unable to speak,[55] and, finally encouraged, falls on his knees and prays mercy "like a lover."[56] Laudine's interrogation of him is typical of the courtly love convention as proposed in the twelfth century:

Laudine. I suppose it would have been no use, if I had had you put to death. But I should be glad to learn whence you derive the force that bids you to consent unquestioningly to whatever my will may dictate. I pardon you all your misdeeds and crimes. But be seated, and tell us now what is the cause of your docility?

Yvain. My lady, the impelling force comes from my heart, which
   is inclined toward you. My heart has fixed me in this desire.
Laudine. And what prompted your heart, my fair sweet friend?
Yvain. Lady, my eyes.
Laudine. And what the eyes?
Yvain. The great beauty that I see in you.
Laudine. And where is beauty's fault in that?
Yvain. Lady, in this: that it makes me love.
Laudine. Love? And whom?
Yvain. You, my lady dear.
Laudine. I?
Yvain. Yes, truly.
Laudine. Really? And how is that?
Yvain. To such an extent that my heart will not stir from you, nor
   is it elsewhere to be found; to such an extent that I cannot
   think of anything else, and I surrender myself altogether to you,
   whom I love more than I love myself, and for whom, if you
   will, I am equally ready to die or live.[57]

This is his declaration of love, and she accepts him very
sensibly when he agrees to serve her.

"And would you dare to undertake the defence of my spring
for love of me?"
"Yes, my lady, against the world."
"Then you may know that our peace is made."[58]

The Betrothal follows immediately, when Laudine says:

"Here and now I give myself to you; for I should not refuse to
accept as lord, such a good knight and a king's son."[59]

Within twenty-four hours ("That very day"[60]) the marriage is reperformed by the Church.

From the hand of the chaplain he received the lady, Laudine de

Landuc, . . . and the wedding was celebrated. There were
plenty of mitres and croziers there, for the lady had summoned
her bishops and abbots.[61]

The marriage-feast lasts a week, apparently, before the ar-
rival of King Arthur concludes it.

According to Miss Barrow, "Secrecy is still required"[62]
during a *fine amor* betrothal. The *Yvain* seems to be an exception merely because the *fine amor* betrothal has been replaced with a fully-witnessed marriage accomplished in a
church ceremony. There is no attempt at secrecy because the
relationship is legal. The lovers are in a situation in which
they may have all of the privileges of *fine amor* with none
of the restrictions of social danger. Yvain even receives a
ring from Laudine which he is still wearing, apparently
openly, a year later when Lunete comes to relieve him of it.[63]

It was expected that marriage should ennoble the lover
and not enervate him. Gawain, in trying to persuade Yvain
to leave his wife for a while, uses that argument:

"What? Will you be one of those . . . who degenerate after
marriage? Cursed be he by Saint Mary who marries and then
degenerates! Whoever has a fair lady as his mistress or his wife
should be the better for it, and it is not right that her affection
should be bestowed on him after his worth and reputation are
gone."[64]

Here is an ideal situation from a moral point of view. Yvain
is in love with and has achieved the lady, but first he has
been married to her. Now Chrétien can have him go through
all the trials of courtly love romances, but he has first made
Laudine an honest woman and Yvain an honorable man.
The formula is superb. Here is no extramarital relationship.
The first husband is dead. Of course Laudine married rather

in haste, but Chrétien motivates that adequately as being necessary to the preservation of herself and her domain.

The motivation of the Ordeal is rather strained, for it is incredible that Yvain, truly in love, would forget to return to his wife of two weeks after a year's separation. When he does so forget, however, Lunete goes to him and takes the ring back, thus denoting divorce. This symbol•for terminating a marriage occurs relatively often in literature, for instance, in Webster's *The White Devil*.

Immediately Yvain goes mad through sorrow, a surfeit of melancholy which is recognized and amplified during the Elizabethan age.

Very few of the aspects of *hereos* are present in this poem. Chrétien uses many more of them in *Cligés*. Yvain has little time for *hereos* between his falling in love and his marriage, and when he goes mad his confused mind has no place for so cultivated and artificial an emotion. Laudine, however, suffers from the separation as any lover should do:

"My lady had marked every day in her chamber, as the seasons passed; for when one is in love, one is ill at ease and cannot get any restful sleep, but all night long must needs count and reckon up the days as they come and go."[65]

After he recovers from his madness, Yvain continues his quest for his beloved in a roundabout way. He now constantly thinks of her, and this is the first step in his reformation, for he had lost his wife because he did not think of her and so forgot his promise. Chrétien emphasizes this point:

The true lover, wherever he may go, holds the heart dear and brings it back again. But Yvain has caused my lady's death, for she supposed that he would guard her heart for her, and would bring it back again before the year elapsed.[66]

Chrétien agrees with the rule of Andreas that "A true lover is constantly and without intermission possessed by the thought of his beloved,"[67] and he uses the breaking of that rule as the motivation of his plot and of Yvain's ordeal.

The Union comes after both Yvain and Laudine have suffered through almost four thousand lines. Yvain, again through the efforts of Lunete, is reunited with his wife. She does not accept him very graciously. When she recognizes him she says to Lunete:

"God save me! You have caught me neatly in a trap! You will make me love, in spite of myself, a man who neither loves nor esteems me. . . . And if it were not a mean and ugly thing to break one's word, he would never make his peace or be reconciled with me."[68]

In return, Yvain addresses his wife as a courtier should address his lady:

"Lady, one ought to have mercy on a sinner. I have had to pay, and dearly to pay, for my mad act. It was madness that made me stay away, and I now admit my guilt and sin. I have been bold, indeed, in daring to present myself to you; but if you will deign to keep me now, I never again shall do you any wrong."[69]

This is by no means the speech of a husband to his wife. Yvain is deliberately—and sincerely, according to the tone of Chrétien—abasing himself before his mistress. Chrétien shows no interest in her condition of being in love. Laudine is Yvain's queen and his judge. Her decisions are based upon calm philosophical analysis. His place, his sorrows, his sufferings have no effect on her. Although she states that she re-accepts him because she is tricked into it,[70] her real reasons are obviously practical and logical.

Of Chrétien's four poems, *Erec* and *Cligés* are tales of married fidelity, "the perfect union of two hearts in matrimony." The third, *Lancelot*, is a wild swing to the other extreme, an attempt of Chrétien's to follow the precepts of Andrean courtly love. And *Yvain*, the fourth chronologically, shows a mature Chrétien presenting an amalgamation of courtly and romantic love, of his own concepts added to those which Andreas describes. Thus Professor Mott can refer to the poem as containing "the most refined courtly love, with all its subtleties, as existing between husband and wife." For the poem proves not only that love can exist between husband and wife, but also that the love so existing can be as ideally happy as that between the most secret of illicit lovers. This, then, is a confirmation of Chrétien's concept seen also in his *Cligés*. There is a distinct difference between Chrétien and Andreas as to the purpose of love and of *fine amor*. Andreas is primarily interested in the means, the ritual, and Chrétien is equally interested in the conclusion, the intent of the courtship. Andreas tends to emphasize the *hereos* and the speeches to be used in the development of the courtship, Chrétien the compatibility and inner motivations of his lovers. Andreas is not interested in why his lover wants to seduce the beloved, but Chrétien spends pages analyzing the reasons for love. Yet Chrétien himself uses many verbal clichés and stereotyped patterns to describe his characters' activities. He has had a training similar to Andreas's, but he puts it to a different use.[71]

The love with which Geoffrey Chaucer deals in his *Troilus and Criseyde* is in the tradition of *Courtoisie*, and yet not in it. Andreas had codified *fine amor*, and many writers had tried to follow his analysis, especially in the Arthurian romances. But those who used his work as a basis found that

they had to sacrifice verisimilitude. For the love described by
Andreas was a formalized inhuman love, a conception which
"merely embodies an ideal which appealed to patrician
women and to some men as an escape from the brutal life
of the time."[72] And a writer who hewed undeviatingly to
that line was forced to omit traits of character, of the woman
primarily but also of the man.

Chaucer, a humanist in the sense that his characters are
so real-seeming as to be individuals, could not have his
Criseyde a goddess condescending to fornication with little
or no emotion. His Criseyde is burningly human, on a pedes-
tal to Troilus but not to the auditor, marble from a distance
but flesh and blood in proximity. To Chaucer's audience she
was a symbol of infidelity in courtly love, but to Chaucer
she was more than a symbol, she was a woman. And so he
recreated her within the framework of the rather formalized
plot given him, striving to make her actions credible and
her infidelity justifiable in terms of her emotional nature.
The love which he thus delineates is courtly in a sense, but
in a larger sense it is romantic love. Chrétien had been dis-
satisfied with his *Lancelot* and its love bound by unyielding
rules; Chaucer, unlike Chrétien even in his *Yvain*, treated
of a love which was unbounded by any larger conventions
although he applied many of the rules which Andreas had
mentioned. Fenice surrendered herself to her lover only after
difficult obstacles to the preservation of her good name had
been overcome; Laudine felt little emotion and condescended
to the gift of a kiss or herself when she felt that such a gift
was justified by the circumstances. Both were governed by
reason. The Criseyde of Chaucer could for a time govern
herself by reason, but when she was forced to participate
immediately in a situation, her reason fled and she was con-

trolled by her emotions. She suffered as much as Troilus, and
it is a misunderstanding of the poem to believe that she did
not.

The two lovers follow a courtship in many ways typical
of those which preceded and succeeded theirs, both in *fine
amor* and in romantic love. Although their ages are not
given, it may be gathered that Criseyde is somewhat older
than Troilus, since she has been married before. Professor
Tatlock thought that the previous marriage had not been a
love-match and that Criseyde had not known love.[73]

The girl in Chaucer's writings is invariably between twelve
and twenty before she marries. If she is older, she is not
ordinarily desirable. The Merchant said when he was thinking of a wife: "I wol no woman thritty yeer of age."[74] Apparently a woman would be old at that time. Therefore
Criseyde would be probably between twelve and thirty years
of age, a little older than twenty because of her widowhood.
She is no more than thirty because she is still exceedingly
beautiful, and beauty and youth fled early from a person of
the fourteenth century.

The rank of the lovers in *Troilus and Criseyde* is dissimi-
lar. Troilus is a prince, a son of Priam. Criseyde is not of
such noble blood. Although there is no statement that she
is a commoner, she is conscious of the difference in rank,
especially since her father has been so recently a traitor.
Therefore she is exceedingly careful, when she first grants
Troilus her love, to assure him that he will not be in control of the situation:

> "But natheles, this warne I yow," quod she,
> "A kynges sone although ye be, ywys,
> Ye shal namore han sovereignete
> Of me in love, than right in that cas is."[75]

Here is apparently a perfectly good reason why Criseyde should not have married Troilus, although Professor Tatlock feels it insufficient motivation in this case since so many romances do cause lovers of similarly divergent rank to marry.[76] Chaucer's explanation is nevertheless valid enough to be credible: a king's son could not marry a person of Criseyde's rank and in her present semi-ostracism since her father's defection to the Greek camp.

Troilus is a soldier, as were Cligés and Yvain before him. His achievements in war are great before he falls in love with Criseyde, and by reason of his love they become greater:

> But for non hate he to the Grekes hadde,
> Ne also for the rescous of the town,
> Ne made hym thus in armes for to madde,
> But only, lo, for this conclusioun:
> To liken hire the bet for his renoun.[77]

After she has accepted him as a lover,

> Benigne he was to ech in general,
> For which he gat hym thank in every place.
> Thus wolde Love, yheried be his grace,
> That Pride, Envye, and Ire, and Avarice
> He gan to fle, and everich other vice.[78]

It is the courage shown in his fighting with the Greeks which helps to attract Criseyde, and it is significant that she first begins to fall in love when she sees him returning from battle and hears the acclamations of the crowd:

> His helm tohewen was in twenty places,
> That by a tyssew heng his bak byhynde;
> His sheeld todasshed was with swerdes and maces,
> In which men myght many an arwe fynde
> That thirled hadde horn and nerf and rynde;

> And ay the peple cryde, "Here cometh oure joye,
> And, next his brother, holder up of Troye!"[79]

But it is not his courage alone which appeals to Criseyde. He
has other ideal traits. When she begins to consider him as a
possible lover, she

> gan to caste and rollen up and down
> Withinne hire thought his excellent prowesse,
> And his estat, and also his renown,
> His wit, his shap, and ek his gentilesse;
> But moost hir favour was, for his distresse
> Was al for hire, and thoughte it was a routhe
> To sleen swich oon, if that he mente trouthe.[80]

This is no Rosalind sardonically declaring that "Men have
died from time to time, and worms have eaten them, but not
for love." Criseyde, in her simplicity and sincerity, believes
that Troilus really could die for love of her, as he too believes. Such a concept could not find root in one who had
any degree of *Weltschmerz,* but only in an idealist, one who
was so honest himself that he could not see the dishonesty
in others.

Set a thief to catch a thief. Yes, and set an ingenue, Criseyde, to catch an ingenu, Troilus. For both are obviously in
love for the first time. Still, she is as cautious as might be.
Chaucer is careful to say that she does not fall in love at
first sight. She "only inclines towards Troilus, moved both by
his manhood and his devotion."[81] Unlike Shakespeare's characters, she analyzes the entire process as she goes through
each one of the stages, maintaining her intellectual superiority, keeping her reason sovereign of her emotions, as long as
she can. True, she feels love strike her as she watches Troilus
pass her window and she cries "Who yaf me drinke?" But

that is the cry of a girl who feels an emotion despite her
intellectual control, and Chaucer is at pains immediately
to add:

> For I sey nought that she so sodeynly
> Yaf hym hire love, but that she gan enclyne
> To like hym first, and I have told yow whi;
> And after that, his manhod and his pyne
> Made love withinne hire herte for to myne,
> For which, by proces and by good servyse,
> He gat hire love, and in no sodeyn wyse.[82]

The Inception begins when both of them fall in love, each
unaware that the other also sees and loves. Troilus sees her
in a crowd in the temple, and Criseyde sees him from her
window as he walks through an admiring throng. The difference between the two, however, is great. Troilus, who
like Benedick has been a mocker of love, is immediately
struck, almost literally, to his knees. He falls in love at first
sight. Criseyde, who has known nothing of love, either for
or against the disease, is able to analyze her feelings and to
exercise much more caution in the developing affair. Chaucer shows the differences between the lovers even more in the
Development than before. Troilus suffers from *hereos* soon
after he has seen Criseyde. Chaucer had already set forth details of *hereos* in the *Knight's Tale,* which Professor Tatlock
described as atypical. "There is nothing to indicate that the
Knight would be interested in a love story, and since he had
devoted his life to the Crusades, why should he tell such a
tale? Here Chaucer forces an already-composed tale on one
of his characters. The *Knight's Tale* is much more Chaucer
than the Knight. Consider, too, the philosophy, in which the
Knight would not apparently be interested."[83] Therefore,

when the Knight speaks of Arcite's *hereos* he is apparently
the spokesman for Chaucer.

> So muche sorwe hadde nevere creature
> That is, or shal, whil that the world may dure.
> His slep, his mete, his drynke, is hym biraft, . . .
> His hewe falow and pale as asshen colde,
> And solitarie he was and evere allone,
> And waillynge al the nyght, makynge his mone; . . .
> [He was] chaunged so, that no man koude knowe
> His speche nor his voys, though men it herde.
> And in his geere for al the world he ferde,
> Nat oonly lik the loveris maladye
> Of Hereos, but rather lyk manye,
> Engendred of humour malencolik.[84]

From the time that Troilus has fallen in love with Criseyde,
he suffers from the same disease, with almost identical symptoms:

> And fro this forth tho refte hym love his slep,
> And made his mete his foo, and ek his sorwe
> Gan multiplye, that, whoso tok kep,
> It shewed in his hewe both eve and morwe.[85]

> . . . .

> And whan that he in chambre was allone,
> He doun upon his beddes feet hym sette,
> And first he gan to sike, and eft to grone.[86]

He feels anxiety when he cannot have Criseyde:

> The felyng of his sorwe, or of his fere,[87]

and loses it when she yields:

> Agon was every sorwe and every feere.[88]

He desires death if he cannot have her:

> "now wolde God, Criseyde,
> Ye wolden on me rewe, er that I deyde!"[89]

He says he has a fever:

> Therefor a title he gan him for to borwe
> Of other siknesse, lest men of hym wende
> That the hote fir of love hym brende,
> And seyde he hadde a fevere and ferde amys.[90]

When he first sees Criseyde, his heart pains him:

> Therwith his herte gan to sprede and rise.[91]

He almost goes mad for love of her:

> But thanne felte this Troilus swich wo,
> That he was wel neigh wood . . .[92]

He is pale:

> The fyr of love . . .
> . . . brende hym so . . .
> That sexti tyme a day he loste his hewe.[93]

He swoons when Criseyde reproaches him[94] and cannot speak when the time comes to part:

> And specheles thus ben thise ilke tweye,
> That neither myghte o word for sorwe seye.[95]

And he keeps alone except when with her.[96]

Troilus really suffers from *hereos,* as does Criseyde. Chaucer does not so emphasize the agonies of her love for Troilus as he does his for her, but obviously they are as real. When they are finally separated:

Ful ofte a day she sighte ek for destresse.[97]

. . . .

Ful pale ywoxen was hire brighte face,
Hire lymes lene, as she that al the day
Stood, whan she dorste, and loked on the place
Ther she was born, and ther she dwelt hadde ay;
And al the nyght weping, allas, she lay.[98]

She does not suffer so before the affair, but Chaucer clearly
feels that she suffers greatly just before she yields to Diomed
as quoted above. And the suffering he describes parallels the
symptoms of *hereos* so closely as to give the impression that
that is her disease, and that therefore she is truly in love with
Troilus at that time.

The go-between for the lovers is Pandarus, whose allegiance is to both, although he seems to prefer Troilus. According to Andreas and to his contemporaries, lovers are allowed
one go-between between them, and a confidant apiece.[99]
Pandarus appears to fulfill all three functions, as he says:

"Wherfore I am, and wol ben, ay redy
To peyne me to do yow this servyse;
For bothe yow to plese thus hope I
Herafterward; for ye ben bothe wyse,
And konne it counseil kepe in swych a wyse
That no man schal the wiser of it be;
And so we may ben gladed alle thre."[100]

His main activities, however, are attempts to persuade Cri-
seyde to do Troilus' will, whereas he never tries to persuade
Troilus to accede to Criseyde's wishes. When Criseyde leaves
Troy, Pandarus does not go with her. He remains with
Troilus and clearly shows his allegiance. Criseyde has no
confidant except her uncle, and when he is away from her,

as when she is in the Greek camp, she would naturally have difficulty in making decisions. It may be that some of the cause of her defection is the lack of a confidant. Her father, the only person in the Greek camp whom she knows besides Diomed, is of little help to her in matters of love.

Troilus is in the fifth book of *Troilus and Criseyde* immensely helped by Pandarus' advice, and Pandarus is, importantly, the last speaker of the poem. He is obviously sincere when he says:

> "If I dide aught that myghte liken the,
> It is me lief; and of this tresoun now,
> God woot that it a sorwe is unto me!
> And dredeles, for hertes ese of yow,
> Right fayn I wolde amende it, wiste I how.
> And fro this world, almyghty God I preye
> Delivere hire soon! I kan namore seye."[101]

The go-between of the Duke of True Lovers expresses the function of the position at this time:

". . . you must tell me truly of your state, without reserve, and naught must you conceal from me of your condition which you would not do from a priest to whom you would make confession, and certes, very foolish would you be to keep sealed up in your heart the trouble which robs you of your peace of mind and your health. . . . And greatly do you misconceive our close fellowship if you fear that in aught I would betray you, and that I would not screen you more than I would myself. When you have told unto me the trouble which has cruelly taken possession of you, doubtless you will find your grief diminished, for very great hurt comes to him who suffers from love-sickness without speaking of it to anyone."[102]

He, too, acts as confidant as well.

The guerdons used in the Betrothal of Troilus and Criseyde are not exchanged as promises of marriage, but merely as symbols of vows of troth in the peculiar arrangement that obtained in courtly society. The exchange of rings, for instance, has long been a symbol of marriage between a loving pair. Chaucer, however, when he tells that Troilus and Criseyde exchanged their rings, says that they do so not seriously: he wants no hint of matrimony, or at least no more than a hint.

> Soone after this they spake of sondry thynges,
> As fel to purpos of this aventure,
> And pleyinge entrechaungeden hire rynges,
> Of whiche I kan nought tellen no scripture.[103]

At the same time Criseyde gives Troilus a brooch with a ruby set in it.[104] Later she gives Diomed a brooch[105] that had been Troilus's and which Troilus thinks is his when he sees it.[106] Apparently that brooch had been given to Criseyde at the parting.[107] Earlier, before the seduction, she had sent Troilus a ring by Pandarus.[108] The three rings and two brooches seem to be the only gifts that Troilus and Criseyde exchange. She gives more presents to Diomed than she does to Troilus:

> Hire glove he took, of which he was ful feyn.[109]
>
> .   .   .   .
>
> And after this the storie telleth us
> That she hym yaf the faire baye stede,
> The which he ones wan of Troilus;
> And ek a broche—and that was litel nede—
> That Troilus was, she yaf this Diomede.
> And ek, the bet from sorwe hym to releve,
> She made hym were a pencel of hire sleve.[110]

She does not appear to give Diomed the ring which Troilus
had given her, although that may well be only because Chaucer forgot to mention it. But Criseyde gives Diomed a glove,
a horse, a brooch, and a sleeve, and Troilus receives only
a brooch and a ring from her. Apparently Diomed gives
nothing in return, and Troilus gives more than he receives.
Again, whether that was intentional or not on Chaucer's
part it is impossible to say. In general, the gift was used to
aid the romance, to keep a beloved reminded of her lover.[111]
Troilus, however, sends no gifts to Criseyde and gives her
none until after she has sent him a ring. To this extent she
seems to have been the aggressor in both affairs.

The Betrothal scene in Book III incorporates the same
exchange of vows as those used by Yvain and Laudine and
is similar to the ceremonies between Alexander and Soredamors and Cligés and Fenice:

> "Now yeldeth yow, for other bote is non!"
> To that Criseyde answerde thus anon,
> "Ne hadde I er now, my swete herte deere,
> Ben yold, ywis, I were now nought heere!". . .
> Criseyde, al quyt from every drede and tene,
> As she that juste cause hadde hym to triste,
> Made hym swich feste, it joye was to seene,
> Whan she his trouthe and clene entente wiste;[112]

and the witness, Pandarus, speaks as in blessing when he
brings them together:

> . . . "Kneleth now, while that yow leste,
> There God youre hertes brynge soone at reste!"[113]

Finally, after their night together, they exchange rings.[114]

All of these steps in the Betrothal approximate those of a
true clandestine spousal as described in Chapter V below. Of

the nine points there mentioned, in this passage of *Troilus and Criseyde* there are at least six: consent of both parties, a witness, a contract or oath, a kiss, the blessing, and the exchange of gifts. The ceremony does not differ greatly from that of a valid marriage. But by the use of the word "pleyinge" to describe the interchanging of the rings, if by no other means, Chaucer shows that this is no true betrothal in the sense of spousals which would bring marriage rights.[115] The passage is remarkable, however, in that it shows how closely the *fine amor* of Andreas could be made to approximate an actual marriage. It is a step between the similar scenes in Chrétien and those of the sixteenth-century drama.

In the course of the Ordeal of Book IV Troilus resuffers the agonies that preceded his period of happiness with Criseyde. And in the Parting of Book V Chaucer shows the recognition of the finality of the separation and the death of Troilus, a death which had become necessary in a romance in which marriage or permanent union was not possible. The division of the five stages to the affair is perfectly even, one book to each topic.

Chaucer has taken, in *Troilus and Criseyde,* a story handed to him with many of the trappings of *fine amor* and has subtly altered the rules and the actions so that the characters behave like consistent human beings and are not bound by the conventions which they portray, although they stay in general within their limits. Thus the love of Troilus and Criseyde is courtly love, it is romantic love conditioned by rules of courtship, and their final separation and her perfidy are matters not necessarily extraneous to both conventions. Chaucer took the story of a faithless woman bound by the traditions of courtly love in an affair with a young man also playing a serious game whose rules took little cognizance of human feeling. By making his characters real and allowing them to actuate the plot, he has caused the lovers to free themselves from the bonds of courtly love and still accept in large part the conventions. To them under Chaucer, the code is a means of communication, a series of symbolic attitudes. These they transcend but do not negate when a strict interpretation of such rules would hamper their individuality.[116]

George Gascoigne, in *The Pleasant Fable of Ferdinando Jeronimi and Leonora de Valasco* (1573),[117] presents an example of courtship carried on in the Andrean manner. Here is no story of romance ultimately solved, but instead the unblushing seduction of another man's wife.

Master F. J., having been invited to court Frances, the virtuous daughter of the Lord of Valasco, proceeds to fall in love with her brother's unvirtuous wife, Elinor, who has had many previous affairs and is perfectly capable of handling the affair with F. J. Her first few letters written in answer to his are the composition of her current paramour, her Secretary, and much of her early activity with F. J. shows a similar ennui.

When the Secretary leaves town, however, Elinor slakes her lust upon F. J., and he lives happily until the return of the Secretary. Then she ridicules F. J. and ousts him. He leaves the Castle of Valasco, despite the declared love of Frances, the girl he was invited to court, to spend the "rest of his dayes in a dissolute kind of lyfe: & abandoning the worthy Lady *Frauncischina,* who (dayly being gauled with the griefe of his great ingratitude) dyd shortlye bring hir selfe into a myserable consumption: whereof (after three yeares languishing) shee dyed." Dame Elinor, the perfidious, however, "lived long in ye continuance of hir acustomed change."[118]

The division of the five stages of the affair is quite uneven, and the seventy-one-page story is handled as follows:

	Number of Pages	Percent
Inception	1	1
Development	23	35
Betrothal	10	13
Ordeal	36	52
Separation	1	1

The emphasis is obviously on the Ordeal, as it was in the *Yvain* of Chrétien.

The Inception of the story is abbreviated. The first meeting is not described. The Development does not begin until after F. J. has gained sufficient courage to write to his beloved. The couple are of high enough rank to be candidates for a love affair in the courtly mode, since he is a knight and she is the daughter-in-law of a lord. They both appear to be young, although she is apparently older—at least she is more ex-perienced—than he. Other traits of his characer, since Dame Elinor accepts him as a lover and Lady Frances loves him, are probably similar to the ideals described by Dame Pergo in her narrative of her lover: "I could by no meanes mislike of him by any good reason (considering that he was of byrth no way inferiour unto mee, of possessions not to bee disdained, of parson right comelye, of behaviour Courtly, of manner mod-est, of mynde lyberall, and of vertuous disposition."[119]

The second half of the Development, which usually fol-lows the suffering from *hereos,* in earlier tales, includes here both *hereos* and the active courtship leading to the seduction. It begins on the second page of the story with F. J.'s first let-ter, and it continues for twenty-three pages.

F. J. describes his symptoms of the disease in his writings

to Dame Elinor, and his analysis may or may not be true. The author's description, however, comes after the first letters. F. J. does not seem to be at all in love until after the affair has proceeded to actual courtship. His suffering comes not during his period of silence but later, and seems to be in direct relation to his closeness to Dame Elinor. He is induced to love by the eyes of his beloved:

Even so *Ferdinando Jeronimi* lately overcome by the beautifull beames of this Dame *Elynor* . . . (as in a traunce) he lifted up his dazled eies, and so continued in a certen kind of admiration.[120]

This leads him directly to externally observable *hereos,* which appears after he has had an interview with his beloved:

And at supper time, the Lord of *Valasco* finding fault yt his gestes stomacke served him no better, began to accuse the grosnesse of his vyands, to whom one of the gentlewomen which had passed ye afternoone in his company, answered. Nay sir, quod she, this gentleman hath a passion, the which once in a day at the least doth kill his appetite. . . . Fayre ladie quod *Ferdinando,* you either mistoke me or overheard me then: for I told of a comfortable humor which so fed me with continuall remembrance of joy, as that my stomack being ful therof doth desire in maner none other vittaylcs. Why sir, (quod the host,) do you then live by love?[121]

Soon after this, when he has had a misunderstanding with his mistress, he retires into a garden in melancholy and sits "downe under a tree to allay his sadnesse with solitarines." Searchers "founde the Knight with hys armes foulded in a heavy kinde of contemplation . . ." and this leads to sleeplessness, as he tells Dame Elinor the day after the argument: "It is not yet xx. houres, since without touch of brest, she gave him such a nip by the harte, as did altogether bereave him his nightes rest with the bruse therof."[122]

As go-between the lovers for the most part use their letters, but on one occasion F. J. uses Mistress Frances to convey a message to his beloved, and Dame Elinor uses her maid to approach F. J. "desiering him to repayre unto their Mistresse." F. J. has no confidant, and he keeps the secret of his love completely to himself. Dame Elinor, apparently, confides the affair to the Secretary, and certainly the maid is privy to many of the activities. Here the conventional two confidants and one messenger have become two confidants for one person, and two messengers. The maid apparently performs both functions.[123]

The Betrothal in this tale is divested of all the ceremonies of a spousal. Indeed it is nothing but a simple seduction. Secrecy has been so far maintained by F. J. in relation to the other characters of the story, although Dame Elinor has made little secret of the affair. The day after the first seduction, when he accompanies Lady Frances and Dame Elinor on a horseback ride, Master F. J. realizes that he has mislaid his sword during the night, and he "coulde not be mery, as on that estemed the preservation of his mistres honor, no lessse then the obteyning of his owne delightes. . . . The Lady *Elynor* (more carelesse then considerative of hir owne case)"[124] tries to persuade him to merriment.

Prouty feels that secrecy is not maintained, and that that lack of secrecy suggests that the tale is autobiographical. He finds such frankness realistic and feels that it "vitiates the principle of secrecy. Though we are treated to a long discussion on this subject, we are allowed to see the two poems which deal with Elinor's seduction."[125] But this would be a violation of secrecy only if the story were true. Otherwise, the author's omniscience would explain the verisimilitude. It would be impossible for any author to tell an engrossing love story without violating the principle of secrecy. This is no proof of realism, of autobiography. F. J. does maintain secrecy as a lover should.

During this third period he "made an Idoll of hir in his inwarde conceyte"[126] more than he has done in deification during the period of Development.[127] There are few misunderstandings, and he is happy until

the unhappy *Secretary* whom I have before remembred, was returned from *Florence,* on whom *Ferdinando* had no soner cast his eies, but immediatly he fell into a great passion of minde, which might be compared unto a feaver.[128]

With that he retires to bed, and incited by jealousy he suffers many of the aspects of the disease.

F. J.'s jealousy presents a curious contradiction. According to the codes of love, jealousy should be favorably regarded by the lady, since it emphasized her lover's devotion. On the other hand, suspicion of the lady's faith was not allowed nor was promiscuity on the lady's part. F. J.'s suspicion is unconventional because it is real, exactly as Elinor's faithlessness is real.[129]

Andreas Capellanus states that "Love increases . . . if one of the lovers feels real jealousy, which is called, in fact, the nurse of love. Even if he does not suffer from real jealousy, but from shameful suspicion, still by virtue of this his love always increases and grows more powerful."[130]

By the time of Gascoigne, however, the tradition had changed, as so many others seem to have, and although Monophylo says that upright men "will rather repose a resolute loyalty in their Ladies, than once presume of suspicion of treason,"[131] Chariclea, in the second section of *Monophylo,* expresses a completely different opinion, saying that the jeal-

ousy of a lover always exists and makes his love more painful
than pleasant:

> But because I haue dwelt alwayes in this minde, that notwithstand-
> ing the pleasures distending with loue, is great in the highest de-
> gree, in respect of other felicities, yea and without comparison: yet,
> in common experience it comes not neere the least part of the sor-
> rowes & tormentes, which of it are nouzled and trayned, as a thou-
> sand suspicions, ten thousand ielowsies, with infinite distempered
> feares (the proper substitution of love) with whome . . . is
> brought such passions & panges, that to a man of sound judge-
> ment there seemes no differences betweene the laborinth of this
> endlesse traueyle, and the infernall gulphe.[132]

The jealous lover of the sixteenth century is not praised,
but jealousy was a very real aspect of love in the time of
Gascoigne, apparently, and its presence in this story is not
so much a proof of the identity of Gascoigne and F. J., as it
is a proof that courtly love was abandoning the ideal for the
real, the exalted for the naturalistic.

During this period F. J. thinks constantly of his beloved.
This absorption in her continues through his illness, and is
apparent when Lady Frances speaks to him on his bed.
"Ferdinando (as on in a traunce) had marked very little of
hir curteouse talke, & yet gave hir thankes, and so held his
peace whereat the Ladyes (being all amazed) there became
a silence in the chamber on all sides."[133]

When Dame Elinor comes to visit him, he assures her:

> But in trueth Mistress I am sicke (quod he,) and therewithall the
> trembling of his hart had sent up suche throbbing into his throte,
> as that his voyce (now deprived of breath) commaunded the tong
> to be still.[134]

This loss of speech recurs later,[135] and when she returns to

him for another visit his voice trembles.[136] When she finally
tells him all is well, he is made so happy and so conscious of
his own unworthiness that he swoons.[137] The first quarto
continues:

But I have heard my friend *F. J.* confesse, that he was in a happy
traunce, and thought himself for divers causes unhappely revived.
For surely I have heard him affirme, that to dye in such a passion,
had ben rather pleasant, than like to panges of death.[138]

Upon his revival from the swoon he confesses his jealousy
and shows that he knows of her other affairs. Whereupon
in a passion she leaves him permanently. Gascoigne shows
her lack of the *hereos* of true courtly love by remarking that
when she leaves her lover thus, in anger, "I doubte not, but
shee slept quietlye the rest of the night. As *Ferdinando* also
(perswading himselfe that he shoulde with convenient lea-
sure recover her from this haggard conceipt) tooke some better rest towardes the morning, than hee had done in many
nightes forepast."[139]

Dame Elinor changes her love so quickly as to cause comment by the subtly interfering Frances, who remarks: "I do
much mervayle that ye Lady *Elinor* is now so unwilling to
take any travayle in his behalfe, especially remembring that
but yesternight she was so diligent to bring him to bed."
Obviously Elinor has not loved F. J. or really even the Secretary, for she is unfaithful to both in a period of less than
forty-eight hours. And Gascoigne comments on Lady Elinor's perfidy that "thus we see that where wicked lust doth
beare the name of love, it doth not onelye infect the lyght
minded, but it maye also become confusion to others [F. J.
and the Lady Franceschina] which are vowed to constan-
cie."[140]

The cure for *hereos* he speaks of, as might be expected, to Dame Elinor as having been "by your bountifull medicines applied."[141]

He receives no real guerdon from her, nor she one from him, with the exceptions of the letters exchanged and one "fayre wroughte kerchife" which she gives him. This is, however, not mentioned again. But the Secretary obviously has suffered from her cupidity, for Gascoigne describes the cause of her love for him as being that he had "a well lyned pursse, wherewith he could at every call, provide suche pretie conceytes as pleased hir peevish fantasie." Since "by this meanes hee had throughly (long before) insinuated him selfe with this amorous dame," the lack of permanent success of F. J.'s suit might be partly due to his lack of gifts.[142]

In many ways this work is similar to *Troilus and Criseyde*. The hero, Master F. J., like Troilus, loves and is successful for a time, and apparently is loved in return. Certainly Dame Elinor sheds tears for him.[143] She, on the other hand, is as fickle as Criseyde was thought to have been by the people of the sixteenth century. She has few of the endearing traits of Criseyde, but the hero himself is rather stilted, even more so than is Troilus. And the final dismissal of him to live a riotous life, leaving the loving Lady Frances to languish and die, is not intended by Gascoigne as a noble action. Nobility does not seem to come to F. J. at any time: he does not seem to gain anything from the affair except the physical satisfaction of seduction. Gascoigne gives no hint of ennoblement of F. J. The Secretary might well be compared to Diomed, for he seems to take F. J.'s place when he returns.

The differences, of course, are that Lady Frances is represented as loving Master F. J., whereas Troilus is loved by no woman but Criseyde. Dame Elinor has been unfaithful before her affair with F. J. as well as after it. And F. J. has no confidant with whom he can talk for protection against his emotional turmoil as has Troilus with Pandarus to whom he can confess his condition.

The story is rather lasciviously written. Upon the return of Dame Elinor's husband, F. J., knowingly cuckolding him, is unfair in his happiness, suggesting to the reader that part of his love is caused by his superiority to the husband, his having in secret that which no one else can have.

"Though the husband is a negligible object, F. J.'s frank gloating over his 'deepe invention' of the hunting horn and the horns of the cuckold is very ugly realism. The open adultery of courtly love may be abstractly discussed by Monophylo, but the viciousness of actual practice is only too closely revealed in this poem."[144]

But in the later quartos much of the obscenity, including a quasi-rape, is removed.

Although Gascoigne's moral is carefully drawn—"And to that ende I have recyted this Fable which maye serve as ensample to warne the youthfull reader from attempting the lyke worthles enterprise"[145]—it is obvious that his relish, as he expected his readers' to be, was more in the tale than in the moral.

To this level, then, courtly love had come. Its idealism had become frank sensuality, for the love affair has become the sophisticated seduction of a married woman. The few lines of moral are too brief to justify the full description of the affair which precedes them.

In the hundred and fifty years from Chaucer, *fine amor* had fallen into desuetude. The love of Criseyde for Troilus is until the last book real and strong and romantic in the

sense of modern moral romanticism. The love of Yvain for
Laudine and of Cligés for Fenice has been less real but
nevertheless a faithful one. The love of Dame Elinor for
F. J. is purely lascivious. Chaucer loves the Criseyde he creates, Gascoigne obviously detests the Elinor he creates.

The tradition of *fine amor,* mocked, distorted, and muti-
lated, could not be annihilated. Its persistence in the drama
of the end of the sixteenth century will be the subject of
the succeeding chapters.

Chapter II

INCEPTION: THE FIRST MEETING

THIS STUDY, in order to ascertain the features and routines of courtship as they appear in Elizabethan drama and particularly in the plays of Shakespeare, will compare three fields, which may be exemplified by specific works, with the drama:

1. The traditions of *fine amor* as received by the late sixteenth century and described in the previous chapter. The tradition itself was best exemplified before the fifteenth century by the work of Andreas Capellanus and Chrétien of Troyes in France, and by Chaucer in England. In the material of the early sixteenth century the writings of Gascoigne, whose *Master F. J.* has already been discussed, and Geoffrey Fenton are perhaps more typical for this purpose than are the Italian works which did not originate in England although they strongly influenced English customs.

Etienne Pasquier's *Le Monophyle,* published in 1554, is a disquisition on love intended to show the tradition of *fine amor* then prevalent in the French court. Geoffrey Fenton translated this as *Monophylo* in 1572. The book is divided into two parts, for no discernible reason except that one day ends at the conclusion of the first part. The entire work is a discussion of love overheard and to a certain extent participated in by the author. Monophylo is the character with whom the author most sympathizes. He is represented as love-sick in the ideal fashion of *hereos.* Glaphyro is a good courtier who is polite to ladies for courtesy's sake rather than because he is in love. Phylopolo is the young courtier who tends to fall in love with any woman. The three debate, under the arbitration of Madame Charyclea, various qualities of love. The debate comes to no real conclusion except that, as mentioned, Monophylo seems to have the best of it.

2. The exhortations of preachers and other moralists. However, it may appear that the work of Shakespeare himself will prove as moral as that of a Puritan preacher in views toward courtship and marriage; and that Shakespeare, veering from *fine amor's* more licentious aspects, turned to a morality which was a compromise between that and the rabid asceticism of the unworldly.

3. The laws of England. Opinions as to these are given in the writings of Henry Swinburne, a York justice who wrote, sometime about the year 1600, *A Treatise of Spousals,* which for some reason was not published until after his death. In this work Swinburne attempts to ascertain all the legal aspects of marriage which could possibly arise, and some which apparently could arise only in an artist's mind.

This examination may find in drama a heightening of theatrical effect and changes from the dramatic for the sake of verisimilitude. In other words, even the dramatic eagerness of the writer for surprise and novelty would not ordinarily lead him to depart very far from actuality or custom approved in his time. Although he might very well deal with an unusual complication of the law or of tradition in his plot, such as the marriage of a man with two women, he probably would not violate custom to the extent of giving a happy solution to the problem.

Throughout the work the nature of the dramatic treatment of courtship will be clarified by frequent references to the ideals of *fine amor,* moral idealism, law and actuality.

The domestic tragedy, based on lurid fact, often as reported in contemporary scandal sheets, dealing with marital infidelity, is an example of such close relationship of the drama with actuality. It is thus an amalgamation of Christian morality and courtly love as understood in the twelfth century. In the typical plot, of an unhappily married couple, the wife has extramarital relations with a man whose help she employs to murder her husband. The murder is eventually successful, the criminals are easily caught, they repent and are hanged. *Arden of Feversham* (1591) and *A Warning for Fair Women* (1599)[1] are of this type. Thomas Heywood's *A Woman Killed With Kindness* (1603) varies from the pattern principally in that there is no attempt by Mrs. Frankford and Wendoll to kill Master Frankford. He strongly emphasizes infidelity and the usual thesis of the wages of sin.[2] Such plays, dealing only with the married state, are in general beyond the scope of this paper, which is primarily concerned with the forms and rituals preceding marriage.

In this, the second chapter, I shall discuss the first meeting of lovers principally as it occurred in Shakespeare's plays, and I shall attempt to find the qualifications prerequisite to this meeting. In the dramas these qualifications are essentially similar to those Andreas discusses. Tradition demanded that all lovers be relatively similar, just as modern tradition demands a certain type in the lover. The similarity extended through physical and mental traits to nationality, rank, and even profession. The lovers sympathetically portrayed on the English stage at this period tended to be English in thought and action even if not in name. (Englishmen seem to have been rather prejudiced on that point.) The

Courtesan of Thomas Heywood's *2 If You Know Not Me You Know Nobody* (1605) says:

> I haue tride ere now
> The sweatie Spaniard, and the carowsing Dane,
> The foggy Dutch-man, and the fiery French,
> The briske Italian, and indeede what not:
> And yet of all and all, the Englishman
> Shall goe for me: I yo'are the truest Louers,
> The ablest, last night, and the truest men
> That breath beneath the Sunne.[3]

The audience took a certain pride in seeing an Englishman on the stage out-court a foreigner. Capital is made of this feeling in the plot of William Haughton's *Englishmen For My Money* (1596).

It was necessary that the meeting lovers be young—there are few examples of middle- or old-age marrying youth and living together happily. Othello is considerably older than Desdemona, and he implies in the course of the play that that might well be one reason for her supposed unfaithfulness.[4] A marriage in which the couple varied widely in their ages was seldom successful.

There was an age below which it was not legal for the child to marry, a minimum age limit. There was, apparently, no maximum age limit for Elizabethans, and therefore for lovers in the dramas, and there could not be if the theories of marriage were to be sustained. Man did not marry, according to the thought of the time, solely for the pleasures of a bed. Marriage, says Thomas Becon, is:

an hie, holye and blessed order of life, ordayned not of man, but of God . . . wherein one man and one woman are coupled and knit together in one fleshe and body in the feare and loue of God, by the free, louinge, harty, and good consente of them both, to the entent that they two may dwel together, as one fleshe and body of one wyl and mynd in all honesty, vertue and godliness, and spend theyr lyues in equal partaking of all such thinges as god shal send them with thankes geuynge.[5]

Such an attitude was obviously that of Shakespeare's contemporaries in the drama. They did not, however, deal often with the courtship and marriage of older people, possibly because those aspects would have been more difficult for them to handle with verisimilitude: the writers had had experience in the matters of youth, and they could speak of them with authority.

The dramatists all knew the legal minimum age, and their characters had achieved, invariably, that minimum before they fell in love. This law had not changed since the time of Andreas. Hugo of St. Victor (1097-1141) had said that men of less than fourteen years and girls of less than twelve might not, according to the laws, enter into marriage.[6] At the other extreme of time is Lord Hardwicke's Marriage Act, which states, according to Edvard Westermarck, that such early marriages were made void:

In England, by the common law, marriages of minors who had attained the age of consent—fixed at fourteen years for males and twelve for females—were valid without the consent of parents until the year 1753, when Lord Hardwicke's Marriage Act (26 George II., c. 33, para. 11) declared such marriages void.[7]

In between the periods of the early twelfth century and 1743, Henry Swinburne discussed the relative ages and the exceptions to the rules in his *A Treatise of Spousals*.[8] His opinion, which he admitted was not without many exceptions, was:

That a Man so soon as he hath accomplished the Age of Fourteen years, and a Woman so soon as she hath accomplished the Age of Twelve years, may Contract true and lawful and individual Matrimony, in case there be no other impediment to hinder the same.[9]

Nevertheless, Swinburne found that the courts permitted marriage at an earlier age if both parties had achieved puberty before the time of marriage.[10]

In general, the age for marriage as suggested by Swinburne seems to have been considered the same by the dramatists of the period. Mall, in Henry Porter's *1 Two Angry Women of Abington* (1598), is somewhat older than twelve or fourteen before she is married, but by the time of the play she is worried about her age:

> Being fourteen and toward the tother year,
> Good Lord, thought I, fifteen will ne'er be here!
> For I have heard my mother say that then
> Pretty maids were fit for handsome men:
> Fifteen past, sixteen, and seventeen too,
> What, thought I, will not this husband do?[11]

Mall's mother, believing fifteen the minimum age, is apparently conservative. Mathea, the youngest girl in William Haughton's *Englishmen For My Money,* claims to be fifteen. Her father claims she is twelve.[12] When she marries, within twenty-four hours of these claims, without his consent, he makes no effort to break the contract. Even at twelve, then, if her father really believes that that is her age, she would apparently be legally permitted to marry a man of her own choosing.

Moll, in *The Puritan Widow* (1606), which may have been written by Thomas Middleton, declares that "your northern wench in her own country may well hold out 'till she be fifteen, but if she touch the south once, and come up to London, here the chimes go presently after twelve."[13] London was of course the setting for most of the plays as far as laws and customs were concerned. Viola may be living in Illyria, but her customs are those of sixteenth-century London.

Shakespeare's references to the age of his lovers are definite, but they are generally made unintrusive. Miranda, for instance, in *The Tempest,* is apparently about fifteen, for she can remember a time, twelve years previous to the action of the play, when she was in Milan.[14] She is obviously more than twelve, and just as obviously less than twenty. Viola, in *Twelfth Night,* claims to have been thirteen when her father died.[15] At that time she was with her brother Sebastian. Possibly they began their sea voyage as a result of their father's death. If so, the age of fifteen would not sit heavily on Viola. Marina, in *Pericles,* is fourteen. At least she was that age when she left Cleon.[16] And since Pericles has not shaved in fourteen years at the end of the play,[17] it is apparent that he stopped shaving when he lost his wife and newborn daughter. Perdita, in *The Winter's Tale,* is sixteen.[18] Her lover, Florizel, is somewhat older, since he had been alive when his father had left him, nine months before the action of the play and more than that before her birth.[19] Mistress Anne Page, of *The Merry Wives of Windsor,* is less than seventeen, since she is to come into an inheritance when she achieves seventeen.[20] Troilus, in *Troilus and Cressida,* is the only lover whose precise age is given. He is twenty-two.[21]

Chilton Latham Powell, in *English Domestic Relations, 1487-1653,* says: "Shakespeare evidently wished to emphasize the child-parent contention in *Romeo and Juliet,* since he altered the original story to make Juliet under the legal

age for marriage. . . ."[22] This statement is simply not true.
Juliet was considerably over the marriageable age. "The legal
age for marriage, which might follow spousals immediately
or after an interval of any length, was fourteen for males
and twelve for females," says Powell on another page.[23]
Powell has evidently missed Lady Capulet's statement that

> Younger than you,
> Here in Verona, ladies of esteem,
> Are made already mothers. By my count,
> I was your mother much upon these years
> That you are now a maid,[24]

which follows almost immediately upon the statement that
Juliet is at least thirteen years and forty-nine weeks old,[25]
when the legal age for marriage was twelve. Juliet was, her
mother apparently felt, almost an old maid.

Writers of the time, especially preachers and other moralists, objected to marriages at such a youthful age. Becon,
who seems to view marriage quite from the modern conservative viewpoint, says:

forasmuch as maides no les then yonge menne after they come once
to xiiii yeres of age, are so desirous to be maried, . . . notwithstanding suche untimely mariages are not to be commended . . .
it shalbe conuenient for al honest maides, if they tender the health
and cōseruation of their bodies . . . that they labor to the vtter-
most of their power to suppresse that luste and desire in them.[26]

and Fenton's Glaphyro, speaking of the wisdom to be used
in selecting a spouse, says:

neyther can I alowe in this behalfe, the consideration of the Ro-
maines, who gaue lybertie to their daughters at twelue yeares, and
leaue to their sonnes at fortene to marrie: respecting more the
abilytie of the body, then capacitie of the minde, as esteeming those

ages most fitte for copulation to multiplye the world. At those
yeares they suffered man and woman to alyenate their bodie, and
yet in all other contractes, they forbad alyenacion of lands and bene-
fite vntill twentie and fiue yeares.[27]

Despite such statements, one religious and dealing with
reality and the other courtly and dealing with the unreality
of literature, the age of consent seems to have been generally
accepted as twelve and fourteen. Yet few characters of
Shakespeare could have married at that age. None are definitely that young. Shakespeare seems to have written with a
margin of moral safety.

Courtly love had had its beginning in the nobility and
therefore it was popular eventually with all classes because
of the eternal desire of the lower to emulate the activities of
the upper classes. If the bourgeoisie of the late sixteenth
century had not adopted the principles of *fine amor* to their
own use, at least they were anxious to see them represented
on the stage, and, from their reading, they knew that the requirement as to the rank of the beloved was quite strict—
even though they desired to break it down. Andreas, in *The
Art of Courtly Love,* had specifically advocated similarity of
rank in lovers wherever practicable.[28] Chaucer, no member of
the nobility himself, had in *The Wife of Bath's Tale* recognized that class inequality gave privileges to the higher-rank-
ing person. The unnamed knight, the hero of the tale, rapes
a girl who is obviously not of the nobility. The trouble she
makes for him is as nothing to the shame that would have
come to the same knight if he had acted similarly with one
who was a lady.

Knights, of whom so many of the romances were written,
were not necessarily of the nobility themselves, but often,
in the course of the tale, quite generally they succeeded in

proving to their audience that they were kings' sons in disguise. It is quite true that courtly love adapted itself to a caste system. According to E. A. Freeman, "The chivalrous spirit is above all things a class spirit. The good knight is bound to endless fantastic courtesies towards men and still more towards women of a certain rank; he may treat all below that rank with any degree of scorn and cruelty."[29] The twelfth-century knight became the sixteenth-century gentleman who knew "that courtesy is not the same thing for all men, but one thing for superiors, another for equals, and yet another for inferiors."[30]

The argument as to the relative rank of the lover and beloved was developed at some length in Andreas Capellanus's work,[31] and it was the subject of much debate through succeeding centuries. By the time of Elizabeth the outcome of the argument had been decided, but the subject was still debated. Fenton found in England (1572) that there was a difference between the ranks, apparently as Pasquier had found in France when he had written the book (1554) which Fenton translated. When the question of rank is brought up in *Monophylo,* the author says:

yea, this ought to stande in such high consideration with Ladies as not ones to fall into the thought of any noble mynde: the same being the cause whye some making a question whether it were better to offer loue to a gentlewoman or a Marchaunts wife, maintaine that to the gentlewoman belongs a more propertie to loue, as whose fancie is not defiled with vile respect of money, nor hir pleasure subiect to other tribute then loue for loue: and yet I will not excuse those people of their errors, seeing that as we see commonly, so I haue heard that the effect of money is no lesse hatefull to many marchauntes wiues, then to most gentlewomen, on whom in this case may be throwne a more suspition, bicause their estate being great and of nature like to birdes desiring costly feathers, requires a highe proportion, and continuall supply of money.[32]

The tendency advocated here, to avoid matrimony solely for wealth, persisted through the idealistic centers of the Elizabethan age, but the apparent trend in the seventeenth century was to return to marriage for financial security. In any case, the plots of many of the plays are similar to that of Philip Massinger's *A New Way to Pay Old Debts* (1625), in which Tom Allworth recovers his fortune by marrying Margaret Overreach, the daughter of the man who had ruined his father. In this play the wealth motif is combined with the love motif.

Glaphyro, in *Monophylo*, feels that the lover must consider carefully his beloved's "parentage, and maner of bringing vp from hir youth,"[33] and even Monophylo, whose ideas the author accepts almost as his own, says:

if I chaunce to settle in affection with a mayde of base condition, and by a tollerable suggestion of nature, proceede with hir in holye maryage, shall I not runne into a popular obloquie . . . and my parents eschew me and my choyse with vnnaturall grudge, as to haue mingled my discent with a matche of inferiour estate (such is the impression and regarde of dowryes) where they discerne not that in this I haue found my Paradise, and by the other I should haue runne hedlong into hell.[34]

It posed a nice problem, as they were all aware. In the anonymous *Fair Em* (1590), Mariana pleads with her king that he "not seek by lust unlawfully to wrong my chaste determination," to which he sensibly replies:

> I hold that man most shameles in his sinne
> That seeks to wrong an honest lady's name
> Whome he thinkes worthie of his mariage bed.[35]

William is here very careful to say that he will not wrong the name of a woman who is (a) honest, (b) a lady, and (c) worthy of marriage.[36] By implication, although there is of course nothing in the play to prove this, if she cannot fulfill any one of those conditions his restraint will vanish. A lady is, of course, the wife of a member of the nobility, the knightly class, or the gentry. That distinction is still implied in the nomenclature of the United States Army, which invariably speaks of "officers and their ladies, enlisted men and their wives."

But these rules were breaking down in the sixteenth century, and caste distinctions especially were questioned. Thomas Dekker gives a good example of the conflicting forces in *The Shoemaker's Holiday* (1599). Here representatives of the three large classes of Elizabethan society desire and debate mixture of the classes through intermarriage.

The highest class consisted of the titled nobility, the landed gentry, and important members of the learned professions. These were the only classes with leisure, according to Andreas, for the practice of courtly love. The clergy, the learned men of his day, he considered "the noblest class of all."[37] The lowest class of the Elizabethan period were unskilled laborers, uneducated peasantry, and artisans whose trades required little skill and brought little pay. Between these extremes was a great middle class of merchants, tradesmen, and craftsmen, whose thoughts and interests centered in material profits.[38] Sir Hugh Lacy, of the titled nobility as Earl of Lincoln, opposes the marriage of his nephew, Sir Rowland, with Rose, daughter of Sir Roger Oately, Lord Mayor of London but of the bourgeoisie, a merchant who has been knighted. Sir Roger, on the other hand, opposes violently the marriage of Rose to either Sir Rowland or to

Hans the shoemaker, who fortunately is Sir Rowland in disguise. Thus when Sir Hugh speaks to his nephew he argues:

> I would not haue you cast an amorous eie
> Upon so meane a proiect, as the loue
> Of a gay, wanton, painted cittizen,
> I know this churle, euen in the height of scorne,
> Doth hate the mixture of his bloud with thine,
> I pray thee do thou so.[39]

Sir Roger, consulted by Sir Hugh in an attempt to separate
the lovers before they can marry, assures his superior in rank:

> Too meane is my poore girle for his high birth;
> Poore Cittizens must not with Courtiers wed,
> Who will in silkes, and gay apparell spend
> More in one yeare, then I am worth by farre,
> Therefore your honour neede not doubt my girle.[40]

But when he learns his daughter has fled with Hans, Sir
Roger roars:

> A Flemming butter-boxe, a shoomaker.
> Will she forget her birth? requite my care
> With such ingratitude? scorn'd she young *Hammon*,
> To loue a honnikin, a needy knaue?[41]

Dekker's view, however, is clear from his conclusion: the
King marries Rose to Sir Rowland Lacy in a decision accepted by all. The class segregation is powerless against all-
powerful love.[42]

The situation of Fenton and Anne Page in Shakespeare's
Merry Wives of Windsor is similar to that of Sir Rowland
and Rose in *The Shoemaker's Holiday*. Fenton, in discussing
Page's objections to his marrying Anne, says to her:

> He doth object I am too great of birth,
> And that, my state being gall'd with my expense,
> I seek to heal it only by his wealth.[43]

It is evident that Shakespeare agrees, at least in this instance, with Dekker, for Fenton and Anne marry at the conclusion of the play, proving Dekker's thesis of the power of love.

Other writers tended to echo these sentiments. The anonymous author of *Fair Em* causes Manville to say:

> A Millers daughter, says the multitude,
> Should not be loued by a Gentleman.
> But let them breath their soules into the ayre,
> Yet will I still affect thee as my selfe,
> So thou be constant in thy plighted vowe,[44]

and in the same scene Mountney generalizes:

> . . . I hope full well you know
> That loue respectes no difference of state,
> So beautie serue to stirr affection.[45]

This is precisely Dekker's argument as presented by the King in *The Shoemaker's Holiday:*

> Dost thou not know, that loue respects no bloud?
> Cares not for difference of birth or state?[46]

which is merely a rhymed paraphrase of Andreas Capellanus in *The Art of Courtly Love:*

"I know well that Love is not in the habit of differentiating men with titles of distinction, but that he obligates all equally to serve in his (that is, Love's) army, making no exceptions for beauty or birth and making no distinctions of sex or inequality of family."[47]

But because of the increasing influence of the middle class, there had to be some substitute for noble blood to make a person acceptable. On the other hand, some people apparently felt that noble blood alone was not enough. As a combination of the two attitudes, and as a member of a class whose cause he embraces, Andreas speaks for the clergy, the nobility of the fourth estate:

Now the clerk is considered to be of the most noble class by virtue of his sacred calling, a nobility which we agree comes from God's bosom and is granted to him by the Divine Will . . . [It] is not derived from his ancestors, nor can the secular power deprive him of it . . . if any clerk should wish to enter into the lists of Love let him speak and apply himself to Love's service in accordance with the rank or standing of his parents.[48]

Euphues in the sixteenth century generalizes a change in the standard which would make a man take his nobility from birth, voicing a very usual Renaissance concept of emancipation when he says in his requirements for Ephoebus:

First, that he be of honest parents, nursed of his mother, brought vp in such a place as is incorrupt, both for the ayre and manners with such a person as is vndefiled, of great zeale, of profound Philosophy, whereby he may atteine learning, and haue in al science a smacke, whereby he may readily dispute of any thing. That his body be kept in his pure strength by honest exercise, his wit and memory by diligent study.[49]

The substitute for education was the long-praised military service which took its honor from before the days of chivalry, but in the sixteenth century this service was of no more value than was schooling.

Ideally, the two abilities of scholarly and military prowess

are combined in Shakespeare. The best-known example is
Hamlet, whom Ophelia describes as

> The courtier's, scholar's, soldier's, eye, tongue, sword,
> Th'expectancy and rose of the fair state,
> The glass of fashion and the mould of form,[50]

but Bassanio, in *The Merchant of Venice,* is known as a
scholar as well as a soldier, and he is so recommended to
Portia by Nerissa.[51] The Duke, Vincentio, in *Measure for
Measure,* who is eventually to marry the *de facto* heroine of
the play, tells Lucio: "Let him be but testimonied in his own
bringings-forth, and he shall appear to the envious a scholar,
a statesman, and a soldier."[52]

It is significant that none of Shakespeare's heroes is a
scholar only: none inhabits an ivory tower. Most are primarily soldiers in one form or another, but all of them appear able to read and write fluently when the occasion appears. The hero, then as now, was not a soldier of the ranks,
but he was a leader, as Othello, Macbeth, or Julius Caesar,
or as the knight of the Middle Ages whom he recalls.

In *The Duchess of Malfi* (1614) Julia, apparently a noble-
woman, at least a lady, who has erred in her moral ways,
persuades Bosola, a professional soldier, to pay court to her
on the grounds that "ignorance In court-ship cannot make
you do amisse." There is, for her, a natural breeding in such
a person as Bosola, which comes in part from his experience
as a soldier.[53] But neither Julia nor Bosola is a sympathetic
character, and therefore neither necessarily speaks the author's mind. It is much more probable that Webster would
have disagreed with Julia's attitude and have selected a
well-educated melancholic in preference to a blunt illiterate.

His protagonist of the same play, Antonio, is a thoughtful man, although he is capable of fighting when necessary.

Of Shakespeare's heroes in the love-plots, most are of the nobility or the higher middle class. Those who are of lower rank than the nobility have no visible means of livelihood, as Bassanio and Benedick, except, when it is made clear, the relatively precarious income of military service. Orlando, of *As You Like It,* is of much lower rank than Rosalind, who is the daughter of a duke. David L. Stevenson explains this courtship by saying: "It is only in Arden, one is made aware, that an unpropertied youth turned wrestler could meet and woo the outcast daughter of the duke."[54] It seems more likely, however, that Orlando, not really turned wrestler— he spends more time in the play writing verses than he does wrestling—might be compared with Rose of *The Shoemaker's Holiday,* and Rosalind with Sir Rowland Lacy.

Some differences of rank between lovers are merely, in Shakespeare, pretended in the course of a disguising, as in *The Winter's Tale,* and they logically resolve themselves in the *denouement* of the play. He has in his plays no marriage impossible from the standpoint of differences of rank, principally because he seldom raises the issue. Laertes's advice to Ophelia that she should not hope to marry Hamlet because

> He may not, as unvalued persons do,
> Carve for himself, for on his choice depends
> The safety and health of this whole state,[55]

is shown to be fallacious when Gertrude, who would necessarily know whether such a marriage would be possible or not, says over Ophelia's grave: "I hop'd thou shouldst have been my Hamlet's wife."

Helena, in love with Bertram in *All's Well That Ends Well,* feels that her love is hopeless because

> I am from humble, he from honoured name;
> No note upon my parents, his all noble.
> My master, my dear lord he is, and I
> His servant live and will his vassal die.[56]

That Shakespeare's dramatic attitude is similar to Dekker's is obvious from the marital solution of the play, a solution in which the author does not show any evidences of having strained his own credulity.

Occasionally the mixing of classes in marriage causes tragedy. One of the objections to Othello's marriage, he at least feels, is Desdemona's supposed higher rank:

> I fetch my life and being
> From men of royal siege; and my demerits
> May speak (unbonneted) to as proud a fortune
> As this that I have reach'd.[57]

The Cardinal does not state his objection to the marriage of the Duchess of Malfi to Antonio, but it is clear that his ostensible objection is to his rank. This is the primary cause of the play's tragic conclusion.

In general, while rank could be a bar, as Andreas suggests, before love's inception, once love had been felt by the participants, all barriers of rank were overcome. "For . . . no matter how much nobler one of the lovers is than the other, after they have begun to love they should walk in Love's court with equal steps."[58]

Love could come to a person through any of the senses, according to Ferrand. who wrote in 1640: " 'The evident causes of Love, according to the doctrine of the Morall Philosophers, & Platonists, are five; to wit, the five senses.' "[59] As might be expected from the courtly love tradition, the eyes were the most powerful inducement to love both subjectively and objectively: love entered by the eyes, and the eyes of the beloved were an inducement to love. "The objectivity of Elizabethan thinking is indeed nowhere more apparent than in the psychology of love. Affection normally enters the soul through the eye. By often gazing, according to Burton's quotation from Ficinus, men drink or suck in love between them."[60] The beloved also needed attractive eyes for courtship.

Monophylo found the eyes especially powerful:

. . . as there is diuersitie of beauties, so also euerie one enclining according to his perticuler fancie, some delightes in the properties of the minde, other takes pleasure in the personage, to some the state and maiestie of the continuance are a singuler felicitie, and to other, the facilitie and promptnesse of speeche, is the onely cause to kindle affection, but aboue all, the eye hath a supreme power, about the which the little *Cupid* flies and fleetes in ten thousand sortes and shapes.[61]

This concept was used by the dramatists of the time. Romeo finds power in the eye of Juliet when he says, under the balcony, as she looks at the sky: "Her eye discourses," and soon adds, "There lies more peril in thine eye Than twenty of their [Capulets'] swords."[62] Even the women admit the power in other women. Helena tells Hermia that her "eyes are lode-stars;" Lysander rhapsodizes to Helena:

> Reason becomes the marshal to my will
> And leads me to your eyes; where I o'erlook
> Love's stories, written in Love's richest book.[63]

Ford, as late as 1627, carried on the tradition in *'Tis Pity She's a Whore* when he has Giovanni say of Annabella:

> Such a pair of stars
> As are thine eyes would, like Promethean fire,
> If gently glanced, give life to senseless stones.[64]

The eyes could, however, be used by the man, also, in developing love in the beloved. Romeo found his eyes powerless in his campaign with Rosaline. He complains:

> She will not stay the siege of loving terms,
> Nor bide th' encounter of assailing eyes.[65]

Prospero, delighted at the immediate love of Ferdinand and Miranda in *The Tempest*, declares:

> At the first sight
> They have chang'd eyes.[66]

The speech of Phebe, then, in *As You Like It,* especially since it is by an unsympathetic character, pokes fun at a tradition which is nevertheless accepted by the lovers in the play. Phebe is a recalcitrant and here she is speaking to Silvius, whom she is repulsing:

> And if mine eyes can wound, now let them kill thee!
> Now counterfeit to swound; why, now fall down;
> Or if thou canst not, O, for shame, for shame,
> Lie not, to say mine eyes are murtherers!
> Now show the wound mine eye hath made in thee.
> Scratch thee but with a pin, and there remains
> Some scar of it; lean but upon a rush,
> The cicatrice and capable impressure
> Thy palm some moment keeps; but now mine eyes,
> Which I have darted at thee, hurt thee not,
> Nor I am sure there is no force in eyes
> That can do hurt.[67]

Phebe is no Rosalind to be taken seriously. She is a parody of the scornful shepherdess in Italian pastorals.

The speech of both the beloved and the lover should have more than mere charm of words. Castiglione advocates that one "eschue as much as a man may, and as a sharpe and daungerous rocke, too much curiousnesse, and (to speake a new word) to use in everye thing a certaine disgracing to cover arte withall, and seeme whatsoever he doth and saith, to doe it without paine, and (as it were) not minding it."[68]

When, in *The Raigne of K. Edward the Third* (1590), the King thinks of the Countess, his beloved, he soliloquizes:

> Shee is growne more fairer far since I came hither,
> Her voice more siluer euery word then other.[69]

Helena admits to Hermia that all find

> . . . your tongue's sweet air
> More tuneable than lark to shepherd's ear
> When wheat is green, when hawthorn buds appear.[70]

Ovid says of Julia in *The Poetaster* (1601):

> . . . he
> Which hears her speak, would swear the tuneful orbs
> Turned in his zenith only.[71]

Maria speaks of her beloved in *The Family of Love* (1602) when he addresses her from a trunk in her bedroom and she had thought him out of town:

> That accent sounds sweet music; 'tis my love!
> That tongue breathes life into my senseless spirits:
> Gerardine? o rapture![72]

Florizel, in *The Winter's Tale,* speaks specifically of Perdita's voice:

> When you speak, sweet,
> I'ld have you do it ever. When you sing,
> I'ld have you buy and sell so; so give alms;
> Pray so; and, for the ord'ring your affairs,
> To sing them too.[73]

Pleasant speech was important to later dramatists. Antcnio, speaking of the Duchess of Malfi, whom he serves as a steward and does not know that he will later marry, says:

> For her discourse, it is so full of Rapture,
> You onely will begin, then to be sorry
> When she doth end her speech, and wish (in wonder)
> She held it lesse vain-glory, to talke much,
> Then your pennance, to heare her.[74]

The voice of Beatrice, in *The Changeling* (1622), causes Alsemero to love her:

Beatrice. Which of the sciences is this love you speak of?
Alsemero. From your tongue I take it to be music.
Beatrice. You're skillful in it, can sing at first sight.[75]

These two factors had long been recognized as powerful inducements in awakening love. The recognition of the attractiveness of eyes and speech is, perhaps, the reason why a woman, to be considered modest (i.e., not looking for a lover), should lower or veil her eyes in public and speak only when spoken to. She should not use unadvisedly the advantages of two of beauty's most powerful weapons.

The main difficulty in having the lover recognize the beauty of voice was that a person often lost his voice as soon as he felt love. Suffolk says of Margaret in *1 Henry VI:*

Fain would I woo her, yet I dare not speak.
I'll call for pen and ink and write my mind.
Fie, de la Pole! disable not thyself.
Hast not a tongue? Is she not here thy prisoner?
Wilt thou be daunted at a woman's sight?
Ay, beauty's princely majesty is such
Confounds the tongue and makes the senses rough.[76]

So Claudio speaks of Benedick. He pretends to decide that
Benedick is in love because "his jesting spirit . . . is new-
crept into a lutestring, and now govern'd by stops."[77] Orlando, when he first sees Rosalind, in *As You Like It,* cannot
understand:

What passion hangs these weights upon my tongue?
I cannot speak to her, yet she urg'd conference.[78]

Rosalind behaves identically when she is alone with Celia:

Celia. Why, cousin! Why, Rosalind! Cupid have mercy! not a
word?
Rosalind. Not one to throw at a dog.[79]

The appeal of such lovers is their reality: lovers today feel
the same way.

The third physical aspect, that of dress, was not so important as the first two, although it could affect love. It is possible, Shakespeare showed over and over again, for a person
to fall in love with another person even though one or both
are in disguise. Thus, for instance, Florizel's affection for
Perdita, whom neither knows to be a princess, seems not to
be altered by her costume as a shepherdess. Thaisa falls in
love with Pericles even though his armor is rusty. Her father's
comment might have influenced her:

Opinion's but a fool, that makes us scan
The outward habit by the inward man.[80]

Andreas' member of the higher nobility speaks to his intended beloved on this subject, declaring that he has "put on
these worn-out clothes that you see to find out clearly whether
you honor a man of good character because of his clothes, or
the clothes because of the good character of the man."[81]

According to Castiglione, the dress of the lover should be
grave and not gay,[82] and in fashion; and the dress of the beloved such as to show her beauty and grace, not vain or friv-
olous.[83] Sir Thomas Elyot said of dress, in *The Governour:*
"So is there apparaile comely to every astate and degree, and
that whiche excedeth or lackethe procureth reproche, in a
noble man specially. For apparaile simple or scante, reproveth
hym of avarice. If it be alway exceeding precious, and often
tymes chaunged, as well in to charge as straunge and newe
facions, it causeth him to be noted dissolute of maners."[84]

But the dramatists seem to have varied considerably from
that ideal in their heroes, and in fact to have taken notice
mainly of slovenliness of dress, as Andreas mentions above.
This occurred, however, in the lover after he had fallen in
love, and therefore should denote a change from a former
and by implication better condition of dress. It is interesting
that the comments on dress appear to have been mainly critical. Dekker, the champion of the bourgeoisie, agrees with the
ideas of Elyot through the words of Agripyne in *Old Fortunatus* (1599):

Yet by my troth, we poor women do but smile in our sleeves to see
all this foppery: yet we all desire to see our lovers attired gallantly.
. . . But this apish monkey fashion of effeminate niceness, out
upon it! Oh, I hate it worse than to be counted a scold.[85]

Palamon, too, in *The Two Noble Kinsmen,* despises foppery:

> Why am I bound
> By any generous bond to follow him
> Follows his tailor, haply so long until
> The follow'd make pursuit? Or let me know
> Why mine own barber is unblest, with him
> My poor chin too, for 'tis not scissor'd just
> To such a favorite's glass?[86]

Other comments are uncomplimentary, of people in love. Mistress Glister accuses Maria of loving Gerardine in *The Family of Love:*

What? have not I observed the rising and falling of the blood, the coming and going of the countenance, your qualms, your unlacings, your longings? most evident tokens.[87]

Speed rallies his master for being in love:

> O, that you had mine eyes! or your own eyes had the lights they
> were wont to have when you chid at Sir Proteus for going
> ungarter'd!
> *Valentine.* What should I see then?
> *Speed.* Your own present folly and her passing deformity; for he,
> being in love, could not see to garter his hose; and you, being in
> love, cannot see to put on your hose.[88]

Ophelia is frightened when Hamlet assumes the garb of the affected lover. She tells Polonius of

> Lord Hamlet, with his doublet all unbrac'd,
> No hat upon his head, his stockings foul'd,
> Ungart'red, and down-gyved to his ankle.[89]

The woman and the man were both expected to dress well, neatly and in good taste until they were in love. Before love, they dressed so as to attract a member of the opposite sex: in Shakespeare's plays any slovenliness of dress was symptomatic of their love-sickness—their preoccupation.

After having fallen in love, they could afford to be slovenly in their dress in order to show that all their thoughts were concentrated on the beloved, as Speed apparently believes.[90] The lover had no time to affect an interest in dress, indeed his lack of interest was often affectation in itself.

The normal hero of a love affair had no visible means of support, but he did have an avocation. Most of the men, from Sir Rowland Lacy to Hamlet, had been soldiers at one time. "In feudal society, even more than now, warfare was conceded to be the most honorable employment; if Sir Rowland were to go to fight in the Low Countries, his uncle would have achieved the double purpose of separating him from Rose and directing the gadabout into a reputable occupation."[91]

Agripyne characterizes her ideal lover:

Me thinkes, a souldier is the most faithfull louer of all men els: for his affection stands not vpon complement: his wooing is plaine home-spun stuffe; theres no outlandish thred in it, no Rethoricke: A souldier casts no figures to get his mistris heart, his loue is like his valour in the field, when he payes downright blowes. . . . I loue a souldier best, for his plaine dealing.[92]

Bosola and Julia discuss the same theme in *The Duchess of Malfi:*

Bosola. Know you me, I am a blunt souldier.
Julia. The better,
       Sure, there wants fire, where there are no lively sparkes
       Of roughnes.
Bosola. And I want complement.
Julia. Why, ignorance in court-ship cannot make you do amisse.[93]

Henry V seeks to win Katherine not as a king but as a plain soldier:

But before God, Kate, I cannot look greenly nor gasp out my eloquence, nor I have no cunning in protestation; only downright oaths . . . I speak to thee plain soldier . . . take me, take a soldier; take a soldier, take a king.[94]

For many of the stage courtiers soldiering was pure avocation, but it brought with it honor which even Pistol recognized. Actually, at this time, "political conditions conspired with the unwarlike character of all the Tudors to shift the emphasis from military to civil service, and the knight became the gentleman, a man dedicated essentially to the pursuits of peace."[95]

But the dramatists were concerned with the ideal, generally of the past, and not with their present, real and tawdry. Thus the soldiers in Shakespeare's works are numerous. Romeo, while apparently not a soldier, demonstrates his fighting ability in the duel with Tybalt. And so it is with many of the protagonists in Shakespeare's plays.

Mental courage was of course identified with soldiering. If the lover were not a soldier he took, as Romeo, some other means of proving his courage. Pericles shows his courage in facing King Simonides:

King. Traitor, thou liest!
Pericles.   Traitor?
King.   Ay, traitor.
Pericles. Even in his throat—unless it be the King—
          That calls me traitor, I return the lie.
King. (aside) Now by the gods, I do applaud his courage.[96]

But the mere fact that he had been a soldier or was an ex-

soldier with an honorable discharge was sufficient testimony
to his courage.

> For gentle love and noble courage are
> So near allied that one begets another;
> Or Love is sister and Courage is the brother.
> Could I affect him better than before,
> His soldier's heart would make me love him more.[97]

Most of Shakespeare's lovers display courage at some time
before the conclusion of the play. Romeo fights and kills Tybalt after showing that he does not wish to fight but arousing
in the audience the feeling that he should fight to prove to
Tybalt his bravery. Earlier, under Juliet's balcony, he proves
his courage to Juliet merely by his daring to be in the garden
belonging to his enemies, the Capulets. Pericles, in a strange
court and in disguise, outfaces a king. Hamlet, despite the
warning of a sixth sense and the fears expressed by Horatio,
fights Laertes. Benedick, urged on by his beloved Beatrice,
challenges his best friend Claudio to a duel. "Courage . . .
was conspicuously an outward-looking virtue, as the Renaissance valued it. It looked both ways, to be sure; on the one
hand steeling a man to patient endurance of misfortune, to
equanimity before success, on the other spurring him to great
enterprises. But it was chiefly praised as a spur to action." It
was seldom called "fortitude," a word which had in it too
much of Christian forbearance and stoic passivity, but "courage," or even, and preferably, "valor." "This was the virtue
particularly needed by the gentleman in his capacity as defender of his country and the right. . . . This was of course
par excellence the virtue of the knight. . . . The gentleman,
though no less ready to prove his mettle in great and dangerous undertakings, saw no virtue in meeting danger for its own

sake."[98] This is precisely the case of Romeo when he refused to fight Tybalt.

Occasionally the hero shows his valor when he first meets his beloved. So Orlando is first seen by Rosalind when he is about to encounter Charles, the wrestler. This, since she speaks so often of it, is one of his attractions for her. Desdemona has fallen in love with Othello through mere accounts of his exploits:

> She lov'd me for the dangers I had pass'd,
> And I lov'd her that she did pity them.[99]

In all of the plays this trait is emphasized. Valentine shows courage in persuading the outlaws to accept him as their leader. Perhaps his lie that he has killed a man seems in poor taste in a man of valor, but it is motivated by his desire for keeping secret his love for Silvia. He could not tell the true reason for his leaving the court, because the true reason involved his beloved. Ferdinand, in *The Tempest,* shows his courage in his meeting with Prospero.

Logically, the display of courage should come either at the time of the first meeting of the lovers or, at least, before the declaration of love. Otherwise it could not be considered a prerequisite to love. Benedick is just returned from successful combat at the beginning of *Much Ado About Nothing,* for which Beatrice rallies him. Ophelia recognizes the exemplar of valor in Hamlet when he leaves her to mourn him as the ideal courtier, scholar, and soldier.[100]

In general, the lover was supposed to be chaste. "The virtues that were by common consent considered the most important for the gentleman were justice, prudence, courtesy, liberality, temperance, and fortitude."[101] A lover in the dramas

of the class of knighthood or gentility would have found
these virtues also essential. Glaphyro says:

beautie lyeth not altogither in the bodie, but hath also hir resi-
dence in the partes of the minde: the one is called beautie simplie,
and the other good behauiour, which consistes not onely in good
maners and outward fashions of conuersation, but also hath a
speciall perticipation wyth vertue, euen as the beautie of the bodie
restes not altogither in the lineamentes and features of the face,
but also in a good composition and vniuersal proporcion of all
the other parts of the bodie.[102]

Thus the Nurse describes Romeo as "an honest gentleman,
and a courteous, and a kind, and a handsome, and, I warrant,
a virtuous."[103] Bellafront, in *1 The Honest Whore* (1604),
tells Hippolito that what he has revealed to her is "That
which I love thee for (thy virtues)."[104] Don Pedro speaks of
Benedick as "of a noble strain, of approved valour, and confirm'd honesty."[105] And the Friar of *'Tis Pity She's A Whore*
perhaps epitomizes these general traits when he speaks of
Giovanni, the protagonist, as

>   . . . that miracle of wit
>   Who once, within these three months, wert esteem'd
>   A wonder of thine age throughout Bononia.
>   How did the University applaud
>   Thy government, behaviour, learning, speech,
>   Sweetness, and all that could make up a man![106]

The man, then, in order to be prepared for a love affair in
the drama of the period, had to be at least fourteen and probably one or two years older than that; of good rank, at least
knighthood or its sixteenth-century equivalent in the social
position of gentleman;[107] by avocation a soldier; well-dressed
without ostentation or affectation; of undisputed and proven

courage; and generally virtuous in the Christian sense of virtues as the concept had been transmitted through the age of
chivalry.

The girl had to be at least twelve, and she was usually
somewhat older than that; of a rank above the laboring
classes; well-dressed without affection; and beautiful both
physically and mentally. It was expected that she be chaste.

Heywood's ideal is in his description of Mrs. Frankford:

> First, her birth
> Is noble, and her education such
> As might become the daughter of a prince:
> Her own tongue speaks all tongues, and her own hand
> Can teach all strings to speak in their best grace,
> From the shrillest treble to the hoarsest base [*sic*].
> To end her many praises in one word,
> She's beauty's and perfection's eldest daughter,
> Only found by yours, though many a heart has sought her.[108]

Webster's Duchess of Malfi is even more beautiful, according to Antonio, who loves her:

> For her discourse, it is so full of Rapture,
> You will onely will begin, then to be sorry
> When she doth end her speech: and wish (in wonder)
> She held it lesse vain-glory, to talke much,
> Then your pennance, to heare her: whilst she speakes,
> She throwes upon a man so sweet a looke,
> That it were able to raise one to a Galliard
> That lay in a dead palsey; and to doate
> On that sweete countenance: but in that looke,
> There speaketh so divine a continence,
> As cuts off all lascivious, and vaine hope.
> Her dayes are practis'd in such noble vertue,
> That sure her nights (nay more her very Sleepes)

Are more in Heaven, then other Ladies Shrifts.
Let all sweet Ladies breake their flattring Glasses,
And dresse themselves in her. . . .
All her particular worth growes to this somme:
She staines the time past: lights the time to come.[109]

The Duchess is a widow, but such was nevertheless the ideal woman of the period.

The lovers first met in a place selected by the dramatist as one which could force plot complications. Therefore the location was generally semi-public: in a ballroom, a court or even a forest. Secondly, the location was under the control of the enemy, who usually, for many reasons, was personified in the beloved's father.

Romeo meets Juliet at a relatively public ball and is in danger of an encounter with Tybalt because the ball is in the Capulets' house, and they are enemies to Romeo's family. Ferdinand meets Miranda on an island under the complete control of her father Prospero. Claudio meets Hero in public on property under the control of her father, who eventually in the play proves to be Claudio's enemy for a time. The same is true of Valentine, who meets Silvia at her father's court where he is at first accepted and from which he is later banished. Orlando meets Rosalind at a wrestling match in which he is to be a participant, in a public place under the control of her uncle, who strenuously objects to Orlando's family. Oliver meets Celia in the forest which is under the jurisdiction of Rosalind's father, who could have disliked Oliver because of his evil treatment of his brother, Orlando.

The lovers are seldom formally introduced to each other. It was quite clearly the intention of the author that they love at first sight and not wait for introductions. The requirements mentioned above in this chapter, of nobility, courage, and chastity, would have been visible in the face. Many of Shake-speare's characters believe that there is an affinity between physical and moral beauty. When Marina finds Pericles sick on his bed and desires to be excused from telling her history because, she says, he will not believe her, he urges:

> Falseness cannot come from thee; for thou lookest
> Modest as Justice, and thou seem'st a palace
> For the crown'd truth to dwell in.[110]

So Polixenes says of the princess Perdita, disguised as a shepherdess and not even herself knowing her rank:

> This is the prettiest low-born lass that ever
> Ran on the greensward. Nothing she does or seems
> But smacks of something greater than herself,
> Too noble for this place.[111]

Romeo is immediately struck when he sees Juliet:

> Did my heart love till now? Forswear it, sight!
> For I ne'er saw true beauty till this night!

and Juliet during the same scene reveals what has happened to her:

> Go ask his name.—If he be married,
> My grave is like to be my wedding bed.[112]

If Juliet does not know his name, they have probably not even introduced themselves to each other. They would obviously not have been introduced by anyone present: the Capulets would have refused, and Romeo's friends could not have done it, since they do not recognize what has happened when they speak in the next scene.

Most of Shakespeare's lovers appear to fall in love at the first meeting. Beatrice, who has apparently been in love with

Benedick before the action of *Much Ado About Nothing,*
may have had a formal courtship earlier:

Pedro. Come, lady, come; you have lost the heart of Signior
  Benedick.
Beatrice. Indeed, my lord, he lent it me a while, and I gave him
  use for it—a double heart for his single one. Marry, once before
  he won it of me with false dice; therefore your Grace may well
  say I have lost it.[113]

In the case of the others, and possibly even including Beatrice
and Benedick although apparently not Hero and Claudio, the
matter is of love at first meeting, if not before. There seem
to be few exceptions to this in Shakespeare, and the evidence
for it is strong.

Angelo falls in love with Isabella,[114] Lucentio with Bianca,[115] and Rosalind with Orlando at first sight.[116] Rosalind
declares her love by giving her lover a guerdon immediately.[117] Orlando falls in love with Rosalind at the same time,
as he explains when he admits he cannot speak.[118]

Dekker used the tradition in *1 The Honest Whore.* Bellafront says to Hippolito: "I No sooner had laid hold upon
your presence, But straight mine eie conveied you to my
heart."[119] She and Hippolito are, however, introduced, and
they meet in her own home which is under her control.

Much was made of Marlowe's saw: "Whoever lov'd, that
lov'd not at first sight?"[120] and this was even paraphrased by
those who pretended to love. Franceschina, in *The Dutch
Curtezan* (1604) by John Marston, has a purpose in pretending love when she says:

. . . did you ever heare of any that loved at the first sight?
Malheureux. A thing most proper.
Franceschina. Now fait, I judge it all incredible, untill this houre
  I saw you pritty fayre eyes yout.[121]

Occasionally a hero falls in love without seeing his beloved, either from a picture, as William the Conqueror in *Fair Em:*

> No sooner had my sparkeling eyes beheld
> The flames of beautie blasing on this peece,
> But sodenly a sence of myracle,
> Imagined on thy louely Maistres face,
> Made me abandon bodily regarde,
> And cast all pleasures on my woonded soule:
> Then, gentle Marques, tell me what she is,
> That thus thou honourest on thy warlike shield,[122]

or by verbal description by someone who had seen her, as happened to Mucedorus (1590):

King of Valentia.   But what desire,
>   Or young-fed humour Nurst within the braine,
>   Drew him so privatly to Aragon?
Anselmo. A forcing Adamant:
>   Loue, mixt with feare and doubtfull ielousie,
>   Whether report guilded a worthlesse truncke,
>   Or Amadine deserued her high extolment.[123]

So naturally Henry VI could be persuaded to love by a description:

> Your wondrous rare description, noble Earl,
> Of beauteous Margaret hath astonish'd me.
> Her virtues, graced with external gifts,
> Do breed love's settled passions in my heart.[124]

There is generally danger, real or imagined, in the hero's being present at the place where he meets his beloved. Romeo is in danger when he meets Juliet, Ferdinand when he meets Miranda, Orlando when he meets Rosalind, Viola when she meets the Duke, and both Proteus and Valentine are in danger—although from different sources—when they fall in love with Silvia. There are exceptions to this, as Benedick and Beatrice in *Much Ado About Nothing,* but in general Shakespeare seems to find dramatic strength in the formula of combining love and physical danger.

When the lover meets the beloved in such a location under such circumstances, he falls in love immediately and, in Shakespeare, generally the love is returned as soon as it has developed in the lover, although the man may not recognize at the time that he is beloved. If the beloved does not see the lover, as Bianca apparently does not see Lucentio in *The Taming of the Shrew,* it will be impossible for her immediately to love.

The violence of the love in the development of the play can be judged by the violence of the return of the love. Romeo and Juliet, for instance, are so strongly attracted that they cannot keep apart. Juliet makes no modest refusals before accepting her lover, although she excuses herself for acting as precipitously as she does. All that keeps them apart the first night is that Juliet's bedroom is as crowded with the Nurse and Lady Capulet as the ballroom below had been earlier. The violence of such love is emphasized by Shakespeare because it is so important to the plot. The love of Rosalind and Orlando, of vital importance, is shown immediately through actions of Rosalind, who will take the initiative in the courtship throughout the play, as does the active Romeo of his play. The love of Oliver and Celia is relatively unimportant to the action of *As You Like It,* and so it is related as having occurred offstage. But even in this case, from the description by Rosalind, the love is violent. The love of Ferdinand and Miranda flames as soon as they encounter.

In three of these cases, those of Romeo, Oliver, and Ferdi-

nand, there is really little need for any of the courtly pining
and *hereos*. But in most of the plays the lover finds it impossible to declare his love immediately, either because of the
place or the lack of introduction, or because of the scorn of
the beloved or the exigencies of disguise. Therefore he retires to his home to develop the symptoms of the disease
of *hereos*, which increase until he is able to speak of his love
to his mistress in one of a number of ways which will be
dealt with in Chapter IV. His *hereos* will be the subject of
the succeeding chapter.

Chapter III

DEVELOPMENT: THE LOVERS APART

Now THAT the lover has seen his beloved and recognized her as such, he retreats from the encounter stricken with *hereos,* the illness which traditionally comes to all who fall in love. This grows progressively worse as the two continue apart, and it endures until the cure can be effected. The lover may not recognize the disease by name—the word is not used in Shakespeare, and the *New English Dictionary* does not list it—but he does very soon realize that he is suffering from lovesickness. The interesting feature of the Elizabethan treatment is the emphasis on the woman's suffering from *hereos* herself. Previous literature had represented women as having the disease, but the authors, telling of the courtship from the viewpoint of the lover, had been less interested in the condition of the beloved. Now, however, the bourgeoisie felt the woman relatively more important than before, an attitude which they inherited from the nobility of earlier times. This courtly attitude, combined with the inherited middle-class belief in woman's share in home affairs, caused in bourgeois literature, especially the drama, the new emphasis on the feelings of the woman in *fine amor*. The Criseyde of the four-teenth century, the Dame Elinor and Ferinda of the early sixteenth century, became the suffering Mariana and Helena of Shakespeare. Certainly they were different characters, but in that very difference lies the importance of the change.

This, together with the shift to a new kind of love, brought to the stage a view of courtly love which has persisted to the middle of the twentieth century: that its rituals be accepted but its desired culmination of clandestinely relieved lust be rejected.

Shakespeare and the earlier generation of Elizabethan dramatists received from their environment and from their associates the tradition of courtly love, but it had been changed, for reasons already suggested, so that the writers of the late sixteenth century made a relatively sharp distinction between courtly and romantic love.

Romantic love, as used in this paper, is, then, the ritualistic courtship by which a man and woman proceed to express a desire for physical and mental relationship which can be fulfilled only after a public ceremony of recognition of the union. A somewhat oversimplified definition of the distinction is that courtly love is sincere, but with its focus upon seduction; romantic love is sincere, but with its focus upon marriage.

Glaphyro is the speaker for the traditional *fine amor* attitude when he says in *Monophylo:*

for a man to fall in maryage into the handes of hir whom he had long pursued in loue, is the thing which aboue all other he ought most to feare: for where afore he professed the state of hir seruant and slaue, with a prompt readinesse to runne vnder hir commaundements, his condicion being now chaunged by reason of maryage, he altereth also his authoritie, chalengyng an empyre and souereigntie ouer hir, wherunto she is hardly brought considering hir experience in hir former preheminence.[1]

This would seem to be anomalous, for what man, having been a slave, would not desire to be king? But Glaphyro's point is not that the man should not desire to control his wife but that he will have difficulty in so succeeding. And his reasons are not so important as is his conclusion. Glaphyro is a man interested in the chase and, undoubtedly, in the capture, but not, to strain the metaphor, in the kill. He does not wish to be encumbered with the prize for any length of time.

Such a concept as Glaphyro's had long been fought by the Church and by other organized forces of society as tending to break down the social structure through a weakening of the prestige of the family.[2] The U.S.S.R., in the twentieth century, tried for a time a plan of free love, but that country's government soon found that the resulting anarchy destroyed the family and thereby tended to undermine the larger social consciousness necessary to the maintenance of the state. It was some time after the October Revolution that Lenin began limiting free love, and now the rigor of the laws in the U.S.S.R. has so increased that divorce is almost impossible.[3]

Such, too, was the pressure of sixteenth-century English society. And although Glaphyro's argument would have interested everyone and found acceptance by some, yet the social disapproval in both France and England was so persuasive that the author could take a strong moral position against such a concept. Although Fenton does not completely agree even with Monophylo, he comes much closer to agreement with him than with Glaphyro. And Monophylo, the most sympathetic of the characters, favors romantic love:

Loue is then a power lying betweene the two worse extremities, not setting his originall vpon this common lust, and yet, though long he doe reiect it, at last he doth admit it: the same being the cause (as I beleeue) why all our church lawes in the conformation of a true mariage (wherein ought to consist the marke and ende of true friendship) require not but the consent of the parties: as though this true loue of mariage ought not to pass but vnder a conformitie of mindes, and not by any lust or suggestion of the fleshe.[4]

This, romantic love, is not vitally different from courtly

love except in its culmination. Both Glaphyro and Monophylo would have proceeded by a similar road to the union of mind and body—through conversation and physical achievement. But Glaphyro was not interested in burdening himself for life, physically, mentally, and financially, with one woman. Monophylo and most Elizabethans of the later sixteenth century apparently were.

Therefore, if this last theory as to romantic and courtly love be correct, there should be little difference in the *hereos* suffered by each of the lovers. There had been no serious challenge to the classification of *hereos* as described by Galen and Rhazes. The central distinction between Glaphyro and Monophylo lay in the culmination desired, and this dichotomy had further split by the time of Shakespeare so that there were really three separate groups of lovers.

1. One lover believed the entire pursuit an intellectual game, and he set out gaily to play to win. The reward was the ennoblement of himself. Any other achievement he desired was only as some slight evidence that he had interested the lady more than had other men.

He intended to keep his love at the level of adoration, on a non-physical plane. This is the "pure" love discussed by Andreas, deriving ultimately from Plato, which

binds together the hearts of two lovers with every feeling of delight. This kind consists in the contemplation of the mind and the affection of the heart; it goes as far as the kiss and the embrace and the modest contact with the nude lover, omitting the final solace, for that is not permitted to those who wish to love purely.[5]

If he sincerely believes in the game he plays, the lover worships his beloved religiously and veers from any conscious desire to touch her more than for the occasional "holy" embrace. He is the follower of Cardinal Bembo, who in *The Courtier* addresses Love as, "Thou most beautifull, most good, most wise, art derived of the unitie of the heavenly beautie, goodnesse and wisedom, and therein dost thou abide, and unto it through it, (as in a circle) turnest about."[6] Love to him is as much the supreme cosmic force, the expression of God, as it is now to the Christian Scientist. He believes that to love beauty and goodness and wisdom is to love God, and vice versa.

Such men found that the trait in women they most admired was their power to cause a man to be ennobled and thereby to approach God. "This Platonic 'religion' of love and beauty extended a wide sway over Renaissance courtly society from the circles of Isabella d'Este, Vittoria Colonna, and Elizabetta Gonzaga in Italy, to those of Marguerite of Navarre in varying degrees of sincerity involved."[7]

However, the natural increase of love eventually brought most of these men to the point of requiring some union with the beloved. Mental union for most was impossible, and presently the lover declared his desire for physical consummation as an expression of the love. Such consummation, as many of the love-philosophers realized, was necessary. What else could be the culmination of an affair? Andreas himself had admitted the possible necessity of physical relations if either lover desired them on the grounds that "all lovers are bound, when practicing Love's solaces, to be mutually obedient to each other's desires."[8] Even Monophylo is forced to believe in physical relations, although his love is presented as ideal and intellectually real.[9]

Cardinal Bembo describes as spiritual the culmination of love as it transcends earthly beauty to a contemplation of heavenly beauty:

For like as through the particular beautie of one bodie [love] guideth [the soul] to the universall beautie of all bodies: Even so in the least degree of perfection through particular understanding hee guideth her to the universall understanding. Thus the soule kindled in the most holy fire of true heavenly love, fleeth to couple her selfe with the nature of Angels, and not onely cleane forsaketh sense, but hath no more neede of the discourse of reason, for being chaunged into an Angell, she understandeth all thinges that may be understood: and without any veil or cloud, she seeth the maine sea of the pure heavenly beautie and receiveth it into her, and enjoyeth the soveraigne happinesse, that can not be comprehended of the senses.[10]

This is the Platonic doctrine of non-physical love, and if this ideal could be achieved the lover had reached, as Cardinal Bembo admits implicitly, a deific state at which he transcended mortal failings. But such a state was beyond the power of mortal men, and such men as the Cardinal describes could exist only in ideal and unreal literature.

This lover might well be designated, as Plato described the most perfect lover in the *Phaedrus,* the non-physical lover. He loves the beautiful, and when his soul is one which has lately come to earth after a view of Divinity,

when he beholds a fact of aspect divine well copying the Beautiful, or an ideal bodily form, first he shudders, and something of the terror he then had comes over him; anon, as he gazes at the object, he reveres it as if it were a god, and if he were not afraid that men would think him downright mad, he would bow down to his love with offerings as if it were a graven image and a god indeed.[11]

The non-physical lover desires such a love and wishes to accept as its apex a spiritual union. But most men cannot successfully carry out such an intellectual course.

The kiss was a common greeting, adopted long before by

the barbaric Europeans from the admired oriental society.[12]
But even that touch could denote more than a mere greeting;
it could arouse a man to lust or even love: "yea oftentymes a
sweete kisse receiued of a delicate Ladie, breathes such a poy-
son, as there is no arte to purge it."[13] Also, at this time, the
kiss was a part of a spousal. Thus a kiss could be the equivalent of a handshake, an inducement to physical excitement,
or a formality in the marriage or spousal ceremony.

A kiss, then, had no meaning or all meanings. It was not a
definite culmination. But any act of physical contact beyond
the mere kiss tended to lead to the folly of arousing emotions beyond immediate control.

Therefore, whether the participants wished to realize it or
not, the desire of the courtly and romantic lovers, as well as of
the lovers who considered the entire relationship intellectual,
was for physical fulfillment as expression of monogamous
love. This is the decision of the debaters in Fenton's *Monophylo,* and it is the attitude expressed on the stage of the late
sixteenth century. Fenton logically proves the concept by
analogy:

what is he in the worlde that loues not chiefelye for that ende, and
yet (sir) not to assure my self vpon so fraile a iudgement, I praye
you tell me, if the loue of a man to a woman pretended not but to
the minde, why shoulde we feele the same to passion vs, sometime
with a white winde of ioye, and from thence to a storme of sor-
rowe, and then sodainely become as ouerwhelmed with quail-
enesse of feare. And in the friendeship of man to man, we are
touched with no such torment, sauing that in this last we holde our
selues satisfied to be beloued of them, and the same beeing knowne
vnto vs, we haue alreadie touched the poynt of our pretence.[14]

2. A lover of the second group wished to possess the lady
without the necessity of marriage. He believed that this was

more possible in an affair with a married woman than in one
with an unmarried girl. His desire to avoid marriage led him
to haunt the society of married women. He was the courtly
lover, the continuer of the *fine amor* tradition of the past
centuries who persisted in smaller numbers and with less
praise than before.

To Plato he would have been the physical lover, completely
non-intellectual and seeking the physical possession of his
beloved with little or no consideration of her mental qualities.

3. A lover of the third group had as his object matrimony.
He fell in love with a girl to whom he felt he had been fated,
and he attempted to find some means of marrying her for
the establishment of a family. True, the other lovers might
well feel that they had been fated to the girl they loved, but
the idea that the union should be marital had a newly assumed importance in the late sixteenth century.[15] Troilus had
not mentioned matrimony, Gascoigne's F. J. avoided it.

All these lovers suffered, in varying degrees, *hereos*. The
belief of the dramatists under discussion that a lover of the
third class suffered more severely than the others is merely a
comment on the lover's sincerity, not on his susceptibility. He
is the hero to a bourgeoisie assuming increasing importance.[16]

An example of this division of the lovers of the late sixteenth century into these three groups could best be found
in a character who has experienced at least two of the aspects.
Romeo, when he loves Rosaline, is suffering from *hereos,* but
the disease is quite clearly artificial. He is in love with her
because he feels he should be in love with someone. When he
falls in love with Juliet his *hereos* becomes "real" in the
sense that it is sympathetically portrayed, is returned, and,
by implication, is viewed sympathetically by the audience.
Shakespeare succeeds in following strictly the courtly tradi-

tion in the two loves by having Romeo, in the affair with
Rosaline, change his love, in accordance with one of Andreas'
rules,[17] and leave her without a repentant thought after meeting Juliet, and by having him, in his relation with Juliet, obey
another rule[18] beyond requirement by committing suicide
after he has lost her. To Romeo, Rosaline is the object of the
game of *fine amor* and Juliet the sincere object of a romantic
love which he feels to be his entire life. Romeo exemplifies
traits of the first and third types of lovers described above.

Lovers of all three types could suffer *hereos,* and in each
case to a similar degree. Those of the second type, with some
exceptions, were inclined to avoid *hereos* so that the author
could point out to the audience their insincerity. Roderigo, in
his pursuit of Desdemona, is an example of the second type.
He pretends to some of the manifestations of the disease, as
when he insists, "I will incontinently drown myself,"[19] but
his emotions are closely controlled by the cynic Iago, whose
"Put money in thy purse," once Roderigo accepts it as valid
advice, becomes a reminder to the audience of the falseness of
Roderigo's love. For even the lover in *fine amor,* says Andreas,
should not become involved financially. "If any woman is so
possessed with a feeling of avarice as to give herself to a
lover for the sake of pay, let no one consider her a lover, but
rather a counterfeiter of love, who ought to join those shameful women in the brothel."[20] So Roderigo, so badly misjudg-
ing Desdemona in believing she could be purchased, forces
the audience, sympathetic to Desdemona, to find fault with
Roderigo in believing her avaricious. The man who would
ask that his gifts be returned before he "will give over [his]
suit and repent [his] unlawful solicitations"[21] has an attitude
toward love which both Shakespeare and Andreas decry. Thus

Roderigo is fubbed by Iago and mocked by the author for his adulterous love.[22]

The lover, after his cataclysmic vision of his beloved described in the previous chapter, suffered first internally from the effects. The two parts of the body most severely affected were the heart and the mind. The function of other organs, such as the tongue and the eyes, might later be impaired, but the first two so afflicted were invisible to any observer.

Of the physical organs the heart, the seat of the affections, suffered the most. According to Burton, the heart is controlled by the mind: ". . . the *brain* must needs primarily be misaffected, as the seat of *reason;* and then the *heart,* as the seat of affection."[23] In Elizabethan writings and earlier, the heart was often confused with inclination or desire or impulse, and opposed to the mind for a contrast of intellect with emotion. Its advantage was that it was hidden, and therefore its love was somewhat secret, although the eyes unfortunately were a window to the heart, and unless their shades were drawn, the curious might easily peer in. Thus Monophylo was plainly in love, the author declares, because "by the onely heauie and deade cariage of his eye, might be discerned the secret passion and disposition of his heart."[24] The heart could receive persons or impressions of persons which it could usefully retain. Jonson's Ovid, forbidden his Julia, soliloquizes: "She's in thy heart; rise, then, and worship there."[25] It was further separable from the body in its figurative sense, for Helena tells Hermia of "A foolish heart that I leave here behind . . . With Demetrius."[26] It could palpitate under the stress of emotion, as Leontes found when he became jealous of Hermione and Polixenes: "I have tremor cordis on me; my heart dances, But not for joy; not joy,"[27] and in the same

sense it could suffer physical pain, even when it belonged
to a more ardent mocker of love:

Rosalind. . . . O, how full of briers is this working-day world!
Celia. They are but burrs, cousin, thrown upon thee in holiday
foolery. If we walk not in the trodden paths, our very petticoats
will catch them.
Rosalind. I could shake them off my coat. These burrs are in my
heart.[28]

Apparently it was capable of some kind of procreation: the
Duchess of Malfi says quite seriously, "Goe, go brag You
have left me heartlesse—mine is in your bosom, I hope
'twill multiply love there."[29]

These were the emotional reactions to the love generally
caused by the image of the beloved transmitted through the
eyes of the lover.[30] The impression was received through the
lens and imprinted, as on a photographic plate, on the heart.
The picture could be identified with the actual object, which
might well explain why Lucentio in *The Taming of the Shrew*
and Proteus in *The Two Gentlemen of Verona* wanted pictures of their beloveds. If the picture were imprinted on the
heart, as Jonson's Ovid comments, that was a welcome substitute for the actual person.

The mind, too, was influenced by the beloved. One of the
rules of Andreas Capellanus was that the lover think constantly of his beloved,[31] and the tradition seems to have persisted through the Elizabethan age; a man could not consider
his beloved everything if he ever thought of anything else.

Monophylo had outlined the aspect for his century in the
generation before Shakespeare as

to haue the thought cleare from all corrupt motions, as neyther to
aspire by ymagination, nor attempt by pollicie, howe so euer the

season or oportunitie doe fauor: for who maketh profession of
true loue ought so to brydle hys sturring lustes to all other women,
that so much lesse he performe any desire, which you say to be
natural, but also the will or disposition of so doing doe not once
fall into hys mindc.[32]

The behavior of most characters of Elizabethan romantic or
love dramas shows that they have but one love. When they
have more than one or exhibit any degree of profligacy, the
author himself censures them or so presents them that the
audience will do so.

Angelo is treated as perfidious by Shakespeare and is forced
back into a marriage with Mariana which it is apparent
neither will long enjoy. Similarly, Bertram is finally captured
by Helena through his very lusts. He is depicted as luxurious
in order to motivate adequately his attempted adultery, which
the Elizabethan audience would not have condoned otherwise.[33] Proteus, changing women too rapidly in *The Two
Gentlemen of Verona,* gets into trouble because his second
love is already betrothed. Such cases are selected at random.
Shakespeare's sympathetic characters do not actually love two
women at thc samc timc, and that poinl is quite clearly made
in cach play concerned. Even fickle Cressida is shown as faulty
in not loving Troilus. Thus, when she falls in love with
Diomedes, she does not violate Andreas's rule[34] by loving
both Troilus and Diomedes at the same time. She loves in
succession, not concurrently, and the fault lies in her haste
and time-serving.

Hippolito, in *2 The Honest Whore* (1605),[35] is the most
obvious example of such duplicity. He dotes on a mistress
while married. But the point even there is made that he does
not love his wife at the same time that he does the mistress.

The hero invariably loves only one person at a time, and

while he is in love with her he spends all his efforts in seeking her favors. This concentration is so intense that he often
becomes absent-minded and incapable of dealing adequately
with other matters. Edward III, talking with Audley and
Darby, cannot concentrate on war:

> *King.* Then let those foote trudge hence vpon those horse
>   According too our discharge, and be gonne.—
>   Darby, Ile looke vpon the Countesse minde anone.
> *Darby.* The Countesse minde, my liege?
> *King.* I meane the Emperour:—leaue me alone.[36]

Phebe behaves in the same way in *As You Like It*. When
Rosalind, disguised as Ganymede, causes Phebe to love her,
Silvius can attract her attention only with difficulty:

> *Silvius.* Sweet Phebe—
> *Phebe.*   Ha! what say'st thou, Silvius?[37]

And Romeo epitomizes the trait of concentration in his exit
line to Benvolio, who is trying to take Romeo's mind from
concentration on Rosaline: "Farewell. Thou canst not teach
me to forget."[38]

The characters seldom discuss this absolute fidelity, apparently because it is taken for granted. The lover has to
think constantly of his beloved. If he does not, if he considers mundane matters of war or clothing, he is not in love.

The lover, as soon as his head and heart have been affected
by his beloved, sets her so high that he no longer considers
her human, and he states and apparently believes that she is
superhuman. This deification of the beloved occurs often in
speech and action. As Tristram literally worshipped his Ysolt
in the grotto in which he had built an image of her,[39] so many
late sixteenth-century dramatic characters deify their beloveds.

Their speech might be extravagant in some cases, but it would be incredible if it were so in all; the persistence of the belief in deification obviates such a conclusion. Other characters, describing the condition of the lover, believe that he worships his beloved. The identification of the adored woman with a goddess is frequent, and she becomes the object of various forms of religious ritual. So Monophylo, describing a luckless friend who has fallen in love with an ugly girl,[40] says that

sometimes (in an ydolatrous regarde to hyre) he blasphemes openly all other women, as not to holde value and comparison with hir, in whome (if loue be to be measured by that beautie you speake of) there is no one sparke or part of such perfection: sometimes againe he sets hir in his minde as an oracle or Goddesse of contemplacion, raysing hir even vnto the highest heauens, with hymnes & prayses, drawing hir excellencies into partes, & (as it were with a pensell) leauing no part vntouched with high reuerence & deuocion.[41]

And he has taken the deification for granted earlier when he says:

. . . if . . . euery one bent his deuocion to hir in whome reposed his whole religion, we should cutte of all the paynes and traueyles which we see at this day reigne amongst worldlings.[42]

Thus it would seem quite natural that Mucedorus address Amadine: "Most gracious goddesse, more than mortal wight, Your heauenly hewe of right imports no lesse."[43] Jonson's Ovid goes even further:

> Here, on my knees, I worship the blest place
> That held my Goddess; and in the loving air,
> That closed her body in his silken arms:
> Vain Ovid! kneel not to place, nor air;
> She's in thy heart; rise, then, and worship there.[44]

Mounchensey, in *The Merry Devil of Edmonton* (1602), says to Millicent, his beloved: "I'll be thy votary, we'll often meet."[45] Wendoll soliloquizes on Mrs. Frankford when he is trying to persuade himself to avoid seducing her:

> . . . prayers are meditations;
> And when I meditate (O God, forgive me!)
> It is on her divine perfections.[46]

Chapman's Rinaldo says to the loving Fortunio:

> For I am witness . . .
> Both to the daily and the nightly service
> You do unto the deity of love,
> In vows, sighs, tears, and solitary watches.[47]

Middleton's Beatrice tells Vermandero:

> I shall change my saint, I fear me; I find
> A giddy turning in me.[48]

Ford's Annabella cannot see the humanity of Giovanni:

> But see, Putana, see! what blessed shape
> Of some celestial creature now appears![49]

And Giovanni himself see his blasphemy in deification when he declares:

> O, that it were not in our religion sin
> To make our love a god and worship it![50]

There should, then, be no difficulty in assuming that Shakespeare's characters were not merely speaking in hyperbole when they made similar declarations.

Proteus. Was this the idol that you worship so?
Valentine. Even she; and is she not a heavenly saint?
Proteus. No; but she is an earthly paragon.
Valentine. Call her divine.[51]

Proteus, a sixteenth-century realist in that he cannot recognize a human being as divine, is an unsympathetic character in *The Two Gentlemen of Verona*. He it is who leaves one beloved to fall immediately in love with the beloved of his best friend, thus voiding his previous spousal *de futuro,* and developing the central theme of the play—love versus friendship. He soon shows how impure his second love really is by his attempted rape of Silvia.

The views of such a character might well be taken rather lightly, and, since Valentine is presented as a young hero in love, his ideas are probably considered more valid than Proteus's by the author and his audience.

Lucentio, another sympathetic even though formalized character, says of his Bianca: "Sacred and sweet was all I saw in her."[52]

Romeo's attitude toward Juliet is perhaps too well known to require quotation here. He addresses her as "saint"[53] and begins his courtship of her at the ball with:

> If I profane with my unworthiest hand
> This holy shrine.[54]

Juliet's reaction to Romeo is similar, and her language so closely approaches that of Giovanni recently quoted[55] as to confirm that women, too, could love to deification:

> . . . if thou wilt, swear by thy gracious self,
> Which is the god of my idolatry.[56]

Lysander speaks of Helena as an impartial observer:

> Demetrius, I'll avouch it to his head,
> Made love to Nedar's daughter, Helena,
> And won her soul; and she (sweet lady) dotes,
> Devoutly dotes, dotes in idolatry,
> Upon this spotted and inconstant man.[57]

His objection is not to her deification but to its object. Is Rosalind, then, mocking when she uses the word to describe Orlando's conduct?

. . . There is a man haunts the forest that abuses our young plants with carving "Rosalind" on their barks; hangs odes upon hawthorns, and elegies on brambles; all, forsooth, deifying the name of Rosalind.[58]

Helena says of Bertram:

> But now he's gone, and my idolatrous fancy
> Must sanctify his relics. . . .
>   . . . Thus, Indian-like,
> Religious in mine error, I adore
> The sun, that looks upon his worshipper
> But knows of him no more.[59]

Miranda and Ferdinand tell the audience they are in love by declaring deification:

Miranda. I might call him
        A thing divine; for nothing natural
        I ever saw so noble,

and Ferdinand, not hearing her, soliloquizes:

> Most sure, the goddess
> On whom these airs attend![60]

D'Urfé, in the contemporary *L'Astrée*, concluded:

le bien dont amour recompense les fidelles amans, est celuy-la mesme qu'il peut donner aux dieux, et a ces hommes qui s'esclavant par dessus la nature des hommes, se rendent presque Dieux.[61]

There is nothing strange in the fact that the lover should look upon his beloved as being more than mortal. The long tradition of the woman's sovereignty and the man's servitude, the Platonic concept of man and woman as having been divinely divided from an original union, and the natural habit of man to deify that which is superior, would all tend to the literal deification of the beloved, especially in the period of *hereos*. The unusual aspect here in the late sixteenth century, as in other matters of *hereos,* is the woman's susceptibility to the disease.

The state of mind induced by deification would lead to physical manifestations of *hereos*. The lover, loving in truth, assumes many of the aspects of the religious. As many nuns of the earlier times were accused of confusing the spiritual Jesus with the physical man in their adoration, so the lover, adoring a physical woman, confusedly elevates her to the mystic realm of deification.

The internal sufferings from *hereos,* since they are not visible either to other characters or to an audience, are manifested by speech or action. Deification is, of course, most easily shown by speech, but the affecting of the heart and the absorption could also be stated, as shown above. Whether such are mere statements of fact or are overstatements is of dubious importance; they are mentioned in circumstances of seriousness and are accepted as true by characters in the various works.

The external manifestations of *hereos* are more easily recognized than the internal, but these, too, according to stage traditions of the sixteenth century, are revealed in speech rather than stage make-up, and action is conveyed in the same way. Thus it is even now possible to interpret the activities of the sixteenth-century stage lovers through the words which they and their fellow-characters spoke.

Apparently the most common external symptoms of *hereos*

are weeping and sighing. So the lover acts when he cannot win his beloved; when he cannot see her; or when he is, after achievement, separated from her in the Ordeal. At present, or in the present discussion of the lover, between the period of his first meeting with his beloved and his first opportunity to further his suit, the mood of sadness is as strong as it could be in the post-nuptial separation of the Ordeal.

The Elizabethan wept easily; tears could be evoked as part of the game of love as well as for sincere or romantic emotion. Thus Friar Laurence exclaims to Romeo:

> Jesu Maria! What a deal of brine
> Hath wash'd thy sallow cheeks for Rosaline!
> How much salt water thrown away in waste,
> To season love, that of it doth not taste!
> The sun not yet thy sighs from heaven clears,
> Thy old groans ring yet in mine ancient ears.
> Lo, here upon thy cheek the stain doth sit
> Of an old tear that is not washed off yet.
> If e'er thou wast thyself and these woes thine,
> Thou and these woes were all for Rosaline.
>
> .   .   .   .
>
> O, she knew well
> Thy love did read by rote, that could not spell.[62]

Still, when Romeo is sincerely in love with Juliet and banished from her before they have been able to consummate their marriage, he expresses his *hereos* in much the same way. When the Nurse inquires for her "lady's lord," the Friar points him out, "There on the ground, with his own tears made drunk."[63] It cannot be assumed that the tears for Juliet are any more real than those for Rosaline. Both express frustration. Romeo has admitted early of Rosaline that

> She will not stay the siege of loving terms,
> Nor bide th'encounter of assailing eyes,
> Nor ope her lap to saint-seducing gold.[64]

And the mere distinction between the psychosomatic and the romantic does not necessarily affect the degree of the suffering.

Dekker recognizes that sometimes the weeping requires previous training. It was, apparently, part of the education of some courtiers that they learn to produce tears at will. Agripyne does not praise such insincerity, but she recognizes its existence when she speaks of the "spruce silken-faced courtier, that stands every morning two or three hours learning how to . . . sigh by his glas."[65] Perhaps Romeo, in his weeping for Rosaline, is exhibiting the results of such training. But Shakespeare does not say so, and the only evidence that such weeping could have been insincere lies in the quick change of love, which, by courtly rules, was perfectly legal, and in the Friar's comments, more humorous than sympathetic. He treats in a similar derisive temper Romeo's condition when he is separated from Juliet, and therefore the only good evidence that there is now a difference in Romeo's condition is that of his degree of constancy and his achievement. Such evidence does not prove the weeping insincere, and it is quite clear that Shakespeare does not intend to differentiate the two cases of *hereos*.

Silvius, who is Shakespeare's picture of a pastoral lover, knows the rules of *hereos*. When Phebe prompts him to define love, he replies, "It is to be all made of sighs and tears,"[66] and the quick concurrence of Phebe, Orlando, and Rosalind seems to show that Shakespeare adopts the convention whether or not he believes it to be a reflection of reality.

Even Jonson's Propertius, when he has been separated from

his beloved by her death, shows lasting sorrow, and when a group comments on his feelings he chides them:

> Speak they of griefs, that know to sigh, and grieve:
> The free and unconstrained spirit feels
> No weight of my oppression.

On this Ovid comments:

> Worthy Roman.
> Methinks I taste his misery; and could
> Sit down and chide at his malignant stars,

and Julia adds, not wavering from her love for Ovid:

> Methinks I love him, that he loves so truly.[67]

How could one distinguish true from simulated love, sincere from insincere? As has been shown, Romeo himself is by no means certain of the difference until he meets Juliet. Apparently the distinction could be shown most accurately only in the results, and best through the single-mindedness of the lover. A lover could suffer *hereos* from either true or simulated love. If he is able, through self-persuasion, to be constant to one woman, achieved or unachieved, he is in love so long as he shows the traits of *hereos* pertinent to the situation. Since *hereos* is the proof of love, the disease and the love could not very well be separated, nor could the veracity of sincerity of the feeling be adequately analyzed either by the sufferer or the onlooker. Therefore, so far as can be inferred from the dramatic works of the period, the man is in love until he stops loving or is cured of his disease. If he does not change, he is in love for ever.

Weeping is not the exclusive prerogative of the lover, for the woman, too, is susceptible to *hereos*.[68] Such a relatively new concept had developed from the equalization of the sexes, for in earlier ages the sovereign position of the woman in courtship had kept her immune to the disease. Dame Elinor, for instance, in Gascoigne's work, had suffered little. With the belief that marriage was the cure of *hereos* had come concurrently the idea that both man and woman might love to such a degree as to exhibit the familiar symptoms. Juliet is fully as much in love as is Romeo, for when the Nurse finds Romeo weeping on the floor of the Friar's cell, she comments:

> O, he is even in my mistress' case,
> Just in her case! . . .
> Even so lies she,
> Blubbering and weeping, weeping and blubbering,[69]

and Lady Capulet emphasizes the real cause of Juliet's weeping when she misunderstands and expresses wonder at Juliet's inordinate affection for Tybalt:

> Evermore weeping for your cousin's death?[70]

Claudio lies about Beatrice's expressions of love for Benedick in the entrancing scenes of foolery designed to persuade Beatrice and Benedick to admit their love for each other. The important fact for the present purpose is that Benedick finds Claudio's tale credible. He does not find anything absurd in Beatrice's actions as described by Claudio:

Then down upon her knees she falls, weeps, sobs, beats her heart, tears her hair, prays, curses—"O sweet Benedick! God give me patience."[71]

On the contrary he finds that these actions form incontrovertible evidence of her love for him. Here again, then, Shakespeare's characters imply that love may be shown by such evidence of *hereos* as weeping, and, conversely, that weeping, unless there is some other visible cause—as Juliet's mother found—to explain it, connotes unfulfilled love. Beatrice's deportment as described by Claudio might very well have denoted merely her impatience with the acerbity of Benedick's tongue. But the action of the play shows clearly that Benedick and all the other characters accept such behavior as pure *hereos*.

Even Rosalind, who is sure that no one has ever died for love, has the disease, and when Orlando leaves her for a while, she turns in dismay to the disguised Celia and complains: "I'll tell thee, Aliena, I cannot be out of the sight of Orlando. I'll go find a shadow and sigh till he come."[72] Helena, at the beginning of *All's Well That Ends Well,* when she feels she is alone, soliloquizes concerning her lack of success with Bertram and the impossibility of her marrying him. This the Steward, overhearing, reports to Bertram's mother, adding: "This she delivered in the most bitter touch of sorrow that e'er I heard virgin exclaim in."[73] Even Annabella, in *'Tis Pity She's a Whore,* written in a less idealistic age, shares this evidence of *hereos* with her beloved brother:

> For every sigh that thou hast spent for me
> I have sighed ten; for every tear shed twenty.[74]

It is quite evident that weeping was constantly regarded as an expression of the disease and not limited to any group or period of authors before the Restoration. For one thing, it is one of the most obvious of all the symptoms of *hereos:* it can be seen by merely looking at the sufferer. This external evidence is necessary, for the lover feels obliged to communicate in some way his condition to his beloved. Ideally, the communication would be of some such sort as Benedick's to Beatrice: by means of an unsolicited go-between, because that would remove from the situation any suspicion of falsity or insincerity adopted merely in order to win the credulous woman. But the ideal occurs seldom, and the methods of revelation to the woman who insisted on being blind to her lover's condition are various. They will be discussed later.

Contrasted with the necessity for weeping is the powerful demand for secrecy. The lover must never permit anyone to know that he is in love, and of necessity he must not reveal the identity of his beloved.[75] Therefore the lover tries to weep in solitude. Burton says of the melancholic, which, as will be shown, is an aspect of *hereos:*

they delight in floods and waters, desert places, to walk alone in orchards, gardens, private walks, back-lanes, averse from company.[76]

After all, this solitude too would arouse notice of and comment on what the lover does while alone:

Benvolio. So early walking did I see your son.
> Toward him I made; but he was ware of me
> And stole into the covert of the wood.
> I—measuring his affection by my own,
> Which then most sought where most might not be found,
> . . . gladly shunn'd who gladly fled from me.
Montagu. Many a morning hath he there been seen,
> With tears augmenting the fresh morning's dew,
> Adding to clouds more clouds with his deep sighs.[77]

Such solitude is obviously no secret. Fenton casually comments on Monophylo's solitude as a trait of love:

that euen the groues and medowes wherein he was withdrawne to recorde his desolate state, seemed to impart with his sorowe, and yeelde pittie to his cryes and scorching sighes.[78]

In *The Two Gentlemen of Verona,* Speed, cataloguing for his master the evidences of Valentine's love, mentions that he walks alone.[79] Jonson's Ovid, separated from Julia by force, tells her:

> Farewell all company, and, if I could,
> All light with thee![80]

Even when such a manifestation is mocked, it is ridiculed in the way a fact or truth is ridiculed, not calling into question its validity but rather its pure idiosyncracy. Dekker, in *The Witch of Edmonton* (1621), has the First Clown speak so of Cuddy:

I'll lay my ears *Banks* is in love, and that's the reason he would walk melancholy by himself.[81]

Solitude does not necessarily denote lovesickness, but it is a sign of melancholy,[82] of which *hereos* is one of the causes. If the subject is young, and if a little investigation reveals tears and other more specific manifestations of lovesickness, the prognosis of *hereos* might validly be guessed. Jaques, in *As You Like It,* walks alone, but he does not weep. It would seem, from Rosalind's mocking of his solitude and implied praise of her own, that the lovers prefer having their asceticism an attribute solely of *hereos.*

Ford, too, finds the love of solitude an expression which might cause suspicion of lovesickness when he has Florio say to Giovanni, who is ill from *hereos:*

> Son, where have you been? what, alone, alone still?
> I would not have it so; you must forsake
> This overbookish humour.[83]

Florio mistakes the reason for his son's retreat to solitude by thinking it is caused by his love of books, but he does recognize its danger.

This love of solitude, then, as well as weeping, was universally recognized as a possible sign of *hereos*. When it was combined with weeping, in an eligible youth of either sex, it made the prognosis of *hereos* more likely, although most of the traits of *hereos* were also signs of general melancholy.

Another obvious symptom of love in the Elizabethan period was a loss of appetite. This was a time-honored aspect of *hereos* and led, if sustained, to emaciation and eventually to death. The lack of appetite might pass unnoticed if the victim ate at home,[84] but certainly the emaciation would be evident to all observers.

Valentine pays for his "contemning" of love by his suffering when he falls in love with Silvia. He is then punished "with bitter fasts."[85] Speed notices the change in his master, his tendency "to fast like one that takes diet"[86] after an earlier happier life in which, Speed claims, "when you fasted, it was presently after dinner . . . And now you are metamorphis'd with a mistress, that, when I look on you, I can hardly think you my master."[87] But after Valentine has reached an understanding with Silvia in that "we are betroth'd and the "marriage hour . . . determin'd of," the entire situation changes. When he then tells Proteus:

> Now can I break my fast, dine, sup, and sleep
> Upon the very naked name of love,

his friend immediately comprehends the reason for the change: "Enough! I read your fortune in your eye."[88]

Hamlet, forbidden the sight of Ophelia, according to Polonius:

> Fell into a sadness, then into a fast,
> Thence to a watch, thence into a weakness,
> Thence to a lightness, and, by this declension,
> Into the madness wherein now he raves,
> And all we mourn for.[89]

At the grave of Ophelia, Hamlet challenges Laertes, who of course would be incapable of deep *hereos* because Ophelia is his sister, and offers, among other torments to express his love, to fast for her.[90]

Since fasting is not immediately observable to the audience or to the other characters of the play, it receives rather less recognition in Shakespeare than some of the other traits of *hereos*. There is no attempt made by the dramatist to have each lover show all evidences of *hereos,* and fasting receives less attention than others.

Dekker's Agripyne recognizes the trait when she says: "My lord of Orleans, you look lean, and likest a lover."[91] She implies that a lean and hungry look, Cassius to the contrary notwithstanding, could be interpreted as a sign of love. It is true that many men are lean for other reasons than love,[92] but if the character is in his early maturity, he is expected to be either of a healthy plumpness or in love.

Such were the most external signs of love, some of them openly displayed by the sufferer, and some of them justifiably interpreted as manifestations of a real disease. But it was not so evident to onlookers that the lover suffered from lack of sleep. Yet clearly most lovers in the drama, probably all, are sleepless. Giovanni tells Annabella that he has "spent Many a silent night in sighs and groans."[93] The Duke in Dekker's and Middleton's 2 *The Honest Whore* says of Hippolito, his son-in-law:

> He's no more like vnto *Hippolito,*
> Than dead men are to living—neuer sleepes,[94]

and Shakespeare's lovers are much the same. Valentine claims that

> . . . in revenge of my contempt of love,
> Love hath chas'd sleep from my enthralled eyes
> And made them watchers of mine own heart's sorrow.[95]

Beatrice, according to Leonato, will

> . . . be up twenty times a night, and there will she sit in her smock till she have writ a sheet of paper. My daughter tells all.[96]

Claudio, according to Benedick, will "lie ten nights awake carving the fashion of a new doublet."[97]

But sometimes the poor lover is finally so fatigued that he must sleep or die. Then, as in Hippolito's case, when he prefers sleep to death, "it's dreams: and in those dreams His arms work, and then cries, Sweet."[98]

The lover, when he first loves, finds that dreams are very potent in causing and developing affection, as Glaphyro admits while decrying the strength of love:

> . . . we must not so much stande vpon contemplation of a wauering loue, which possiblyc crept into vs in a dreame or at vnwares, as with deepe aduise and consideration, waigh and maners and conditions of the Ladie with whome we pretende that waye.[99]

The characters of Shakespeare and the early Elizabethan dramatists find much more potency in dreams than did Glaphyro. Romeo feels his closeness to Juliet in his sleep:

> If I may trust the flattering truth of sleep,
> My dreams presage some joyful news at hand.
> My bosom's lord sits lightly in his throne,
> And all this day an unaccustom'd spirit
> Lifts me above the ground with cheerful thoughts.

I dreamt my lady came and found me dead[100]
(Strange dream that gives a dead man leave to think!)
And breath'd such life with kisses in my lips
That I reviv'd and was an emperor.
Ah me! how sweet is love itself possess'd,
When but love's shadows are so rich in joy![101]

Hermia considers that dreams accompany any love:

Then let us teach our trial patience,
Because it is a customary cross,
As due to love as thoughts and dreams and sighs,
Wishes and tears, poor Fancy's followers.[102]

This she finds to be true when Lysander leaves her:

Ay me, for pity! What a dream was here!
Lysander, look how I do quake with fear.
Methought a serpent eat my heart away,
And you sat smiling at his cruel prey.[103]

Andromache, on the fatal day of her beloved Hector, tells him: "My dreams will, sure, prove ominous to the day."[104] Iago claims that Michael Cassio dreamed of Desdemona when he wishes to give evidence to Othello that Cassio loves her.[105]

Most love dreams are in some degree mournful and generally have an exceedingly clear symbolism. This is natural, since the dreams tend to come to lovers under circumstances of *hereos,* when their beloved ones are either not present or not obtainable. If they are not somber in themselves the dreams have ironic overtones, as in the case of Julia, whom Proteus has deserted. She, Silvia tells him, "dreams on him that has forgot her love."[106]

Dreams seldom presage good fortune to the Elizabethan,

and in the more specialized case of lovers' dreams, it appears they never do.

Lack of appetite and its consequent leanness would also induce paleness, if only because paleness accompanies starvation. Besides, many persons of the age prided themselves on their control of their facial color. Blushing was a conscious development, and paleness, too, could to some extent be self-induced. To a lover, however, the heightened or decreased color of his face was a manifestation of *hereos,* and it was not deliberately induced. The blush, by no means a recent development in the sixteenth century,[107] did seem to acquire more popularity than it had earlier, and it seemed to be used both by the lover and the beloved. Some interesting alternations of colorings thus are possible when the blush is contrasted with paleness:

> Loe, when shee blusht, euen then did he looke pale,
> As if her cheekes by some inchaunted power
> Attracted had the cherie blood from his:
> Anone, with reuerent feare when she grew pale,
> His cheekes put on their scarlet ornaments.[108]

Thus speaks Lodowick of Edward and the Countess of Salisbury. But the author makes a nice distinction between the two blushers in the next ten lines, and has Lodowick claim that the Countess blushes for shame and the King for lust.

Juliet, too, is subject to blushes on at least two occasions. The first is when the Nurse tells her abruptly that Romeo is waiting to marry her:

> Now comes the wanton blood up in your cheeks:
> They'll be in scarlet straight at any news.[109]

The second time, by modern concepts also quite naturally, is when Juliet, waiting for Romeo to come to consummate their marriage, thinks of him and the coming meeting. Then she says, in her modesty, "Hood my unmann'd blood, bating in my cheeks."[110]

The redness of the face was not necessarily a sign of love, although it was a sign of high emotion. The Elizabethan dramatist recognized that it could denote scorn or anger, and the heightened color is thus mentioned by Corin when he suggests to Rosalind that she see Phebe and Silvius in

> . . . a pageant truly play'd
> Between the pale complexion of true love
> And the red glow of scorn and proud disdain.[111]

Generally the sign of love was revealed by the absence of blood, as Corin commented above. Every sigh meant that the heart lost a drop of blood. Thus Oberon says of Helena:

> All fancy-sick she is, and pale of cheer
> With sighs of love, that costs the fresh blood dear.[112]

Juliet and Romeo share the affliction in adversity, for when she says to her husband as he leaves early Tuesday morning, suffering for the enforced separation, "Either my eyesight fails, or thou look'st pale," he replies, "And trust me, love, in my eye so do you." And he comments, "Dry sorrow drinks our blood."[113] Bertram's mother finds pallor in Helena a sufficient reason for thinking her suffering from *hereos:*

> Yes, Helen, you might be my daughter-in-law.
> God shield you mean it not! "daughter" and "mother"
> So strive upon your pulse. What, pale again?
> My fear hath catch'd your fondness. Now I see
> The myst'ry of your loneliness and find
> Your salt tears' head. Now to all sense 'tis gross—
> You love my son.[114]

Mistress Glister, according to Middleton, describes the significance of paleness succinctly to Maria:

What? have not I observed the rising and falling of the blood, the coming and going of the countenance, your qualms, your unlacings, your longings? most evident tokens.[115]

And Don Pedro uses paleness as a stage of lovesickness when he tells the mocking Benedick: "I shall see thee, ere I die, look pale with love,"[116] implying that pallor accompanies the affliction.

Paleness could be induced by a sudden emotion, or it could be a relatively constant manifestation, caused by *hereos* and its impeding of the appetite. It was, as Mistress Glister says, a token of love.

The frustration of unrequited love led to such violence as the tearing of the hair. This seems to be a relatively unusual evidence of *hereos,* but Shakespeare describes it in three of his plays in close connection with love. Romeo, after he has been banished, tells the Friar he has been so disturbed as to be justified in tearing his hair.[117] Claudio, describing the condition of Beatrice in her love for Benedick, says that she "tears her hair."[118] And Cressida, threatened with separation from Troilus, says she will "Tear my bright hair."[119]

Such an action to an Elizabethan would ordinarily show that the person was mad or at least had lost all control of his emotions. So, when Shakespearean characters who are more mature tear their hair, they are either truly mad, or like Lear when, losing emotional control, he "tears his white hair,"[120] as Kent reports. This is also true of Constance, in *King John.* When she, in anger, apparently tears her hair, Pandulph accuses her of insanity: "Lady, you utter madness and not

sorrow." But she replies that her pulse doth temperately
keep time:

> I am not mad. This hair I tear is mine;
> My name is Constance; I was Geffrey's wife . . .
> I am not mad. I would to heaven I were![121]

The person who would tear his hair would certainly be
ready, under slight provocation, to go mad. Lear needed
only the shock of the sight of Edgar as Tom of Bedlam, and
lovers, forbidden their loved ones, were in and out of madness if their cases of *hereos* were severe. So Monophylo, in a
moment of sanity, admits that *hereos* is difficult to some
who are "standing inexperienced in such fittes as you note
in me,"[122] and Romeo and Rosalind are of a mind in this.
Romeo says bluntly:

> Love is a smoke rais'd with the fume of sighs;
> Being purg'd, a fire sparkling in lovers' eyes;
> Being vex'd, a sea nourish'd with lovers' tears.
> What is it else? A madness most discreet,
> A choking gall, and a preserving sweet.[123]

Rosalind castigates love more severely but finds the same
meaning in it:

Love is merely a madness, and, I tell you, deserves as well a dark
house and a whip as madmen do; and the reason why they are not
so punish'd and cured is that the lunacy is so ordinary that the
whippers are in love too.[124]

These are, perhaps, figurative meanings, but the evidence
from other authors would seem to imply that they could as
well be literal as figurative. Rosalind may not have intended
that her statement be taken literally, but obviously some

characters, and thus, by implication, some authors and some audiences, did.

Marston, in *Jack Drum's Entertainment,* writes that Pasquill goes completely mad when Katherine, to whom he is betrothed, renounces him after having had her face disfigured by acid. He recovers from the madness when the two are reconciled.[125]

Anselmo, describing madmen in Bethlem, points two out as having been brought to their present state by *hereos,* the first by separation from his beloved:

> . . . this hithermost
> Fell from the happy quietnes of minde,
> About a maiden that he lov'd, and died:
> He followed her to Church, being full of teares,
> And as her body went into the ground,
> He fell starke mad,[126]

and the other through jealousy of his wife:

> . . . This is a married man,
> Was jealous of a friar, but as some say,
> A very virtuous wife; and that spoiled him.[127]

In another play of Middleton's, Folly-Wit, frustrated by a woman, apostrophizes:

> Shall I be madder now than ever I have been?
> I'm in the way, i'faith.
> Man's never at the height of madness full,
> Until he love, and prove a woman's gull.[128]

Madness is the final stage of love-frustration, or of *hereos,* before death. Apparently most men were not driven to insanity, but even if they were so, it was not of necessity permanent. Polonius, in his analysis of Hamlet's condition, which may not have been so foolish as has often been reputed, lists the stages leading to madness:

> . . . he, repulsed, a short tale to make,
> Fell into a sadness, then into a fast,
> Thence to a watch, thence into a weakness,
> Thence to a lightness, and, by this declension,
> Into the madness wherein now he raves.[129]

It is not necessary at this time to discuss the question as to whether or not Hamlet was mad. Madness was loosely attributed to people who acted differently from the accepted norm. But here Polonius implies that there were definite stages leading to the development of madness; and although he does not mention *hereos,* the disease is recognizable.

Many of Shakespeare's heroes suffer the first three aspects: they weep, go without food, and lie awake nights. Some of them go into a weakness, but not to the extent of being bedridden. The lightness which Polonius mentions apparently concerns the mind, not the body, although a man might well lose weight from prolonged fasting. But Polonius means that Hamlet thinks and speaks illogically. This illogicality is not far, if at all, removed from sanity. As Polonius says on another occasion of his prince: "Though this be madness, yet there is method in't."[130] Hamlet seems to him to vacillate between "lightness" and "madness," although Polonius would generally impute to him the latter. The stage which Hamlet had actually achieved, however, seems to be that just precedent to madness, that is, melancholy. The word is used only by Claudius and Hamlet himself in referring to his condition, but Hamlet's use of it is interesting in connection with the idea of madness. It may be, he says, the devil

> Out of my weakness and my melancholy,
> As he is very potent with such spirits,
> Abuses me to damn me.[131]

Hamlet, then, feels that he has not absolute control of his
senses at all times, for "abuses" here is in the sense of "mis-
leads." Since this passage occurs in a soliloquy, he undoubtedly speaks what he considers to be the truth, and therefore
he may feel that he is not always sane.

Madness, says Burton,

> is therefore defined to be a vehement dotage, or raving without a
> fever, far more violent than *melancholy,* full of anger and clamour,
> horrible looks, actions, gestures, troubling the patients with far
> greater vehemency both of body and mind, without all fear and
> sorrow, with such impetuous force & boldness, that sometimes
> three or four men cannot hold them.[132]

Melancholy is more limited in scope than madness, and although it has traits which would not be present in a sane person,[133] in a lover the illness is seldom violent.

Melancholy can be shown both by speech and by position
of the body. One position is that which actors assume when
portraying Hamlet as "the melancholy Dane"—standing with
folded arms:

Valentine. Why, how know you that I am in love?
Speed. . . . you have learn'd, like Sir Proteus, to wreathe your
arms like a malecontent.[134]

.   .   .   .

King.   Longaville
> Did never sonnet for her sake compile,
> Nor never lay his wreathed arms athwart
> His loving bosom to keep down his heart.[135]

Again, the melancholic attempts to hide his face, partly to

keep his paleness from being seen and partly to call attention to himself:

Vail. I can see nothing but his eyes: the rest of him is so wrapt in cloak that it suffers no view. . . .
Glister. What, master Lipsalve, is't you? why thus obscured? what discontent overshadows you?
Lipsalve. A discontent indeed, master doctor, which [is, I love] a certain 'pothecary's wife.[136]

And soon Gudgeon appears in the same costume for the same reason.[137]

Speech would reveal the inner turmoil of the mind. That is the reason Hamlet suggests to Gertrude as proof of his sanity:

> Bring me to the test,
> And I the matter will reword; which madness
> Would gambol from.[138]

This tendency to inaccurate speech is not necessarily a test of madness although it is a manifestation of it. Anyone in love has some similar difficulty, for with his lack of coordination of voice and mind the abstractedness of the mind shows in the expression. Chariclea had noted that, a generation previous to Hamlet's case:

I neuere sawe or knewe any one truely transfigured into the state of a perfite louer, on whome (notwithstanding he had possessed the actuall felicitie in loue) did not attende inward perplexities, and outwarde disquietnesse, confused counsayles and careless execution, broken speeche and vnsounde iudgements.[139]

But by the time the lover had reached the stage of acute melancholy, or had gone beyond it to madness, his vagary of speech was perhaps one method of determining his condition.

The melancholic lover suffered cumulatively from all the aspects of *hereos* mentioned above in this chapter, so that by the time he reached the last or the next to the last stage of lovesickness he would truly be in no condition for practical life. Even without regard for extravagance of speech, there is much evidence that the truly sincere frustrated lovers of the age were quite willing to die rather than continue to suffer.

He that runs head-long from the top of a rock is not in so bad a case, as he that falls into the gulf of love. For hence, saith Platina, comes Repentance, Dotage, they lose themselves, their wits, and make shipwrack of their fortunes altogether: madness, to make away themselves and others, violent death.[140]

Even Burton recognizes that theirs was a very real agony, although he could not sympathize with it. And he more than once expresses the opinion that it can lead to death.

Monophylo analyzed this desire for death quite clearly:

For (to vse a iudgement in simple truth) the pleasure doth not so much mooue vs in our selues, as the desire we haue to be the cause of that wherewith our Mistresses may participate, seeing as we are borne for them and not for our selues, so we liue in them and not in our selues, and die in them, to be eftsoones reuiued in them.[141]

So it was quite logical that Mucedorus, when his Amadine appears to be unattainable, should apostrophize nature and conclude:

> Ye each thing els prolonging life of man,
> Change, change your wonted course, that I,
> Wanting your aide, in woefull sort may die.[142]

Women, too, were subject to this condition. Katherine, in trouble in her love for Pasquill, says:

> Black sorrow, nurse of plaints, of teares, and grones,
> Evaporate my spirit with a sigh,
> That it may hurrey after his sweete breath,
> Who made thee doate on life, now hunt for death.[143]

Shakespeare's characters, then, are consistent with the tradition when they utter such speeches. Helena claims that her

> . . . imagination
> Carries no favour in't but Bertram's.
> I am undone! There is no living, none,
> If Bertram be away. . . .
> The hind that would be mated by the lion
> Must die for love.[144]

Hermione, out of favor with her husband, mentions as one
reason why she is no longer interested in living that "The
crown and comfort of my life, your favour, I do give lost."[145]
The other Helena says of Demetrius:

> I'll follow thee and make a heaven of hell
> To die upon the hand I love so well,[146]

and her friend Hermia, of Lysander:

> . . . I well perceive you are not nigh.
> Either death or you I'll find immediately.[147]

Examples of such expressed wish are relatively prevalent
throughout the plays. As to whether or not they were sincere,
it is quite impossible generally to determine, but on at least
one occasion the sincerity is undoubted, for Romeo and Juliet
die as a result of separation in love. A mere four years later,
in 1599, another Shakespearean character claimed, when her
beloved said he would die if she would not have him:

The poor world is almost six thousand years old, and in all this

time there was not any man died in his own person, videlicet, in a
love cause. . . . Men have died from time to time, and worms
have eaten them, but not for love.[148]

Despite that statement, and perhaps partly because Romeo
preceded Rosalind by almost as many years as Othello succeeded her, it seems that the general tendency in Shakespeare is to view with quite an unjaundiced eye the proceed-
ings of lovers who, through terrific mental stress, may be led
to such a condition as might possibly cause madness or death
or both.

The cure for this disease is the same in the sixteenth century as it had been for so many centuries previous: the seduction of the beloved if the two have not previously been united,
and her return if they have been.[149] For those lovers who
felt that they did not need to consummate their love the mere
presence of the beloved was sufficient to effect a cure. In such
a condition is Pasquier (or Fenton):

> . . . I had not (with *Monophylo*) cause of melancholy conceit, as
> hauing afore mine eies the onely mistresse of my felycities, who by
> happie aduenture, being one of that companie, made me not onely
> forget all my passions of hir absence, but also euen my selfe to
> whom it seemed, hir sweete deliuerye of speache consenting with a
> gracious moouing and disposition of hir eyes, had power to peaice
> euen millions of heartes, yea the deytie it selfe.[150]

The cure for Pasquill was his reacceptance by Katherine,[151]
and the situation of Franciscus, in Middleton's *The Changeling,* is clearly stated, although mocked:

> *Lollio.* So if you love my mistress so well as you have handled the
> matter here, you are like to be cured of your madness.
> *Franciscus.* And none but she can cure it.
> *Lollio.* Well, I'll give you over, then, and she shall cast your water
> next.[152]

Giovanni is cured, too, when Annabella accepts him after he has told her "I fear [I am] so sick 'Twill cost my life."[153]

Shakespeare's Beatrice tells Benedick that it is only her pity which saves him:

I would not deny you; but, by this good day, I yield upon great persuasion, and partly to save your life, for I was told you were in a consumption.[154]

This, then, is the condition of the lover when he is for any reason and for any length of time separated from his beloved. Not all of the examples I have here adduced are applicable strictly to the subject of this chapter, in that they do not always apply to persons in the stage between the first meeting and the acknowledgment of love. But they do all apply to lovers, and, since there may be many alterations of mood and temperament between the first meeting and the grave, the true lover, no matter what his age or his relationship to the beloved, is still susceptible to attacks of *hereos*.

The important addition here, apparently of the sixteenth century, is that the beloved as well as the lover, or the woman as well as the man, might feel all the pangs of love and undergo all its rigors: this in spite of the fact that the woman was still generally placed on a plane higher than the man. Shakespeare even uses the reverse in showing the impartiality of the disease. Thus Helena loves a recalcitrant Bertram; Mariana follows a reluctant Angelo; Ophelia, despite her inclinations, is forced to the position of refusing and desiring Hamlet simultaneously; Viola hopelessly loves the Duke; and Imogen remains faithful through adversity to Posthumus. All of these lovelorn women express varying degrees of *hereos* in their actions and in their language. Most of them are eventually united with the objects of their affection.

When the man hopefully or hopelessly loves the woman, the situation is more traditional, and apparently Shakespeare finds it less interesting, for he seldom makes the love hopeless, and when it is hopeful he seldom draws it out through the stages of *hereos*. Rather, the lover, before he has proceeded very far in his sighs and his sleeplessness, finds, as does Valentine, that his love is returned in a degree equivalent to that which he himself feels. Orlando does suffer in his separation from Rosalind, but the disguised Rosalind seems to bring some surcease from sorrow to him. Benedick has very little time in which to shave and perfume himself before he and Beatrice unite as two magnets. Claudio has only a few hours from the time of his first view of Hero before he is betrothed to her. Ferdinand and Miranda look, love, and declare themselves within a matter of minutes. Perdita and Florizel have met, loved, and been betrothed before they appear on the stage.

Could it therefore be deduced that Shakespeare no longer considered *hereos* of interest to an Elizabethan audience? I doubt it. It would rather seem, from his treatment of the disease, that he did not think the affliction a suitable center to any of his plots. Even in *Troilus and Cressida*, Shakespeare does not put the principal emphasis upon *hereos;* it is the story of a faithless love rather than of a suffering lover.

The loves of Shakespeare's characters are real enough to cause them suffering: the cases, however, of *hereos* are slight and their cure rapid. For the lovers of the late sixteenth century are rather more capable intellectually than were their predecessors, and they soon find some method of communication with their beloved.

This, then, is to be the matter of the succeeding chapter.

Chapter IV

THE LOVERS TOGETHER: PHYSICAL AIDS AND THE REVELATION

AFTER THE LOVER has been separated from his beloved for some time and has developed the disease of *hereos* to such a degree that he feels he must find some means of cure, he considers the various methods of communication with his beloved. This would not be necessary if he were in her presence often enough for her to see the effects of love-longing in him as the disease developed. If he were to avoid its every symptom, he would have to tell her of his love very soon after the first meeting. There were four methods of letting the beloved know that the lover was ill with love: 1. a simple declaration, 2. a go-between, 3. presents, and 4. writings. These will be discussed in succeeding paragraphs.

The first means, that of confessing his love to his beloved immediately, although often used by Shakespeare, would have been scorned by the true courtly lover of earlier ages. Such a course would not be modest in either a man or a woman appearing as a character in Renaissance literature. But in the late sixteenth century the lovers in drama seem to have been more direct, and *hereos* does not develop very far merely because the lovers are quick in expressing themselves.

It is quite often the woman who makes the overture. When Juliet finds that Romeo has overheard the confession of love which she makes to herself, she says:

> Thou knowest the mask of night is on my face;
> Else would a maiden blush bepaint my cheek
> For that which thou hast heard me speak to-night.

> Fain would I dwell on form—fain, fain deny
> What I have spoke.[1]

She recognizes her part in the courtship. As a woman, she must refuse to feel the emotion of love until persuaded by her lover. The "form" of which she speaks is merely that of making it difficult for Romeo to attain her love, echoing the rule of Andreas Capellanus that "The easy attainment of love makes it of little value; difficulty of attainment makes it prized."[2] This she clearly states in the same speech:

> Or if thou thinkest I am too quickly won,
> I'll frown, and be perverse, and say thee nay,
> So thou wilt woo; but else, not for the world.
> In truth, fair Montague, I am too fond,
> And therefore thou mayst think my haviour light;
> But trust me, gentleman, I'll prove more true
> Than those that have more cunning to be strange.[3]

This is a form of modesty which Shakespeare intends to seem more endearing than the traditional modesty of the maiden in courtship. For Juliet is a woman with no defense who offers herself to a man she has not even formally met, and whom she has first seen only a few hours before. If he refuses her, she loses her self-respect. This is the modesty of complete honest frankness. Yet in this scene she is able, through a better command of words, to control the action. She speaks fifty-eight percent of the lines of the scene, Romeo only forty-two percent. Further, it is she who, despite her modesty, formulates the plan for the marriage:

> If that thy bent of love be honourable,
> Thy purpose marriage, send me word tomorrow,
> By one that I'll procure to come to thee,
> Where and what time thou wilt perform the rite.[4]

and she tells Romeo what to do throughout the scene.

This is in the tradition of courtly love in the sense that the woman controls the situation. But the interesting aspect of Shakespeare's treatment of the action is that Juliet is constantly in control despite the fact that she has completely exposed herself to Romeo's possible ridicule or refusal. Here is a situation in which the lovers vie with each other in extravagances of statement, yet each has so completely revealed his thoughts and desires that the words are received by the audience as absolutely sincere. There is an apparent sincerity in ingenuousness. This helps make the scene powerful.

Rosalind handles creditably her encounters with Orlando. Since he finds it impossible to speak in her presence,[5] she later, disguised as Ganymede, persuades him to woo her as though Ganymede were Rosalind. Because Orlando does not penetrate the disguise, he has no difficulty in speaking, and Rosalind is able to conceal adequately her lack of maidenly modesty.

Shakespearean lovers seldom, in the presence of the beloved, lose the power of speech. Yet in order to maintain the love interest, at the same time keeping his lover from looking too foolish for credibility, Shakespeare's romantic hero generally uses one of the three other methods of communicating his love.

The second method is the use of a go-between in a love affair, who carries messages from the lover to the beloved or vice versa. He need be assigned no other dramatic function. According to the courtly tradition, the parties in a love affair were permitted one go-between, who was generally either a servant or a person acceptable to the families of both parties or both. The go-between did not necessarily share the love secrets of the couple. Each lover was permitted in addition

only one confidant in the interests of secrecy. There could thus
be three persons, besides the lovers, concerned in the further-
ance of the affair.[6]

Very often in the dramas of this period the go-between and
the confidant are identical. There is usually at least one go-
between. His function is a dangerous one because the dramatist motivates the secrecy of the affair by having enemies oppose the lovers' union, but if the lover is successful in his
courtship the go-between may be well rewarded. Pedringano,
in Thomas Kyd's *The Spanish Tragedy* (1587), was unfortunate when he acted as intermediary between Bel-Imperia and
Andrea, for Lorenzo controlled him after Andrea's death:

> . . . it is not long, thou know'st,
> Since I did shield thee from my father's wrath,
> For thy conveyance in Andrea's love,
> For which thou wert adjudg'd to punishment.[7]

Pedringano is a servant to Andrea's family, and of the opposite sex to Bel-Imperia, so he cannot serve as her confidant.
She later enlists his aid in arranging her clandestine meeting
with Horatio and, although she feels Pedringano is trustworthy, she does not confide her feelings to him. The confidant is usually of the same sex as the confider: the only apparent exceptions to this rule are members of the clergy. The
confidant may be a servant, as witness Cariola's relationship
to the Duchess of Malfi. The Duchess admits to her:

> To thy knowne secrecy, I have given up
> More then my life, my fame.[8]

Tranio is both servant and confidant to Lucentio:

> Tranio, I burn, I pine; I perish, Tranio,
> If I achieve not this young modest girl.

> Counsel me, Tranio, for I know thou canst;
> Assist me, Tranio, for I know thou wilt.[9]

Juliet's Nurse is her confidante as well as a go-between until the Nurse proves false to Romeo in trying to persuade Juliet to marry Paris. Then Juliet soliloquizes after the Nurse has left:

> Go, counsellor!
> Thou and my bosom henceforth shall be twain,

and immediately proceeds to find another:

> I'll to the Friar to know his remedy.[10]

The Friar eventually becomes Juliet's go-between as well as confidant. Mistress Haughty, in Jonson's *Epicoene* (1609), tells Dauphine that her servant is her intermediary and confidant: "Trusty, my woman, shall be ever awake for you: you need not fear to communicate anything with her, for she is a Fidelia."[11] Vasques, the servant to Soranzo in John Ford's *'Tis Pity She's a Whore,* is also his confidant, as Hippolita recognizes when she tries to alienate him from his master: "Had I one so true, so truly honest, so secret to my counsels, as thou hast been to him and his, I should think it a slight acquittance, not only to make him master of all I have, but even of myself."[12]

All of the above confidants are both servants and go-betweens. But more often the two are separate persons. So in *Romeo and Juliet* Balthasar is Romeo's go-between: he it is who works with the Nurse in the carrying out of the plans for the lovers' night together,[13] and he takes Romeo the message of Juliet's supposed death. But Romeo's confidant is Friar Laurence. Balthasar in the play is solely a servant who acts as go-between merely because it is a part of his duties to his master. He never comments on his master's actions except in a worried way when Romeo appears upset over the news of Juliet's death, and even then his words are ineffectual.

Speed, on the other hand, Valentine's servant in *The Two Gentlemen of Verona*, seems to be a step above Balthasar. He recognizes what is going on in his master's love affair with Silvia, and he shows, when Silvia returns the letter Valentine wrote for her, much more understanding of the situation than his master does. Although a servant, he is privileged to comment as freely as the court fool. And his comments are trenchant. When Valentine is puzzled over Silvia's return of the letter, Speed says:

O jest unseen, inscrutable, invisible,
As a nose on a man's face or a weathercock on a steeple!
My master sues to her; and she hath taught her suitor,
He being the pupil, to become her tutor.
O, excellent device! was there ever heard a better,
That my master, being scribe, to himself should write the letter?[14]

Valentine is of course playing the part of the stupid lover, he whom all the world loves and who is less intelligent in his own affair than all the rest of the world. Speed explains in simple words what has happened. This advice and explanation is a function of the confidant. Speed has acted as go-between for Proteus to Julia,[15] but apparently not in such capacity for his master, Valentine.

Proteus changes go-betweens in the middle of the play. Launce, sent with a pretty dog as gift to Silvia, loses the dog and substitutes his own more famous one. At the same time Proteus has been approached by Julia, in disguise as a page, in search of employment. He dismisses Launce to find the lost dog and commissions Julia his new go-between, to take a ring to Silvia.[16]

In the same play, Lucetta, servant to Julia, is her confidant,

as well as her go-between. This is clearly established at their
first appearance together. Julia's first lines in the play are:

> But say, Lucetta, now we are alone,
> Wouldst thou then counsel me to fall in love?[17]

and she uses Lucetta, apparently, again and again as confidant:

> Counsel, Lucetta! gentle girl, assist me!
> And ev'n in kind love I do conjure thee,
> Who art the table wherein all my thoughts
> Are visibly character'd and engrav'd,
> To lesson me.[18]

Lucetta acts as go-between when she brings Julia a letter
which Speed gave her from Proteus.[19]

Nerissa, "waiting gentlewoman" to Portia in *The Merchant of Venice*, is her confidant, too.[20] Such servants could
serve as go-betweens in an emergency. Often in Shakespeare,
though, the lovers find more need for advice than for inter-
mediaries. So it is with Portia.

The go-between ranged in rank from lowly household servants like Launce in *The Two Gentlemen of Verona* to a
nobleman like Don Pedro in *Much Ado About Nothing*, who
woos Hero for Claudio.[21] There is sometimes little difference
between a go-between and a downright pander: the nature of
the office depends on the intentions of the lover, whether he
seeks marriage or possession without marriage. When King
Edward says to the Countess' father, in *The Raigne of K. Edward the Third,*

> Go to thy daughter; and in my behalfe
> Commaund her, woo her, win her anie waies,
> To be my mistres and my secret loue,[22]

he is asking the father to serve as pander. The Countess is already married. Bryan, in Dekker's *2 The Honest Whore,* acts as pander for his master Hippolito, according to Orlando:

The Irish footman can tell you all hunting houres, the Parke he hunts in, the Doe he would strike; that Irish Shackatory beates the bush for him, and knowes all; he brought that Letter, and that Ring; he is the Carrier.[23]

Hippolito is trying to seduce the Honest Whore, and he uses Bryan as a go-between as well as pander. In the same scene Infelice calls Bryan a "bawd" and "pandring slaue."[24] A third pander is the Curtezan in Middleton's *A Mad World, My Masters.* There she is active in Mrs. Harebrain's affair with Penitent Brothel, even to the extent of carrying on a monolog in her room while Harebrain listens outside and Mrs. Harebrain and Penitent Brothel apparently copulate off-stage. The monolog seems to Harebrain a dialog with Mrs. Harebrain.[25] Curtezan also acts as a go-between when she carries a jewel, which in this case is a guerdon, from Mrs. Harebrain to Penitent Brothel.[26]

Pandarus acts as pander for Troilus in *Troilus and Cressida,*[27] but other attempted seductions in Shakespeare are controlled by the principals themselves without intermediary. Bertram persuades Diana, he believes, in *All's Well That Ends Well,*[28] and he cannot intend marriage with her since he recognizes that his previous marriage with Helena is binding no matter how much he dislikes it. Angelo, in *Measure for Measure,* courts Isabella with no witnesses within hearing, and he dares use no intermediary.[29] In both of the latter plays the plot of substitution of another and already-married woman is used. Shakespeare permits only in *Troilus and*

Cressida the immorality that would occur necessarily if panders of the sense of procurers were used.

Between the extremes of rank of servant and nobility are the friends. They are occasionally servants, although generally servants of the upper classes. But whatever their class rank they have great privilege. Such is Nerissa in *The Merchant of Venice,* who in some ways is as close to Portia as Rosalind to Celia, so equal that were their positions changed as were Rosalind's and Celia's their friendship might well have continued in the same way. To a lesser degree, Tranio is in a similar relation to Lucentio in *The Taming of the Shrew,* and he is even able to change places with his master in the disguise plot of the play.

Occasionally the Elizabethan lover uses a religious as his confidant and go-between. Romeo has two go-betweens toward the end of the play: the Friar sends a message reassuring Romeo as to Juliet's condition and Balthasar carries another message which leads to the tragic misunderstanding. The assumed Friar in *Measure for Measure,* Duke Vincentio, acts as confidant for Isabella.[30] The Friar in *Much Ado About Nothing* acts, to help Hero, in activities similar to those of a confidant. He is really, however, more of general advisor to her family than a private confidant. The Friar of *'Tis Pity She's a Whore* is confidant and go-between for Giovanni.

The go-between was exceedingly useful at most stages of the love affair, but Shakespeare does not seem to have found him as useful as the confidant. Shakespeare's lovers in general seem to have been able to speak without being hindered by the usual dumbness of *hereos* which comes to one in the presence of the beloved.

The third and most common method for a lover to communicate his love was for him to offer the beloved either in person or through an intermediary some precious gift. This could be one of two kinds: those merely intended as presents to a friend, and those intended as binding in a betrothal ceremony. In general, a gift from a man to a woman of the same age is not wasted in Shakespeare: it serves as a declaration of love. "Next to the vows, the exchange of gifts, principally from the man to the woman, was the most important feature of spousals," says Powell of real marriages.[31] It was true also of stage marriages. Love and the opportunity are all that are necessary to marriage in Shakespeare's plays, and therefore the gift generally implies a request for marriage.

Swinburne, in an attempt to define spousals, mentions gifts in a way which is applicable here:

Albeit this word *Sponsalia* (Englished *Spousals*) being properly understood, doth only signifie Promises of future Marriage, yet is it not perpetually tied to this only Sense, for sometimes it is stretched to the significance of *Love Gifts* and *Tokens* of the Parties betroathed; as Bracelets, Chains, Jewels, and namely the Ring; being often used for the very Arrabo or assured Pledge of a perfect Promise.[32]

Many writers apparently believed, with Swinburne, that gifts could be accepted as love gifts, or tokens, or, to use an older word, as guerdons. The guerdon was a distinctive piece of jewelry or apparel given in the Middle Ages by a lady to a knight as evidence of her affection for him, and it was often worn by him prominently as evidence of his affection for her. The girdle worn by Sir Gawain in *Sir Gawain and the Green Knight* was, although he scarcely intended it so, a guerdon, and the magic properties attributed to it were literal statements of an allegorical belief. Any knight believed that he was in less physical danger if he wore the favor of his lady.

A man or woman in the sixteenth century was in danger of
being misunderstood if he or she gave a gift of any sort to an
eligible member of the opposite sex. The misunderstanding
might be to either extreme—that the gift implied betrothal,
or that it was merely a nonbinding gratuity. But the gifts
themselves carried degrees of implications in their value and
their form. A ring was the most obvious of all, and when it
was given the recipient seems to have been justified in regard-
ing it as a declaration of an intention of marriage. Swinburne
says of this:

. . . liberty [has been] granted to contract Spousals by whatsoever form of words, or by any other means, as *Writing, Signs,
Tokens,* &c., Whereby this mutual Consent might appear; and so
at this present, there is no one *Form* of *Deponsation* more lawful
than another, but it is sufficient if the Consent of the Parties do
appear by any form.[33]

The ring will be discussed in detail in Chapter V, because
it is closely allied to spousals themselves.

A picture was a much less significant gift. Its giving did
not imply love, although the receiving of it seems to have
done so. Proteus asks Silvia for her picture, even though he
realizes that she does not love him:

> Madam, if your heart be so obdurate,
> Vouchsafe me yet your picture for my love,
> The picture that is hanging in your chamber,

and he adds the use to which he plans to put it:

> To that I'll speak, to that I'll sigh and weep;
> For since the substance of your perfect self
> Is else devoted, I am but a shadow,
> And to your shadow will I make true love.[34]

Silvia consents, not very graciously, to give him the picture.
To Julia, who is disguised as Proteus' page, she says:

> Go give your master this. Tell him from me,
> One Julia, that his changing thoughts forget,
> Would better fit his chamber than this shadow.[35]

However, the lover liked to have a picture, perhaps to worship, perhaps only to remind him of his beloved. It is not
clear precisely how Proteus did use it, although probably he
sincerely loved Silvia and did worship her picture.

Benedick, when he has been persuaded that Beatrice loves
him, decides that he will give her a chance to win him: "If I
do not take pity on her, I am a villain; if I do not love her, I
am a Jew. I will go get her picture."[36] This would bind Benedick more than it would Beatrice, but it would be neither a
pledge nor a betrothal.

There was besides a wide range of gifts which could be
used in asking for or contracting matrimony. Such gifts are
not always used to demand marriage, but they are always a
request for physical relations. The evidence is overwhelming
that the gifts unless otherwise specifically described are used
for nothing else. In 'Tis Pity She's a Whore Donado has his
nephew Bergetto offer Annabella a jewel which accompanies
a letter. Annabella, knowing its implication, refuses the jewel.
Donado then proffers it as a free gift, with no further implications. Annabella accepts it under those conditions. But when
Giovanni, her beloved, sees her wearing it, she teases him
momentarily for his jealousy.

Thus Donado and Bergetto imply a request for a betrothal
when they offer the jewel, and Annabella so understands it
when she refuses. Giovanni believes the same thing when he
sees her wearing it as, he supposes, a guerdon, but Annabella,

having had the gift explained and the implication removed from it, felt that wearing it put her under no obligation to the giver.

Bel-Imperia, in Thomas Kyd's *The Spanish Tragedy,* had given a scarf to Don Andrea, which he had been wearing on the battlefield when killed, under much the same impression as Sir Gawain when he wore the green girdle. Both believed the gift brought immunity from harm. Horatio had taken the scarf from Don Andrea's body and worn it when he returned from the war. When he tells Bel-Imperia of her lover's death he adds:

> This scarf I pluck'd from off his lifeless arm
> And wear it in remembrance of my friend.[37]

She makes the scarf a guerdon for Horatio by answering:

> But now wear thou it both for him and me;
> For after him thou hast deserved it best.[38]

She then proceeds, in the course of the play, to make an assignation with Horatio where he is killed by treachery. By giving Horatio the scarf Bel-Imperia has given herself. This is one of the oldest of superstitions, that the control of a part gives control of the whole. Symbolically it has been used in most religions. When Horatio possesses a part of Bel-Imperia, her scarf, he possesses all of her; when she gives a part of herself in giving a piece of her clothing, she gives all of herself. So Portia says in *The Merchant of Venice:*

> This house, these servants, and this same myself
> Are yours, my lord's. I give them with this ring.[39]

The specific gift need not be mentioned, apparently, for it is the mere fact that it is given that implies the request. Proteus analyzes his beloved:

> But Silvia is too fair, too true, too holy,
> To be corrupted with my worthless gifts.[40]

The Ghost in *Hamlet* recognizes the importance played by gifts in Claudius' seduction of Gertrude:

> Ay, that incestuous, that adulterate beast,
> With witchcraft of his wit, with traitorous gifts—
> O wicked wit and gifts, that have the power
> So to seduce!—won to his shameful lust
> The will of my most seeming-virtuous queen.[41]

Troilus has difficulty in believing that it is Cressida who gives Diomedes the guerdon, a sleeve, which he had given her:

> No, this is Diomed's Cressida!
> If beauty have a soul, this is not she;
> If souls guide vows, if vows be sanctimonies,
> If there be rule in unity itself—
> This is not she.[42]

Cressida herself, unfaithful though she proves to be, is unable actually to put the guerdon in Diomedes's hands. He has to snatch it from her:

Cressida. Here, Diomed, keep this sleeve.
　　[*She hands it to him.*]
　　. . . You look upon that sleeve? Behold it well.
　　He lov'd me—O false wench!—Give't me again.
　　[*She takes it.*]
Diomedes. Whose was't?
Cressida. It is no matter now I ha't again.

Having the sleeve in her possession, she can with fairness add:

> I will not meet with you to-morrow night.
> I prithee, Diomed, visit me no more.

Diomedes recognizes the significance of the sleeve:

> I shall have it.
> *Cressida.* What, this?
> *Diomedes.*   Ay, that.
> *Cressida.* . . . Nay, do not snatch it from me!
>   [*He takes it.*]
>   He that takes that doth take my heart withal.[43]

That last line Cressida means as literally as any statement in courtship can be intended. The guerdon given with meaning and accepted with meaning signifies a relationship with no restraint between the couple. If Horatio had not induced Bel-Imperia to consent to his keeping Don Andrea's guerdon, he still should have had an understood relationship with her unless and until she had definitely repudiated it. As in law, so in love possession is guilt until proof of the contrary be established. Horatio would never have had the gift in his possession unless Don Andrea had died, so the scarf was definite proof of his death. Whoever had the guerdon had the heart of Bel-Imperia. Don Andrea would never have given it up alive, or if he had Bel-Imperia would have felt justified in leaving him. The guerdon was the symbol of love and was equated with the loved person. Thus, by a slight extension of the concept, whoever possessed the guerdon had the right to claim the love of the giver. Such a situation is discussed by Portia in the last act of *The Merchant of Venice.*

Cressida tries to keep some of her honor when Diomedes asks her who has given her the sleeve.

> *Diomedes.* Whose was it?
> *Cressida.* By all Diana's waiting women yond,
>   And by herself, I will not tell you whose.[44]

She is attempting to abide by the courtly rule of secrecy,[45]

which to Shakespeare's audience at this stage of her career is
foolish to the point of being funny. She was a notorious wan-
ton, and everyone knew it. Diomedes, however, knows how to
find out to whom it belongs:

> To-morrow will I wear it on my helm
> And grieve his spirit that dares not challenge it.[46]

He knows that the only person who would challenge his wearing the sleeve would be the warrior who had given it to Cressida. And Troilus, unseen and unheard by the two lovers,
speaks immediately:

> Wert thou the devil and wor'st it on thy horn,
> It should be challeng'd.[47]

All the observers of the love scene between Cressida and
Diomedes recognize the meaning of the sleeve. Although
there is no word spoken by Cressida as to precisely what she
does promise Diomedes, there is no word necessary. The implication is clear: "He that takes that doth take my heart
withal."

The gift of gloves, perhaps more often than any other
single object, serves as a simple declaration of affection. The
request for close relationship is nevertheless there, as in any
gift.

Anthony, in William Haughton's *Englishmen for My
Money*, explains the symbolism as he gives a pair of gloves
to Mathea from her lover Ned;

> *Mathea*, with these Gloues thy *Ned* salutes thee;
> As often as these, hide these from the Sunne,
> And Wanton steales a kisse from thy faire hand,
> Presents his seruiceable true harts zeale,
> Which waites vpon the censure of thy doome.[48]

These are gloves from the lover which may be worn by the beloved. Other gloves, from the beloved to the lover, are part of her personal clothing and unwearable by the lover as gloves, a treasure instead, a symbolic guerdon. Horatio, in *The Spanish Tragedy*, considers the glove, even single and un-wearable, a treasure. When Bel-Imperia drops her glove, he picks it up:

Horatio. Madame, your Gloue.
Bel-Imperia. Thanks, good *Horatio,* take it for thy paines.
Balthazar. Signior *Horatio* stoopt in happie time.
Horatio. I reapt more grace then I deseru'd or hop'd.[49]

Peculiarly enough, the woman seems to have expected two gloves, the man but one:

Princess. But, Katharine, what was sent to you from fair Dumain?
Katharine. Madam, this glove.
Princess.   Did he not send you twain?
Katharine. Yes, madam; and moreover,
                   Some thousand verses of a faithful lover.[50]

The "of a faithful lover" might have as its subject both the verses and the gloves: the gloves were evidences of a faithful lover, too, as Anthony stated in the above quotation from *Englishmen for My Money.*[51] Gloves of the beloved were fair game when found, and did not have to be returned to the mistress:

Speed. Sir, your glove.
Valentine. Not mine. My gloves are on.
Speed. Why then, this may be yours, for this is but one.
Valentine. Ha, let me see! Ay, give it me; it's mine.
                   Sweet ornament that decks a thing divine!
                   Ah, Silvia, Silvia![52]

Shakespeare's Hero displays as a proud possession a pair of gloves given her by Claudio.[53] Dekker, too, seems to regard the gift of a glove as a valuable love-token. In *The Shoemaker's Holiday* Hammon, a relatively unsympathetic character, tries to marry Rose, who loves Lacy. She demurring, he says:

> What, would you have me pule, and pine, and pray,
> With louely Lady mistris of my heart,
> Pardon your seruant, and the rimer play,
> Rayling on *Cupid,* and his tyrants dart?
> Or shall I vndertake some martiall spoile,
> Wearing your gloue at Turney and at Tilt,
> And tell how many gallants I vnhorst,
> Sweet, will this pleasure you?

Rose immediately accepts his offer:

> Yes, when wilt begin?
> What loue-rimes, man? fie on that deadly sinne.[54]

Hammon is making fun of the courtship conventions of the Lacy milieu. Rose, who is a completely sympathetic character, mocks Hammon's mocking of courtship: she would like to be berhymed. And, by implication, she would like to have her lover wear her guerdon, in this case a glove.

When Hodge, in the same play, goes away to war, he leaves with his wife Jane a pair of shoes which he had made for her. These he regards as a guerdon as well as a practical item, a means of identification in the plot later. Guerdons were means of identification always: the lady could tell which of the knights on the field in a tourney was hers by the guerdon he wore. Dekker, by using the guerdon as a focal part of his plot, shows that even the lower classes still considered them important.

Chapman objected to the externally-worn guerdon because it violated the injunction of secrecy. In *All Fools* Valerio exhorts Dariotto:

> You youths have fashions; when you have obtain'd
> A lady's favour, straight your hat must wear it;
> Like a jackdaw, that when he lights upon
> A dainty morsel, kaas and makes his brags,
> And then some kite doth scoop it from him straight;
> When, if he fed without his dawish noise,
> He might fare better and have less disturbance.
> . . . when you prove
> Victorious over fair Gazetta's fort . . .
> . . . Keep your valour close, and 'tis your honour.[55]

The exhortation to secrecy in the last line is the point of the speech.

Other objects may serve as guerdons, such as the purse which Ferdinand gives to Laurentia in *Englishmen for My Money*,[56] the one from Infelice to Hippolito in *2 The Honest Whore*;[57] the chain from Rosalind to Orlando in *As You Like It*;[58] the one from Young Chartley to Gratiana in *The Wise Woman of Hogsdon*;[59] the handkerchief in *Othello* from Othello to Desdemona;[60] the brooch from Brachiano to Vittoria Corombona in Webster's *The White Devil* (1612).[61]

Most often, however, the specific gift is not named. It is very often called a "jewel," and there is the play on the word as meaning both the object given and the beloved's chastity asked for in return. So Infelice says in *2 The Honest Whore,* when confessing to Hippolito her husband: "I haue stolne that Iewell of my chaste honour (which was onely thine) and given it to a slaue."[62] And Flamineo's quick mind catches a quibble in the words of Brachiano in *The White Devil:*

Brachiano. What valew is this Jewell?
Vittoria. Tis the ornament
　　Of a weake fortune.
Brachiano. In sooth ile have it; nay I will but change
　　My Jewell for your Jewell.
Flamineo. Excellent,
　　His Jewell for her Jewell, well put in Duke.[63]

Maria, in *The Family of Love* by Middleton, describes the present most clearly when she speaks of her "favour that I bid thee wear As pledge of love."[64] That is what the gift was intended to be, and if it were not extremely obvious, it could be worn by the lover without attracting notice and without being associated with the donor. That, of course, would be important in the interests of secrecy.

The present, then, was one of the physical aids for the lover, either given or received. As Powell says, "the exchange of gifts" was "principally from the man to the woman" in spousals, but that does not seem to be necessarily true in a declaration of love. The intrinsic value of the gift was of no significance and therefore the gift of some piece of clothing was as acceptable to the lover as that of money —more so, generally, because the obvious value of money was not sentimental. Indeed, when a lover accepts money from his beloved in a play of the period, he is generally presented as unsympathetic.[65] On the other hand, the lover, usually commanding more money than the woman—Portia and her kind excepted—is in a better position to give rich gifts, and considers himself amply repaid in the receipt of a bit of clothing such as a single used glove. The lover seldom gives money, either, to avoid the possibility of cupidity being suspected in either himself or his beloved.[66]

The twentieth century preserves this attitude toward a

lover's gifts. He seldom makes a present of money, and the
girl who considers the dollar value of a present is scorned.
The beloved who took her engagement ring to the jeweler
for evaluation the next morning, was made the subject of a
cartoon intended to be funny. *Radix malorum est cupiditas*.
said the Pardoner. And we still believe it.

The fourth method of communication between lovers is
the despatch often accompanied by a gift.[67] A letter enables
a tongue-tied lover to speak to his beloved in his own words
without the aid of a go-between. The gentleman of the sixteenth century could write well, and he took pride in this
accomplishment. A good letter could combine the elements
of gift and revelation. It is difficult to write good poetry.
Gascoigne's Dan Barthlemew of Bath is a good poet, and
when Gascoigne told his story it was as much to display
the author's own poetic prowess as to compose a narrative.

Although women in sixteenth-century life were supposed
to be good letter-writers, they seldom show their ability in
the plays. Sometimes they cause their lovers to do their writing for them. Silvia, in *The Two Gentlemen of Verona*, has
Valentine write a letter for her, and then she returns it to
him:

> . . . you writ them, sir, at my request;
> But I will none of them: they are for you.
> I would have had them writ more movingly.
> *Valentine.* Please you, I'll write your ladyship another.
> *Silvia.* And when it's writ, for my sake read it over;
> And if it please you, so; if not, why, so!
> . . . if it please you, take it for your labour.[68]

Speed has to explain to Valentine what she has said: "you
. . . have the reason . . . To be a spokesman from Madam

Silvia . . . To yourself. Why, she woos you by . . . a letter . . . she hath made you write to yourself."[69] He concludes:

> . . . often have you writ to her; and she, in modesty,
> Or else for want of idle time, could not again reply;
> Or fearing else some messenger that might her mind discover,
> Herself hath taught her love himself to write unto her lover.[70]

A letter which Beatrice writes to Benedick is produced in
the last scene of the play as proof that she loves him.[71] Other
letters that the characters assert she has written probably did
not exist, but the fact that Benedick could believe that they
had been written shows that on the stage, at least, women
were capable of writing. Claudio, in the garden scene to gull
Benedick into believing that Beatrice loves him, says:

"Shall I," say she, "that have so oft encount'red him with scorn,
write to him that I love him?"[72]

and Leonato adds that she "rail'd at herself that she should
be so immodest to write to one that she knew would flout
her."[73]

Both Speed and Leonato feel that the woman's writing to
the man would show immodesty. Nevertheless, women on
the stage did not often write during this dramatic period,
and when they did their letters were brief and seldom
rhapsodic.

The letters of the heroes are apparently carefully written
to show both their affection and their creative ability. The
most famous example is Hamlet's to Ophelia, which has
come into the hands of Polonius. It should be, as Dan Barthlemew's, in good poetry, as Hamlet realizes.

"To the celestial, and my soul's idol, the most beautified Ophelia, in her excellent white bosom, these, &c.

Doubt thou the stars are fire;
    Doubt that the sun doth move;
Doubt truth to be a liar;
    But never doubt I love.

"O dear Ophelia, I am ill at these numbers; I have not art to reckon my groans; but that I love thee best, O most best, believe it. Adieu.

Thine evermore, most dear lady,
whilst this machine is to him,
HAMLET."[74]

This is a letter which contains more matter than art, more sincerity than poetry. The verse is obviously extravagant and in bad taste, as both Shakespeare and Hamlet realize.

Orlando's rhymed letter to Rosalind in *As You Like It* is an obvious parody of love missives, particularly those of the shepherds in pastoral drama and romance.

"From the east to western Inde,
    No jewel is like Rosalinde.
Her worth, being mounted on the wind,
    Through all the world bears Rosalinde.
All the pictures fairest lin'd
    Are but black to Rosalinde.
Let no face be kept in mind
    But the fair of Rosalinde."[75]

As Rosalind says, "some of them had in them more feet than the verses would bear,"[76] and the figurative language is absurd.

The letter could serve as a kind of go-between as well as a person. The go-between often replaced the lover because he could talk as the lover could not. Similarly a letter could be

more articulate than a tongue-tied lover. So Suffolk, when
he loses his voice in the presence of Margaret, muses:

> Fain would I woo her, yet I dare not speak.
> I'll call for pen and ink and write my mind.[77]

Beatrice and Benedick both use letters as go-betweens in
Much Ado About Nothing:

Claudio. And I'll be sworn upon't that he loves her;
For here's a paper written in his hand,
A halting sonnet of his own pure brain,
Fashion'd to Beatrice.
Hero.   And here's another,
Writ in my cousin's hand, stol'n from her pocket,
Containing her affection unto Benedick.[78]

Donado, in *'Tis Pity She's a Whore,* uses a letter to express
the love which his witless nephew Bergetto feels for Annabella: "since you are no better a speaker, I'll have you write
to her after some courtly manner, and enclose some rich
jewel in the letter."[79] And Annabella communicates with
Giovanni by letter through the intermediation of the Friar
when she is held prisoner by Soranzo.[80]

These are the four methods of communication which the
lovers use to convey their feelings to their beloveds. Shakespeare's lovers most often simply declare their loves, but
they frequently use the other methods of communication
either in conjunction with the first method, declaration, or
alternately with it.

The revelation of the love could be made either by a go-
between or by one of the lovers in person. In the plays the
revelation is generally either in itself a spousal *de futuro* or
is followed by an immediate spousal. In Shakespeare's works
there seems to be little lapse of time between the declara-

tion of love and the spousal. Romeo and Juliet both declare their love to each other and espouse themselves in the same scene:

Juliet. Deny thy father and refuse thy name!
        Or, if thou wilt not, be but sworn my love,
        And I'll no longer be a Capulet.[81]

The espousal occurs later in the scene, after Romeo has replied to Juliet:

                I take thee at thy word.
        Call me but love, and I'll be new baptiz'd;
        Henceforth I never will be Romeo,[82]

and has thus accepted informally but inextricably Juliet's offer of a vow. The espousal runs threadlike through the scene and culminates:

Juliet. Well, do not swear. Although I joy in thee,
        I have no joy of this contract to-night.
        It is too rash, too unadvis'd, too sudden . . .
Romeo. O, wilt thou leave me so unsatisfied?
Juliet. What satisfaction canst thou have to-night?
Romeo. Th'exchange of thy love's faithful vow for mine.
Juliet. I gave thee mine before thou didst request it.[83]

Ferdinand and Miranda declare their loves and betroth themselves in the same scene.[84] Valentine has told Silvia of his love while they were offstage, but by the time he tells Proteus about it he has accomplished the betrothal too:

Proteus. But she loves you?
Valentine. Ay, and we are betroth'd; nay more our marriage hour

                           ·   ·   ·   ·
        Determin'd of.[85]

Portia's spousal with Bassanio in *The Merchant of Venice*

comes without even a true declaration of love to precede it.[86]

The spousal given at the time of the declaration of love is usually a *de futuro*. It is a promise to marry at some future time, and it may be dissolved upon sufficient grounds or upon consent of both parties. In essence, the *de futuro* spousal parallels the engagement of the twentieth century, and Shakespeare uses it in practically the same way as an engagement. In modern times when a man declares his love for a girl he at the same time asks her if she will marry him. That is a traditional *de futuro* spousal put in terms of twentieth-century custom.

In other ways, too, the modern method parallels the Elizabethan. As we have seen, there is at the time of the spousal the exchange of gifts. At least the man gives the woman a guerdon. Nowadays the guerdon is usually a ring given at the time of what we call betrothal. A gift of some other object is made at the time of marriage. The present of the groom to the bride in modern marriage is often a family heirloom, such as lace belonging to the groom's family to be used for the bride's wedding gown, or a brooch from the groom's mother, or some other apparel which the bride may wear at the ceremony. This is not the first gift, it is the last before the marriage ceremony. But it seems to parallel the first gift of the Elizabethans. Othello apparently used the handkerchief which he gave Desdemona to signify his betrothal. He tells Desdemona later that it had been his mother's:

> She, dying, gave it me,
> And bade me, when my fate would have me wive,
> To give it her. I did so.[87]

Also at the time of the revelation-spousal, the Elizabethan lovers attempt to determine a time or method of marriage.

Unless the marriage is sanctioned by one or more of the parents, the plans have to be made by the couple themselves, and in the latter case they are generally for a huggermugger secret ceremony. Valentine, when he tells Proteus of his arrangements with Silvia, says:

> . . . we are betroth'd; nay more, our marriage hour
> With all the cunning manner of our flight,
> Determin'd of: how I must climb her window,
> The ladder made of cords, and all the means
> Plotted and 'greed on for my happiness.[88]

The unwitnessed betrothal ceremony used at the time of the declaration of love, however, is not any more binding than the fidelity of the lovers makes it. Witnesses are necessary if any such formality is to keep the lovers legally bound to each other. If trust be lacking, which really would be impossible in Shakespeare for two people in love, or if the lover wishes to assure his beloved that he means well, the private spousal of the time of the declaration would be followed by a public spousal which, because witnessed, would be more binding. This assurance Florizel tries to give Perdita in *The Winter's Tale*. He has promised her offstage apparently secretly that he will marry her:

> Lift up your countenance, as it were the day
> Of celebration of that nuptial which
> We two have sworn shall come,[89]

and he therefore attempts to perform a public spousal before the assembled shepherds:

> O, hear me breathe my life
> Before this ancient sir, who, it should seem,
> Hath sometime lov'd! I take thy hand—this hand,
> As soft as dove's down and as white as it.[90]

Olivia, who has great difficulty in persuading Cesario to love her, assures herself of a witness when she gets him to agree—in the person of Sebastian—to a spousal:

> If you mean well,
> Now go with me and with this holy man
> Into the chantry by. There, before him,
> And underneath that consecrated roof,
> Plight me the full assurance of your faith,
> That my most jealous and too doubtful soul
> May live at peace.[91]

In Shakespeare's plays the declaration of love is a declaration of intent to marry. There is no reason why two people in his dramas should not wish to marry if they are in love. No person could love two people, according to both Andreas and Shakespeare, and the only possible impediments are external. The dramatic code of Shakespeare is followed closely by the movie code of the present day in America, which stipulates that a good girl may not kiss more than one man in the course of the play unless she is to be a trollop or has all but one of the men she kisses die. The exceptions to love's being defined, perhaps too simply, as a desire for marriage are very few. Troilus and Cressida do not desire marriage, and as we shall see later, their declaration of love is a travesty of the spousal ceremony. They do, however, declare their love for each other. Bertram performs a bigamous spousal with Diana in his attempt to win her, but he apparently is not sincere at the time, for Dumain, or "First Lord," says of him in the next scene:

He hath perverted a young gentlewoman here in Florence, of a most chaste renown; and this night he fleshes his will in the spoil of her honour. He has given her his monumental ring, and thinks himself made in the unchaste composition.[92]

Almost the only other times that a declaration of love is not accompanied by a spousal are when the love is not returned by the beloved or when one person is unable to answer. Rosalind declares her love for Orlando almost as soon as she sees him, but he is incapable of answering.[93] But in such a case as dumbness the love may be declared by a sign. When Hero cannot talk in her betrothal to Claudio, she answers by a kiss.[94]

During the Middle Ages the courtly lover maintained secrecy in his affair because he feared the interference of the woman's husband. In the Elizabethan drama the secrecy was still important, but the reason for it had changed. The object of fear was the father instead of the husband. In this manner the author maintained one of the more important elements of suspense in a love plot without sacrificing the central characters to immorality.

The sole sharer of the secret of the love is the confidant, one for each of the lovers, and unless he is entirely trustworthy the entire match can be easily broken up. This secrecy we have seen should be maintained even in the stage of *hereos,* because the overt symptoms of the disease might betray the lover's desire.

The Ghost of Andrea in Kyd's *The Spanish Tragedy* tells in the first lines of the play of his past love for Bel-Imperia and his secrecy in that affair:

> . . . in prime and pride of all my years,
> By duteous service and deserving love,
>   In secret I possess'd a worthy dame
> Which hight sweet Bel-Imperia by name.[95]

It is not clear whether Bel-Imperia and Andrea had intended marriage or not. Theirs had been an affair of a type which

Shakespeare avoided. In his plays the love of one person for two people is depicted on the stage only in *Troilus and Cressida*. Bel-Imperia's later assignation with Horatio, which would have made her love bigamous, because it followed so soon upon Andrea's death[96] was not a situation to appeal to Shakespeare.

Wendoll, in *A Woman Killed With Kindness*, who plans to seduce a married woman, naturally argues for secrecy. He assures Mrs. Frankford:

> I will be secret, lady, close as night;
> And not the light of one small glorious star
> Shall shine here in my forehead, to bewray
> That act of night.[97]

In this play the secret is revealed by a man external to the affair, as it is in *The Spanish Tragedy*. Nicholas, the servant to the Frankfords, tells his master of the love.

In *The Duchess of Malfi* Antonio and the Duchess are secretly married, and they maintain the secrecy until the birth of their first child. Antonio finally needs to confide in his best friend, Delio, and he tells him:

> Let me seale your lipps for ever,
> For, did I thinke, that any thing but th'ayre
> Could carry these words from you, I should wish
> You had no breath at all.[98]

In this play, again, the secret is revealed by a man, again a servant. The persons from whom the secret is to be kept, however, are the Duchess's brothers, and the marriage is legal and moral.

In *'Tis Pity She's a Whore* the incestuous affair of Annabella and her brother Giovanni must be kept secret. She is finally married to Soranzo, who finds that she is with child not of his begetting. Soranzo bullies her until his servant Vasques stops him with insincere words, praising the ideal of secrecy:

You would have her confess the author of her present misfortunes, I warrant ye; 'tis an unconscionable demand, and she should lose the estimation that I, for my part, hold of her worth, if she had done it: why, sir, you ought not, of all men living, to know it.[99]

Later, alone with Soranzo, Vasques promises to find out who the father is, and he does find out. Again, the servant is the means of betrayal.

Of the four examples mentioned above, secrecy is strongly exhorted in each, in each the secrecy is eventually violated by a human agent, not by any faulty action of the lovers, and in each the result is a tragic one for the lovers. In *The Spanish Tragedy* the discovery of the relationship of Bel-Imperia and Andrea forces Pedringano to the treachery which initiates the tragedy of the play. Mrs. Frankford dies at least partly because of the repentance caused by the discovery of her fall. It seems improbable that she would have died so soon if she had not been found out. The Duchess of Malfi dies because the secret is revealed to those who oppose her marriage. The violation of the secret of Annabella and Giovanni leads directly to their deaths. In all of the plays secrecy is of literally vital importance.

Secrecy is not so much emphasized in Shakespeare's plays largely because the secrecy is never of an extramarital affair, with the humorous exception of *The Merry Wives of Windsor,* and the revelation of the secrecy never leads to death but invariably is followed by marriage. The deaths of Romeo and Juliet are caused by the keeping of their secret, not by its revelation, which is an irony intended by Shakespeare perhaps more than is generally recognized.

The lovers met as often as possible, either in a neutral place such as Friar Laurence's cell in *Romeo and Juliet,* or in public when secrecy was not required and they could show their affection for each other, as Claudio and Hero in *Much Ado About Nothing.* Shakespeare's lovers almost never have any difficulty with the enemy after they have found out that they love each other. When there is difficulty, they flee, one after the other, to a neutral spot, as a forest in *The Two Gentlemen of Verona* and *As You Like It.* The lovers use these meetings for a renewed declaration of love and for their plans for marriage.

The time before marriage and after the declaration of love is as brief as possible, perhaps because of dramatic necessity. There is never even opportunity for the banns. The hurry of lovers is epitomized in Rosalind's statement of the love of Oliver and Celia, who:

. . . no sooner met but they look'd; no sooner look'd but they lov'd; no sooner lov'd but they sigh'd; no sooner sigh'd but they ask'd one another the reason; no sooner knew the reason but they sought the remedy: and in those degrees have they made a pair of stairs to marriage, which they will climb incontinent, or else be incontinent before marriage. They are in the very wrath of love, and they will together. Clubs cannot part them.[100]

In general, the time elapse is less than a week, as Romeo and Juliet, Ferdinand and Miranda, Petruchio and Katherine, Bassanio and Portia exemplify.

From the time of the declaration of love until the marriage the lover is the servant of the beloved, submitting his entire life to her wishes, in accordance with the behavior of a true courtly lover as stated by Chariclea:

. . . it standes him more in duetie not to offende his Ladie, to
whome he is bounde then she to feare him, whome she maye com-
maunde lyke as in common reason there is always more libertie
alowed in generall respectes to the mayster, than a simple license
to him that professeth the state of a seruant.[101]

So when Phebe says to Silvius: "Tell this youth what 'tis to
love," he answers:

It is to be all made of faith and service,

and all present concur:

Silvius. And so am I for Phebe.
Phebe. And I for Ganymede.
Orlando. And I for Rosalind.
Rosalind. And I for no woman.[102]

It is interesting that Phebe offers service to one whom she
believes a man, for until the marriage the woman is usually in
control, and the man is the servant. But evidently when love
is great the woman does not insist on the courtly formality in
the lover and even attempts to subject herself to him. So
Miranda in her declaration of love to Ferdinand says:

> I am your wife, if you will marry me;
> If not, I'll die your maid. To be your fellow
> You may deny me; but I'll be your servant,
> Whether you will or no.[103]

And Ferdinand has already protested to her:

> The very instant that I saw you, did
> My heart fly to your service; there resides,
> To make me slave to it . . . [104]

Therefore it was natural that the beloved should address her
lover as "servant," and that he should delight in being so

called. For only one man was allowed that title. Chariclea had
acknowledged the titles due the lover and beloved:

> . . . by common voice the woman is esteemed aboue
> him who offereth court to hir (as shee being
> called mistresse, and he seruant) [105]

The term "mistress" is similar to "midomna" and is more
formal than the terms of endearments used by lovers more
intimate. Thus Manville in *Fair Em* says to her when he has
failed in a part of his courtship:

> Ah, Maistres, sometime I might haue said, my loue,
> But time and fortune have bereued me of that. [106]

The terms are used in public places to show some relationship
between the lovers without betraying any great closeness.
Silvia and Valentine caress the words as they speak them to
each other in Thurio's presence:

Silvia. Servant!
Valentine. Mistress? . . .
Silvia. Servant, you are sad. [107]

Here are two children at the game of love and sincerely in
love at the same time, playing with the formality.

When the love is discussed in private, or when the lovers
have progressed beyond the declaration toward marriage, the
endearments increase. But even at the earlier stage, if the
woman loves greatly, she may speak of her lover as she would
ordinarily have him speak of her. Helena has no pride when
she has fallen in love with Bertram, and when she speaks to
the Countess, his mother, of her state, she says:

> My master, my dear lord he is, and I
> His servant live and will his vassal die. [108]

Bertram has not noticed her, and he does not know she loves
him.

Another term used with overtones of meaning beyond the
literal interpretation is "friend," as Monophylo defines it:

. . . and so doubt not at all (sir) that there is any one in loue
who is not extreemely greeued, when his pretended friend or
second himself, findes contentment with any other whatsoeuer.[109]

So Maria, in *The Family of Love,* speaks of her beloved,
Gerardine, as "my absent friend,"[110] and later, when she
sees him, says:

> Be brief, sweet friend, salute and part in one.[111]

Juliet, in addressing Romeo, uses three terms of address of
equal intimacy when she cries to him:

> Art thou gone so, my lord, my love, my friend?[112]

For a woman's "lord" is her husband, her "love" is her accepted lover, and her "friend" is the same. She is showing
an ideal relationship when she calls her husband her lover,
and by that she intensifies the feeling of intimacy and of the
depth of love of the two for each other. Paris uses the companion term to "lord" in addressing Juliet at Friar Laurence's
cell because he has been betrothed to her:

> Happily met, my lady and my wife![113]

Romeo, when he sees Juliet dead, speaks to her as "my love!
my wife!"[114] and when he first speaks to her under the balcony, he bargains:

> Call me but love, and I'll be new baptiz'd.[115]

The frequent iteration of lovers' terms between married

people intensifies the sense of their youth as well as of the strength of their relationship in the audience.

The terms "husband" or "wife," or "lord" or "lady" were generally reserved for use by people who had been formally betrothed *de praesenti,* and were married in fact if not by the church. "Lord" and "lady" could be used before the *de praesenti* ceremony, but they seldom were. The "husband" and "wife" terms were domestic enough so that they were limited to married persons, who might or might not have slept together. Swinburne explains the terms:

Such a Wife was the blessed Virgin *Mary,* that is to say, betroathed to *Joseph,* but neither solemnly married with him, not secretly known by him, at the Conception of Christ; and yet nevertheless termed Wife in the Holy Scriptures: For as well the Sacred Scriptures, as the Civil and Ecclesiastical Laws, do usually give to Women betroathed only, or affianced, the Name and Title of Wife, because in truth the man and woman, thus perfectly assured, by words of *present time,* are Husband and Wife before God and his Church.[116]

Specifically, the terms used could vary as the speaker expressed a desire for a deeper or lesser commitment. But in general the lovers addressed each other immediately after the declaration and acceptance of love as "servant," "mistress," and "friend," and after a *de praesenti* betrothal as "husband" and "wife."

During the period of courtship with which this chapter has been concerned, the lovers have proceeded from *hereos* into the state of happiness in which they have accepted each other and are looking forward to marriage. At most points of this progress the lovers have paralleled Andreas in that they have been searching for an acceptance of each other and have made their offers in a form which is mentioned by

Andreas. Only the simple declaration of love is not traditional. The go-between and the confidant, the guerdon or
present, and the letter are all part of the code of *fine amor*.
The inventiveness of the Elizabethan age in love-making,
insofar as methods of communication are concerned, seems
mainly to lie in the occasional dispensing with *hereos* when
the lovers immediately after meeting declare their loves and
in the double and treble meanings which the lover might put
on his words of courtship in the Elizabethan gaiety of lin-
guistic exploration.

But in the revelation of the love Elizabethans begin to
vary from the code of *fine amor*. Here the purpose of the
declaration must be considered. If the love is to be extramarital, as in *The White Devil, 'Tis Pity She's a Whore,* or
The Spanish Tragedy, the lovers must keep the affair secret.
If, on the other hand, the love is to be consummated with
marriage, as in *As You Like It, Twelfth Night,* or *Much
Ado About Nothing,* every attempt is made to procure an
adequate witness to the ceremony of acceptance. If, again,
the lovers intend marriage but, because of some external
threat such as forbidding parents, must keep it secret, as in
Romeo and Juliet, The Duchess of Malfi, or *The Taming of
the Shrew,* they attempt to merge *fine amor* with honor, ne-
gotiating a ceremony which they feel to be legal but which
is not public. This last is the closest Shakespeare comes, with
the exceptions of *Troilus and Cressida* and *Antony and
Cleopatra,* to a *fine amor* situation with its titillating secrecy.

In general, however, and in all the methods leading to
the Betrothal mentioned in Chapter I, Shakespeare's heroes
and heroines follow the same paths mapped by Andreas and
followed by the romances.

Chapter V

SPOUSALS

MOST LOVE STORIES end with the phrase, "And so they were married and lived happily ever after," or imply as much. In the modern movie romance the two lovers, reunited after many tribulations, embrace as the violins of incidental music rise to a rapturous crescendo; the couples of the cowboy romances face to the west and proceed lingeringly toward the setting sun. There is in neither an actual showing of the marriage ceremony. When such a ceremony is dramatized, either on the stage or in the movies, it is always truncated. No twentieth-century movie or play presents all the ritual. This is probably a concession to superstition. In any case the ceremony itself lacks dramatic interest. For the same reasons no complete marriage ceremonies are dramatized in sixteenth-century plays, although there are *de praesenti* spousals. The setting is seldom the interior of a church, and the action seldom represents an actual church service. The occasional marriage by priest and book, as that of Hero and Claudio in *Much Ado About Nothing,* is invariably incomplete, and it occurs often in a secular location.

It is necessary that spousals be considered in this paper in order that the separation of courtship and spousal may be delineated. Many aspects of spousals have been and are considered preliminary to them, as the casual engagement of today is often not adequately differentiated from the courtship.

For many centuries before the time of Shakespeare a distinction had been made between spousals and marriage. A spousal was a trothplight or betrothal, a promise of marriage to come.

> Spousals are a mutual Promise of future Marriage, being duly made between those Persons, to whom it is lawful. In which definition I observe three things especially: *One,* That this Promise must be mutual; *Another,* That it must be done *rite,* duly; *The last,* By them to whom it is lawful.[1]

The marriage ceremony gives legal warrant and social approval for two people of opposite sex to live together and establish a family relationship. The family had originally been governed by the husband and father, who until recent times had made all important decisions. Previously he had arranged the marriages of his children without consulting their wishes. But a tenth-century Anglo-Saxon betrothal formula required the girl's consent, unconditional and free, to marriage.[2] After this period there was in England a decline, although not rapid, in the number of enforced marriages arranged by the parents.

The doctrine that consent made marriage "had gradually replaced the earlier idea that physical union was necessary for valid marriage. During the twelfth century the Church developed a distinction between two types of spousals. The first of these, *sponsalia per verba de futuro,* was a promise to marry at some future time." Consummation implied present consent at the time of the act and therefore converted "the contract *de futuro* into a valid irregular marriage. The second, *sponsalia per verba de praesenti,* constituted marriage itself; in later times it required no consummation. By the thirteenth century these doctrines were firmly established; they continued to be recognized in English ecclesiastical courts until 1754."[3]

The distinction between spousals *de futuro,* spousals *de*

praesenti, and marriages is clearly given in the 1686 edition
of Swinburne's *Treatise of Spousals* by the editor in his prefatory "To the Reader":

In our Publick Office of Marriage, *Spousals* and *Matrimony* are
united, and performed in one continued Act; when the Minister
demands, *Wilt thou have this Woman to thy wedded Wife, &c.*
And the Man answers, *I will,* and so the Woman *vice versa,* there's
a *Specimen* of *Spousals de futuro.* When the Man repeats the
Words, *J.N. take thee N. to my wedded Wife, &c.* and so the
Woman *vice versa,* there's the form of *Spousals de praesenti,* which
in Substance are perfect Matrimony, (as I said before) though
not as to all Legal Effects. When the Minister adds his Benediction,
and pronounces them to be Man and Wife, then 'tis a perfect
Marriage to all constructions and purposes in law.[4]

Spousals were quite often presented in detail in the
Elizabethan drama. The two basic types developed in the
thirteenth century by the Church were still used: the spousal
de futuro, a promise of marriage at some future time; and
the spousal *de praesenti,* a promise of marriage which was in
itself an oath and constituted marriage. The interesting fact
is that in Shakespeare's plays either form of spousal is invariably followed by a wedding as the twentieth-century audience understands it. The *de futuro* spousal theoretically
could be broken, the *de praesenti* was binding in itself. But
Shakespeare, apparently more conservative than legally necessary, always includes the church rites—or a pagan approximation of them—in the fifth act of the play if not before.

Most courtesy books avoided discussing the form of
spousal, partly because their authors did not advocate marriage as the ideal culmination of a love affair, but partly also
because of the tendency to avoid the obvious. Marriage, to
any century, is the most interesting aspect of life. The statis-

tics of vital concern to the state for a man's record are only three—birth, marriage, and death—and marriage is the only one which the individual can enjoy. Therefore from an early age he knows pretty well the general aspects of the marriage ceremony. So, too, the young adult of the sixteenth century must have known the forms of the spousal and marriage customs of his age.

The precise form of the *de praesenti* spousal cannot be specified. It included a contract given and received, but otherwise it could vary as much as the parties concerned wished. The intent could invariably be gathered at the time of the ceremony. Swinburne, attempting to limit spousals as closely as possible while still keeping within the precedents which had established the laws he tries to explain, finally generalizes:

. . . liberty [has been] granted to contract Spousals by whatsoever form of Words, or by any other means, as *Writing, Signs, Tokens,* &c. whereby this mutual Consent might appear; and so at this present, there is no one *Form* of *Desponsation* more lawful than another, but it is sufficient if the Consent of the Parties do appear by any form.[5]

Usually, however, there are most of nine steps in a spousal in a sixteenth-century drama. These I propose to list and discuss in the order in which they would occur.

1. The consent of the lovers is necessary before the contract may be made. This was the result of a crusade of the Church carried on for centuries in its attempt to stop the bartering of brides. The consent should be obtained, logically, verbally before witnesses.

King John. What say these young ones? What say you, my niece?

Blanch. That she is bound in honour still to do
    What you in wisdom still vouchsafe to say.
King John. Speak then, Prince Dauphin. Can you love this lady?
Lewis. Nay, ask me if I can refrain from love,
    For I do love her most unfeignedly.[6]

There are numerous witnesses to the ceremony, including the King of France, in Shakespeare's treatment.

    2. An agreement as to dowry and other settlements is necessary before the contract may be made. If there is to be no dowry, as occasionally happens, this point would not have to be discussed. When the love is overwhelming and the plot concerned with little but the growth and culmination of passion, Shakespeare avoids any mention of dowry or of other financial matters. Romeo and Juliet do not speak of money at any point in the play. Ferdinand and Miranda avoid the subject completely. But in *The Merchant of Venice,* in which love is important but of less interest than the central plot of the pound of flesh, the dowry is mentioned:

Portia. This house, these servants, and this same myself
    Are yours, my lord's. I give them with this ring.[7]

    When the marriage is one of convenience rather than love, Shakespeare has the participants declare affection for each other, but he also causes the parents sponsoring the betrothal to be quite specific as to the dowry:

King John. Then do I give Volquessen, Touraine, Maine,
    Poictiers, and Anjou, these five provinces,
    With her to thee; and this addition more,
    Full thirty thousand marks of English coin.[8]

    3. The consent of a parent is not necessary, although it is often given. In general, the lovers of Shakespeare's earlier

plays—such as Romeo and Juliet, Orlando and Rosalind, Valentine and Silvia—do not have parental permission at the time of the betrothal. In his last play, *The Tempest,* Prospero, who constantly watches and deifically controls the match, gives his permission to a spousal at the proper time, although this is after the couple have betrothed themselves to each other without their knowing of his consent.

In Shakespeare, as in the popular dramas generally, the young people marry their own choices without regard to parental wishes, as in *A Midsummer Night's Dream, The Taming of the Shrew,* and *The Merry Wives of Windsor.* Polixenes, Florizel's father in *The Winter's Tale,* written in 1611, raises objections to his son's love-match, and the couple espouse themselves without his consent. In Shakespeare's early history plays, the living parent betroths the children:

King John. Philip of France, if thou be pleas'd withal,
          Command thy son and daughter to join hands.
King Philip. It likes us well. Young princes, close your hands.[9]

If the parents are not alive, the lovers are perfectly capable of performing their own ceremony without supervision, as in the betrothal of Richard, Duke of Gloucester, and Anne.[10]

This is true of only the history plays. Both of Romeo's and both of Juliet's parents are alive, but the lovers do not consult them at any time on the matter of their love. On the other hand Portia, apparently an orphan, betroths herself according to her dead father's wishes, giving herself to the man who chooses the correct casket. Perhaps she gives some hints to Bassanio in the song sung while he considers his choice, but otherwise she abides by parental behest.

4. Legally, witnesses are required, and they are generally

present in Shakespeare's plays at the spousals. If there are none present, the contract is not legally binding if either party subsequently refuses to admit the ceremony. If the witnesses present are incompetent, the same would be true.

Swinburne, in his *Treatise of Spousals,* has no definition or limitation of witnesses, but in his *Wils and Testaments* (1640) he discusses witnesses for testaments, and presumably those for spousals would be accepted or rejected for the same reasons. There he mentions three groups of persons who are incompetent to witness wills: those dishonest in manners, those unable to comprehend, and those who because they are related or are servants are prejudiced.[11]

The question of the legality of clandestine marriages was especially difficult since they, by definition, had either an insufficient number of witnesses (two were required) or none at all. Swinburne can find no adequate law and finally decides that the matter is on the consciences of the lovers:

. . . albeit there be no Witnesses of the Contract, yet the Parties having verily, (though secretly) Contracted Matrimony, they are very Man and Wife before God; neither can either of them with safe *Conscience* Marry elsewhere, so long as the other party liveth; for proof is not of the Essence of Matrimony; as if it were, yet their Consciences shall be as a thousand Witnesses before the Tribunal of the immortal God, though it be otherwise in the Judgement of mortal Man.[12]

The words might have been taken from *Fair Em,* written in 1590, at least ten years before Swinburne's work. When Em and Elner argue as to which should marry Manville, he finally intercedes to choose Em:

Manville. To saie the troth, this maide had first my loue.
Elner. Yea, Manuile, but there was no witness by.

Em. Thy conscience, Manuile, is a hundred witnesses.
Elner. Shee hath stolne a conscience to serue her owne turne.[13]

Although Shakespeare has no witnesses of the *de praesenti* spousal of Romeo and Juliet, he does introduce them into most of his other plays. In the betrothal of Petruchio and Katherine, for instance, Gremio and Tranio clearly state that they are acting as witnesses:

Baptista. God send you joy, Petruchio! 'tis a match.
Gremio, Tranio. Amen say we; we will be witnesses.[14]

It is significant that the marriage of Romeo and Juliet is witnessed by the Friar before the lovers proceed to consummation.

5. The contract itself might vary considerably. The intent is more important than the words, and the dramatists seem to have tried to put some of their better poetry into the speeches made on the solemn occasion. Many dramatists use rhyme in these passages, setting them off from the blank verse of the surrounding lines. Webster uses an antiphonal duet in *The Duchess of Malfi,* in a natural approximation of song. The pattern is of a pentameter line followed by a dimeter for four lines, two more dimeter, and then a concluding triplet of which the last line is tetrameter and the two preceding pentameter. The passage has no rhyme, but its rhythmical pattern is ABAB BB AAX. The couple alternate in speaking a pair of lines, and Antonio speaks the last three.

Duchess. Blesse (Heaven) this sacred Gordian, which let violence
            Never untwine.
Antonio. And may our sweet affections, (like the Sphears)
            Be still in motion.
Duchess. Quickning, and make
            The like soft Musique.

Antonio. That we may imitate the loving Palmes
   (Best Embleme of a peacefull marriage)
   That nev'r bore fruite devided.[15]

This is a spousal completely spoken. Occasionally one lover is not able to speak at the ceremony, and then his acceptance can be shown by sign. So in the betrothal of Claudio and Hero, in *Much Ado About Nothing,* Claudio says:

 . . . Lady, as you are mine, I am yours. I give away myself for you and dote upon the exchange.
Beatrice. Speak, cousin; or, if you cannot, stop his mouth with a kiss and let not him speak neither.[16]

    . . . .

. . . the contract itself, whether made in secret, in a private gathering of friends, or in the church service, was the essential feature of matrimony, the ceremony of the church being quite secondary in importance. On this point the publisher of Swinburne's book says, "In all Marriages Solemnized after the most strict manner, the Contract of Parties is the principal Ingredient & most essential Part, all other Matters being only as it were Foreign & Extrinsical to its Nature."[17]

 6. There are constant references in the plays to the clasping of hands either during the contract or immediately after it, in confirmation. The right hands are used, and the sealing of the contract is thus similar to the sealing of any bargain made between individuals. The same handclasp is used in modern marriage ceremonies.

 The Priest of *Twelfth Night* says that the betrothal of Olivia and Sebastian has been

   A contract of eternal bond of love,
   Confirm'd by mutual joinder of your hands,[18]

and Folly-Wit, in Middleton's *A Mad World, My Masters,*

says: "What, is't a match? if't be, clap hands."[19] The same
token is used in royal marriages. At the espousal of Blanch
and Lewis, Dauphin of France, King John arranges the
match and concludes:

> Philip of France, if thou be pleas'd withal,
> Command thy son and daughter to join hands.
>
> *King Philip.* It likes us well. Young princes, close your hands.[20]

Hands are apparently joined even in a marriage by proxy,
for there is evidence that Suffolk and Margaret do so in her
betrothal to King Henry VI:

> *Reignier.* And I again, in Henry's royal name,
> As deputy unto that gracious king,
> Give thee her hand for sign of plighted faith.[21]

7. The contract itself is sealed by a kiss, again as in the
modern marriage ceremony. When Pasquill and Katherine
of *Jack Drum's Entertainment* join themselves in a spousal,
they conclude:

> *Pasquill.* Heauens graunt, being dead my soule may liue nie thee
> *Katherine.* One kisse shal giue thee mine eternally.
> *Pasquill.* In faire exchaunge vouchsafe my hart to take.[22]

At the betrothal of Blanch and Lewis in *King John,* Austria
requests that they kiss:

> *King Philip.* . . . Young princes, close your hands.
> *Austria.* And your lips too; for I am well assur'd
> That I did so when I was first assur'd.[23]

8. Witnesses state at the conclusion of the ceremony that
they have understood the betrothal, and they ask blessings
upon it. Nerissa and Gratiano witness the betrothal of Portia
and Bassanio, and Nerissa concludes:

> My lord and lady, it is now our time
> That have stood by and seen our wishes prosper
> To cry "good joy." Good joy, my lord and lady![24]

Leonato, in giving Hero to Claudio after Don Pedro's wooing of her for his friend, says to Claudio:

"Count, take of me my daughter, and with her my fortunes. His Grace hath made the match, and all grace say Amen to it!"[25]

Mall's betrothal to Francis in Henry Porter's *1 The Two Angry Women of Abington* is witnessed by her brother:

Mall. Why, then, sweet Francis, I am only thine. . . .
      Brother, bear witness.
Philip. Do ye deliver this as your deed?
Mall. I do, I do.
Philip. God send ye both good speed.[26]

9. If possible, gifts are exchanged at the ceremony as earnest of the future or a symbol of the person or property given. Portia, when she gives herself to Bassanio, says:

> This house, these servants, and this same myself
> Are yours, my lord's. I give them with this ring.[27]

The ring here is a particular gift, symbolizing both the marriage and, as mentioned earlier, the dowry. The Priest of *Twelfth Night* who witnesses[28] the spousals of Olivia and Sebastian states that the ceremony was "Strength'ned by interchangement of your rings."[29] Katherine, in *Jack Drum's Entertainment*, concludes her ceremony with Pasquill with "weare this *Ned* for my sake."[30]

An apparent contradiction of the belief that the ring was used at spousals is Swinburne's contention:

. . . whereas I have alledged that the Solemnity of the Ring is

usually observed within this Realm at Marriages, forasmuch, as
that is true indeed, when as the Marriage is celebrated in the face
of the Church, according to the Book of Common Prayer, but not
at the contracting of Spousals, albeit *de praesenti,* for ought I can
learn.[31]

Powell, however, speaks of "the ring of betrothal" as being
"worn on the right hand,"[32] and rings are exchanged by
lovers in many of Shakespeare's plays, *e.g., The Two Gentlemen of Verona,*[33] *Richard III,*[34] *A Midsummer Night's
Dream,*[35] *The Merchant of Venice,*[36] *Twelfth Night,*[37] and
All's Well That Ends Well.[38] And Swinburne speaks of the
token of spousals *de futuro* as being "commonly a Ring."[39]

It is possible that the ring was not exchanged at spousals
in actual life: it certainly is often exchanged in the plays.

Various spousals omit mention of certain details listed
here. But none of those omitted seems to be vital, and some
of those, not mentioned in the dialogue, might have been
presented in the action.

At any time during a play that a number of these nine actions occurs, it is probable that the lovers are going through
a spousal. The characters seldom kiss, take hands, or exchange rings, or go through any of the spousal activities
mentioned above without implying the entire ceremony.

Swinburne finds five variations in the *de praesenti* spousal
accepted by contemporary courts.[40] These variations are
mainly in the verbal contract and not in the actions of the betrothal, and they appear to have been traditional rather than
legal.

The first distinction Swinburne finds is between the simple
and the conditional form of spousal. The conditional is seldom used of the *de praesenti,* although it is of the *de futuro,*
in the dramas. It includes such words as "I will marry you if

my father consent." Margaret, in *1 Henry VI*, espouses herself conditionally to Henry through Suffolk when she says:

An if my father please, I am content.[41]

Katherine, of *Henry V*, uses the same condition:

King Henry. . . . Wilt thou have me?
Katherine. Dat is as it sall please de roi mon père.
King Henry. Nay, it will please him well, Kate. It shall please him, Kate.
Katherine. Den it sall also content me.
King Henry. Upon that I kiss your hand and I call you my queen.[42]

Generally the *de praesenti* spousal in the drama is direct and simple. Ferdinand and Miranda do not consider her father, her dowry, or anything external to themselves when they say:

Ferdinand.   My mistress, dearest!
        And I thus humble ever.
Miranda.   My husband then?
Ferdinand. Ay, with a heart as willing
        As bondage e'er of freedom. Here's my hand.
Miranda. And mine, with my heart in't.[43]

Their spousal is simple, though clandestine.

The second distinction is between present and absent spousals. The betrothal of Romeo and Juliet in the balcony scene is a present spousal *de praesenti* because both lovers participate in person in the ceremony.[44] The spousal of Henry VI and Margaret, which is accomplished through Suffolk as proxy for his king on the battlefield before Angiers, is an absent spousal.[45]

The third distinction Swinburne finds is between public and private spousals. A public spousal is one contracted before sufficient witnesses, as the betrothal of Claudio and Hero in *Much Ado About Nothing*.[46] A private spousal is one which is not adequately witnessed, as the betrothal of Romeo and Juliet or that of the Duchess of Malfi and Antonio, which is witnessed only by Cariola, her servant and therefore not a competent witness.[47]

The fourth distinction is between spousals accomplished by words and those by signs. All of Shakespeare's spousals are made verbally. Occasionally one is attempted by signs, such as the giving and receiving of a ring in corroboration of an implied oath. But in such cases the dialogue makes clear the action and its intent. Olivia sends a ring by Malvolio to Viola. Viola refuses it, and Malvolio eventually throws it at her feet as he leaves. Swinburne believes that one lover or a third person has to explain in the hearing of the lovers the meaning of the token:

. . . [If] the Man saith to the Woman (*I do promise that I will Marry thee, and if thou wilt Marry me, then kiss me or give me, thy hand*), or thus, (The Man saith, *I take thee for my Wife, desiring if thou accept me for thy Husband, to receive this Ring, or to pledge me in a Cup of Wine*); In the former of which Cases the Woman kissing or giving her Hand accordingly, Spousals are Contracted; and in the Second Case receiving the Ring or pledging him, Matrimony is as sufficiently contracted, as if she had expressed her Consent, by the same words, or others of the like importance: Likewise albeit neither of the Parties express any words at all, but some *third* person recite the words of the Contract, willing them if they be therewith content, to joyn their hands together, or to embrace each other; the Parties so doing, the Contract is of like Efficacy, as if they themselves had mutually expressed the words before recited by that third Person.[48]

So Viola feels that the ring signifies a request for betrothal

by signs and that by accepting it she would have assented
to a betrothal, for she says:

> . . . the cunning of her passion
> Invites me in this churlish messenger.[49]

Stage directions for production of the play should have in-
structed Viola to leave the ring in the dust or later to return it to Olivia.

Swinburne's fifth distinction is of spousals sworn or unsworn. Shakespeare's spousals are always sworn, although
the oath is seldom as strong as "Be Heaven my witness."

> *Romeo.* Lady, by yonder blessed moon I swear,
> That tips with silver all these fruit-tree tops—. . .
> *Juliet.* Well, do not swear. Although I joy in thee,
> I have no joy of this contract to-night.
> It is too rash, too unadvis'd, too sudden.[50]

Ferdinand swears to Miranda of his love at the time of their
betrothal.

> O heaven, O earth, bear witness to this sound,
> And crown what I profess with kind event
> If I speak true! if hollowly, invert
> What best is boded me to mischief! I,
> Beyond all limit of what else i'th'world,
> Do love, prize, honour you.[51]

An unsworn spousal would have been rather casually given
and received. Such toying with love, leaving any opportunity
for doubt of the lover's constancy, does not occur in Shakespeare's plays.

An actual spousal of 1600, as preserved in Star Chamber
records, is reported by Professor Sisson. (I have inserted

in brackets the number and a word referring to the aspect of the ritual I have catalogued under the nine points above.)

"Field. . . . And now sweete heart I pray yow tell me your mind plainlie how you are affected towards me & whether yow can be content to forsake all men for my sake & to take me to your husband. [1. Consent]

Agnes (rising from her seat and coming to Field at the foot of the bed). I am content to loue & lyke yow aboue all men & to take yow for my husband.

Field. Your words sweete heart doe greatlie comfort my heart that you can do so. *(takes Agnes' hand, and holding it)* [6. Hand-clasp] I protest before god sweete heart that I loue thee aboue all the women in the world & I take thee to my wife & therevpon I giue thee my faith & trothe & if thou canst doe the like to me give me thy hand *(lets her hand fall).* [5. Contract]

Agnes. (gives Field her hand) I can & I doe & therevpon I give yow my hand & my faith."

Field then kissed Agnes [7. Kiss] and gave her two pieces of gold [9. Gift] "in corroboration."

"& then (they) kissed togither again, *which she thankfullie received,*" as her cousin Agnes remarked enviously. And Joan Coppians pointed the moral: "Now god giue yow ioy cosine for now yow are Mr ffeilds wife." [8. Blessing; 4. Witness][52]

The only details missing in this betrothal were the dowry, which had been settled upon previously, and the consent of the parents, which was in this case impossible.

An excellent example of a simple, present, private, verbal, sworn *de praesenti* spousal is that of the Duchess of Malfi and Antonio. The only deviation from the perfect spousal as proposed by Swinburne is the absence of sufficient witnesses.

Duchess. Kneele.
                    [Cariola shows herself.]

Antonio. Hah?

Duchess. Be not amaz'd, this woman's of my Councell,
       I have heard Lawyers say, a contract in a Chamber,
       (Per verba [de] presenti) is absolute marriage:
       Blesse (Heaven) this sacred Gordian, which let violence
       Never untwine.

Antonio. And may our sweet affections, (like the Sphears)
       Be still in motion.

Duchess. Quickning, and make
       The like soft Musique.

Antonio. That we may imitate the loving Palmes
       (Best Embleme of a peacefull marriage)
       That nev'r bore fruite devided.

Duchess. What can the Church force more?

Antonio. That Fortune may not know an accident
       Either of joy, or sorrow, to devide
       Our fixed wishes.

Duchess. How can the Church build faster?
       We now are man, and wife, and 'tis the Church
       That must but eccho this: Maid, stand apart, . . .
       I would have you lead your Fortune by the hand,
       Unto your marriage bed.[53]

There is nothing in the text to show that a church ceremony succeeds this spousal, yet the Cardinal, the Duchess' brother, hearing of this marriage, does not question its validity. This form of marriage was obviously valid in 1614, the date of the play. And a spousal *de praesenti* was considered marriage. "Marriage required no religious ceremony for its validity, although the omission of it was an offense. The only essential was *verba de praesenti* (as distinguished from a promise to marry at a future date), the man and woman saying to each other, 'I receive you as mine.' No ceremony, no priest, no physical consummation was required; so that after such precontract (as it was called) neither party could marry any other person."[54]

Although this statement appears to be perfectly true, certain aspects of the situation as described here by Arthur Underhill did not often occur. For instance, the fact that no physical consummation was required is likely true, but that there were many *de praesenti* marriages without consummation is unlikely, and that there were any in the drama is even less likely. There are no examples in Shakespeare of a *de praesenti* contract which does not eventually lead either by implication or by actual description to physical consummation. Bertram's marriage to Helena appears to be in the thought of Underhill. But their marriage is consummated before the end of the play. Bertram, however, was bound in marriage without the consummation, and his relations with other women such as Diana would have been stigmatized as adultery.

There was no fast-bound ceremony for a spousal *de praesenti,* but I have tried to show that the ceremony nevertheless existed. As a modern girl prefers a wedding to an elopement, so the sixteenth-century beloved in the dramas felt the seriousness of the spousal, and she and her lover would normally attempt to have it as formal and as stately as possible under their particular circumstances.

Professor Powell says of the same ceremony: "Between persons of age, clandestine marriages were made simply by exchanging such words as 'I take thee for my wife' and 'I take thee for my husband.' Such a contract was in name a mere spousal *de praesenti,* but in effect it was a marriage, and if it was followed by cohabitation, it became automatically recognized as such."[55] The author has confused the spousal *de praesenti* and the spousal *de futuro.* A clandestine spousal *de praesenti* seems to have been binding without cohabitation.[56]

But such secret spousals could cause trouble, as Swinburne suspects, permitting the parties to "alter their purposes, [deny] and [break] their promises, whence Perjuries, Adulteries, and Bastardies, with many more intollerable mischiefs do succeed." He concludes that clandestine marriages would not be valid in law: "It is all one in Law not to be, and not to appear; Wherefore seeing secret Contracts cannot be proved, it is all one in effect, as if they were not." They were, however, valid under the law of God if not under that of man.[57]

Luce, after a clandestine marriage with Young Chartley, in Thomas Heywood's *The Wise Woman of Hogsdon* (1604), says:

> I cannot prove our marriage; it was secret,
> And he may find some cavil in the law. . . .
> To claim a public marriage at his hands
> We want sufficient proof.[58]

Nevertheless, William Harrington in 1528 declared that clandestine marriages were valid. Discussing the consent necessary to matrimony, he added that it

ought to be expressed & shewed in open and in honest places afore & in the p̄sence of honest and laufull wytnesses called specyally therfore, ii at ye leest; for & it be otherwyse yt is to say yf ye man & woman or theyr proctours do make matrymony secretly by them selfe without any recorde or but with one wytnesse yt is called matrymony clãdestinat which for many causes is forboden by the lawe . . . notwithstondying that matrymony is valeable and holdeth afore god.[59]

In 1584 Thomas Cartwright, a Puritan, gave the form of

a spousal in *A Directory of Church-government*. The book
was suppressed and not readily available until its second edition in 1644. It is, however, to be assumed that Cartwright
rather expresses an existing situation than gives advice for ex-
tensive revision.

> Let espousing goe before marriage. Let the words of espousing
> be of the present time, and without condition, and before sufficient
> witnesses on both sides. It is to be wished that the Minister or an
> Elder be present at the espousals, who having called upon God
> may admonish both parties of their duties. . . .
> The Espousals being done in due order, let them not be dis-
> solved, though both parties should consent.[60]

Shakespeare's heroes and heroines seem to follow precisely
the method advocated here by Cartwright. Spousals in the
Shakespearean dramas are not dissolved, and usually they are
without condition.

The general conclusion was that a spousal *de praesenti*
could be equated with marriage, although the Church refused to recognize it unless it were followed by a religious
ceremony. A clandestine spousal *de praesenti,* such as that of
the Duchess of Malfi and Antonio, was valid marriage, as
she states, despite Church objections. Any two people, therefore, could claim a previous *de praesenti* spousal and thus
avoid illegitimate children. The only restraint on these actions would be, as Swinburne says, their fear of God at the
Final Judgment.

A spousal *de futuro* was a promise of future marriage,
generally marked by the use of the future tense in the contract. But the distinction between a *de futuro* and a *de praesenti* spousal was often unclear. Swinburne felt that a contract made by words of the future tense, such as "I will have

thee for my wife," was a spousal *de futuro,* but that one very similar whose words were "very pregnant," such as "I will from henceforth have thee for my wife," was a spousal *de praesenti.* He admitted that many lawyers did not agree, but he found that most agreed that the tense of the verb used in the contract was not so important as the intent of the speakers. He therefore inferred, "when the parties do Contract themselves by such words as may be referred, not only to the *future,* but to the *present* time, as *(I will have thee, &c.)* which also have relations to the *end* and execution of Marriage; this is Matrimony."[61]

The spousal *de futuro* gave the rights of marriage to the contracting lovers with none of its obligations, in that they might live together but were not required to, and the lover might support the beloved but was not required to. A couple which had contracted a future marriage could break the contract if they pleased at any time by mutual consent. Neither could break it without the consent of the other if the spousal had been confirmed with an oath. This was so, so long as the contract had not been ratified by physical union. The question might therefore arise as to whether the *de futuro* spousal, which had been adequately witnessed, had been ratified, and if so what proof there was of such ratification. Swinburne felt that a man who promised future marriage was "forthwith bound to have her for his Wife, yet whiles he hath her not, it is not Matrimony." He was thus sworn to have the woman eventually as his wife, but he might postpone the day as long as he wished.[62]

In case of doubt, however, as to whether the *de futuro* had been physically ratified or the spousal itself was a *de futuro* or a *de praesenti,* the decision of the court would be, Swinburne felt, that the couple were married. For "it is more safe to Judge for Matrimony than against Matrimony; and less peril to join them which be free, than to separate them which be bound."[63]

The *de futuro* spousal in Middleton's *The Family of Love* is altered to matrimony by physical relations. Early in the play Gerardine, the lover, pretends to leave town in a plot to permit his marriage to Maria. He persuades her to a *de futuro* contract just prior to his departure:

> *Gerardine.* Be [thou] constant:
> My absence may procure thy more enlarge,
> And then—
> *Maria.* Desire's conceit is quick; I apprehend thee:
> Be thou as loyal as I constant prove,
> And time shall knit our mutual knot of love.
> Wear this, my love's true pledge. *(Throws it down.)*
> I need not wish,
> I know thou wo't return.[64]

Here she promises to wait for Gerardine, and she gives him a guerdon as earnest of her love.

Later Gerardine apparently gets Maria with child,[65] a perfectly moral action according to the contemporary laws of spousals. He thereby converts the *de futuro* spousal into marriage: ". . . by the presumption of Law Spousals are translated into Matrimony, by carnal Copulation."[66]

When Glister, her uncle and guardian, finds that Maria is going to father the child on him, he is forced to give her a dowry and permit her public marriage to Gerardine in order to preserve his good name.

Walgrave, one of the three lovers of William Haughton's *Englishmen for My Money,* betroths himself *de futuro* to Mathea, the youngest of the three sisters. He says to all three:

> . . . Will you performe your words;
> All things are ready, and the Parson stands,
> To ioyne as hearts in hearts, our hands in hands;
> Night fauours vs, the thing is quickly done,
> Then trusse vp bagg and Bagages, and be gone;
> And ere the morninge, to augment your ioyes,
> Weele make you mothers of sixe goodly Boyes. . . .
>
> *Heigham.* What say you sweetes, will you performe your wordes?
> *Mathea.* Loue to true loue, no lesser meede affordes?
>
> Wee say we loue you, and that loues fayre breath
> Shall lead vs with you round about the Earth:
> And that our loues, vowes, wordes, may all proue true,
> Prepare your Armes, for thus we flie to you. [*they
> Embrace.*][67]

The Parson who is waiting, however, does not witness any
ceremony between Walgrave and Mathea, for she is unable to
leave her house that night. Therefore Walgrave goes to her.
He disguises himself as Susan, a friend come to visit, and
after a slight flirtation with his father-in-law spends the night
in bed with Mathea. This action, with the spousal quoted
above, is sufficient, according to Anthony, who has acted
as go-between and counselor to the couples, for matrimony:

> The day is broke; *Mathea* and young *Ned,*
> By this time, are so surely linckt togeather,
> That none in *London* can forbid the Banes.[68]

Therefore, when the two lovers come downstairs later that
morning in the general melee of sorting out the couples and
finding that they have all been married, Walgrave leads
Mathea by the hand up to her father, saying:

> Nay blush not wench, feare not, looke chearfully.
> Good morrow Father; Good morrow Gentlemen:

. . . and heere stands *Matt* my wife.
Know you her *Frenchman?* But she knowes me better.
Father, pray Father, let me haue your blessing,
For I haue blest you with a goodly Sonne;
Tis breeding heere yfayth, a iolly Boy.[69]

Under such circumstances, there is nothing Mathea's father
can do but permit, as Anthony says, the banns. The implication is that there will be a marriage ceremony after the time
of the banns, and that the child will be perfectly legitimate.

In this case the woman is party to the plot, and the opposition to the marriage could only come from the parent or a
disappointed second lover who is gulled. Such an action was
in direct opposition to the objections of Luther and other
Protestant reformers who

maintained that a marriage contracted without the consent of
parents should be regarded as invalid, unless the consent were
given afterwards. This principle was gradually accepted by most
legislators in Protestant countries, but with the modification that
parental consent could be refused for good reasons only and, in
case of need, the consent of the authorities could take its place.[70]

In *Englishmen for My Money* the father is forced into
later consent, and the *de facto* marriage, which he perhaps
might have been able to have invalidated because it was contracted without his consent, becomes validated. His consent
is forced because he believes that Mathea will have a child
and he must protect the name of his daughter. In both *The
Family of Love* and *Englishmen for My Money* the morality
is somewhat unsatisfactory, for each lover risks the good
name of his beloved in forcing marriage, depending on the
father's consideration for his daughter or himself as being
great enough to force his consent to the lover's wishes. The

father, who is less sympathetically treated by the dramatist, is thus more considerate than the lover, and that the lover should expect the father to be so is in itself unmoral. The action of the lover, in depending on the more unsympathetically-depicted father to have more integrity and family honor than he, and capitalizing on it, is immoral.

When love conquers parental opposition in Shakespeare it does so with a minimum of trickery. The lovers persuade the parent that their marriage would be desirable in itself, not that such marriage would be better than lasting shame. Such are the marriages of Rosalind to Orlando and Ferdinand to Miranda.

A more complicated *de futuro* spousal is in Cyril Tourneur's *The Atheist's Tragedy,* a decadent work as compared with Shakespeare's, and probably intended for the private theaters. Tourneur's plot investigates the possibilities of legal variations in matrimony. Charlemont and Castabella betroth themselves for future marriage before a witness, Languebeau Snuffe, whose single testimony is valid because he is a chaplain. Charlemont says to his beloved:

> And, for the satisfaction of your love,
> Here comes the man whose knowledge I have made
> A witness to the contract of our vows,
> Which my return, by marriage, shall confirm.[71]

Languebeau Snuffe confirms this as a *de futuro* spousal when he speaks of having been "already informed of your matrimonial purposes."[72] Later in the same act, Castabella is betrothed against her will to Rousard, whom she is forced to marry.

Since the spousal with Charlemont was only *de futuro,* the subsequent marriage is not bigamous:

. . . when as either Party having contracted Spousals *de futuro,*
doth afterwards Contract Matrimony or Spousals *de praesenti,* with
another Person; or else contract Spousals *de futuro* with another
Person, and then they lye with the same Person; . . . in both
these Cases the former Spousals are dissolved by the later.[73]

Castabella then is necessarily faithful to Rousard when
Charlemont returns from the wars and meets her at his tomb:

Charlemont. Touch my lip. Why turn'st thou from me? . . .
        Has absence changed thee?
Castabella. Yes.
        From maid to wife.[74]

And there is no more talk of kissing at that time.

The spousal of Florizel and Perdita in *The Winter's Tale*
is *de futuro,* but Shakespeare does not have his characters val-
idate it through physical union: they must work their marriage out in a more orthodox fashion. When Florizel speaks
of the spousal to Perdita, he says:

> Lift up your countenance, as it were the day
> Of celebration of that nuptial which
> We two have sworn shall come.[75]

The spousal has been confirmed by oath, as he says in the
last line quoted above. This he emphasizes later, after his
father has forbidden a public spousal, to Camillo, his father's
counselor:

> Not for Bohemia nor the pomp that may
> Be thereat glean'd; for all the sun sees or
> The close earth wombs or the profound seas hide
> In unknown fadoms, will I break my oath
> To this my fair belov'd.[76]

Therefore when he flees with her overseas to her father's

court he preserves her chastity and is thus forced to admit that their spousal is still merely *de futuro* when he meets Leontes, her unwitting father:

Perdita. The heaven sets spies upon us, will not have
           Our contract celebrated.
Leontes. You are married?
Florizel. We are not, sir, nor are we like to be.[77]

Eventually, of course, they are able to work out this situation to a marriage, because Shakespeare does not have his characters break their espousal oath, but they do this only after Perdita has been proved worthy of her husband in birth.

Occasionally an author brings into his plot the situation of a woman who has been seduced without a preceding *de futuro* spousal. Dekker treats such a situation in *1 The Honest Whore* in a fashion as moral as Shakespeare's, although of course Shakespeare never allows such a situation to arise. Bellafront, the honest whore, has been turned to that profession by the rake Matheo. At the conclusion of the play all important characters meet at Bedlam, where Bellafront pretends to be a mad inmate. The Duke, as *deus ex machina,* arbitrates the claims of various lovers, and addresses Bellafront as "Maid."

Bellafront. Maide, nay, that's a lie: O, 'twas a very rich jewel, called a Maiden head, and had you not it leerer.
Matheo. Out you mad asse! away.
Duke. Had he thy Maiden-head?
           He shall make thee amends, and marrie thee. . . .
Matheo. I thinke I rifled her of some such paltry jewell.
Duke. Did you? then marry her, you see the wrong,
           Has led her spirits into a lunacie. . . .
Matheo. Well then, when her wits stand in their right place,
           I'le marrie her.[78]

That, if Bellafront accepts it, is a conditional spousal *de futuro,* adequately witnessed. She leaps at the words.

Bellafront. I thanke your Grace: *Mathaeo,* thou art mine: . . .
Matheo. Cony-catcht, guld, must I saile in your flie-boat,
    Because I helpt to reare your maine-mast first?[79]

But he accepts the situation and performs a simple *de futuro* ceremony before the witnesses immediately:

    Come wench, thou shalt be mine, give me thy gols,
    Wee'l talke of legs hereafter: see my Lord,
    God give us joy.
Omnes. God give you joy.[80]

The best available example of a spousal *de futuro* is marred only because it is conditional upon the death of the husband of the beloved. In Thomas Heywood's *The English Traveller* (1625) Young Geraldine loves Wincott's wife, and at his first opportunity alone with her establishes a *de futuro* spousal conditional upon Wincott's death:

    [If] we two be reserved to after-life,
    Will you confer your widowhood on me?
Wife. You ask the thing I was about to beg;
    Your tongue hath spake mine own thoughts.
Young Geraldine. Vow to that.
Wife. As I hope mercy.
Y. Ger. 'Tis enough; that word
    Alone instates me happy. Now, so please you,
    We will divide, you to your private chamber,
    I to find out my friend.
Wife. Nay, Master Geraldine,
    One ceremony rests yet unperformed:
    My vow is past, your oath must next proceed;
    And as you covet to be sure of me,
    Of you I would be certain.

Y. Ger. Make ye doubt?
Wife. No doubt; but Love's still jealous, and in that
　　　　To be excused; you then shall swear by Heaven,
　　　　And as in all your future acts you hope
　　　　To thrive and prosper; as the day may yield
　　　　Comfort, or the night rest; as you would keep
　　　　Entire the honour of your father's house,
　　　　And free your name from scandal or reproach;
　　　　By all the goodness that you hope to enjoy,
　　　　Or ill to shun—
Y. Ger. You charge me deeply, lady.
Wife. Till that day come, you shall reserve yourself
　　　　A single man; converse nor company
　　　　With any woman, contract nor combine
　　　　With maid or widow; which expected hour,
　　　　As I do wish not haste, so when it happens
　　　　It shall not come unwelcome. You hear all;
　　　　Vow this.
Y. Ger. By all that you have said, I swear,
　　　　And by this kiss confirm.
Wife. You're now my brother;
　　　　But then, my second husband.[81]

Later Geraldine obtains sufficient evidence that Delavil, his friend, has slept with Mrs. Wincott, and he is thereupon justified in breaking the betrothal: ". . . when as the Party doth after the Contract made, commit *Fornication*, . . . the Innocent Party is at liberty, and may dissolve the Contract."[82]

The spousal *de futuro* was a dangerous contract in that it left the parties to it in a position of some jeopardy. Indeed, its advantages seem to have been considerably outweighed by its disadvantages. It approximated a conditional betrothal, and it permitted the lovers to separate if they desired to marry elsewhere, so long as they had not ratified the spousal by physical union. If either broke the betrothal without the consent of the other, that person forfeited all presents given and had to return double the value of presents received.[83] The breaker of a contract in civil law could not make claims, but that does not mean he had the legal right to break the contract, either. A jilted person could always forbid banns on the basis of a pre-contract. Even if a person had forfeited his gifts or returned those of the betrothed two-fold, he was in danger of having his children classed as bastards if he later married. He could only be safe by getting a release—and the betrothed did not have to give it to him simply because he returned twice the value of his gifts.

The words for such a spousal had to be carefully chosen. Even in the dramas most of the spousals cannot be differentiated as *de futuro* except by afterevents. "Of all the people in the world lovers are the least likely to distinguish precisely between the present and the future tenses."[84]

Bigamy and adultery were subjects of many of the dramas of the age. They naturally separate into two distinct classes, however. Although adultery was an extramarital arrangement made willingly by a married person, bigamy was invariably unwillingly committed. The adulterous person believed his second love to be greater than his first for a while, the bigamous person usually knew that his first love was the better.

Gertrude, Hamlet's mother, when she committed adultery[85] with Claudius apparently preferred his love to her husband's. Certainly she was not bigamous, she did not marry Claudius until after her husband's burial. There are evidences that she loves Claudius, or belives she loves him, for some time, because her marriage to Claudius is regarded as incestuous,[86] and a woman who was not blinded by love would have avoided such a situation. During the course of the play, however, when she learns of her first husband's murder, she repents her adulterous action. Hamlet's words to her in her bedroom cleave her heart in twain; she listens to her son and decides to side with him against her second husband.

When Claudius, in the next scene, asks her "How does Hamlet?" she has so changed allegiance that she lies: "Mad as the sea and wind when both contend Which is the mightier."[87] By these few words, which she does not much amplify, she shòws the audience that she will obey her son, and that, therefore, there has been a change in her attitude toward her husband. Her obedience to Hamlet will probably be complete, even to her refusing to sleep with Claudius:

Queen.   What shall I do?
Hamlet. Not this, by no means, that I bid you do:
      Let the bloat Kink tempt you again to bed;
      Pinch wanton on your cheek; call you his mouse;
      And let him, for a pair of reechy kisses,
      Or paddling in your neck with his damn'd fingers,
      Make you to ravel all this matter out.[88]

When she gives her son her oath of constancy,

      Be thou assur'd, if words be made of breath,
      And breath of life, I have no life to breathe
      What thou hast said to me,[89]

she has completely changed.

The plot of the king and queen in *Hamlet* is apparently that of adultery repented.[90] That the term of adultery extends beyond the death of the husband and into marriage with the adulterer does not change its essential illicitness for the dramatist.

Adultery was sufficient grounds for dissolution of a

spousal,[91] and the supposed adultery of Hero in *Much Ado About Nothing* gives Claudio cause for breaking their *de praesenti* spousal. Claudio is justified in considering her supposed act adultery because they have been through a betrothal as binding as marriage, one which would have permitted their cohabiting:

> *Leonato.* Dear my lord, if you, in your own proof,
>   Have vanquish'd the resistance of her youth
>   And made defeat of her virginity—
> *Claudio.* I know what you would say. If I have known her,
>   You will say she did embrace me as a husband,
>   And so extenuate the forehand sin.[92]

Therefore any relations which Hero might have had with another man would be extramarital.

Adultery was usually the theme of the domestic tragedies, and when it occurred the sin was punished at the conclusion of the play. The writers of such tragedies appear to have been strongly aware of the ills developing from adultery, and their final comments are exhortations to marital chastity. Mrs. Frankford, who repents her affair with Wendoll after she has been found out by her husband, addresses the audience:

> O women, women, you that yet have kept
> Your holy matrimonial vow unstained,
> Make me your instance: when you tread awry,
> Your sins, like mine, will on your conscience lie.[93]

This is a far cry from the attitudes of the courtly lovers of preceding ages. Such a speech could never come from the mouth of Isolde or Guenevere. Here, as so often in the writings of that age, is an expression of a bourgeois morality essential to a monogamous society. Such exhortations as Heywood's, awkward though they be, are sincere. The entire

play is constructed to enforce the moral which Mrs. Frankford expresses.

Ales, of *Arden of Feversham*, repents her adultery with
Mosbye after she has been caught involved in the murder of
her husband. She then addresses Mosbye:

> Ah, but for thee I had neuer beene strumpet.
> What can not oathes and protestations doe,
> When men haue opportunity to woe?
> I was too young to sound thy villanies,
> But now I finde it and repent too late,[94]

and her final words are:

> Let my death make amends for all my sinnes.[95]

Othello suspects Desdemona of treachery, and finds sufficient proof for his purposes. He expresses the strength of his
love for Desdemona when he kisses her just before he kills
her:

> O balmy breath, that dost almost persuade
> Justice to break her sword![96]

and when she argues and pleads with him for her life, he
tells her:

> O perjur'd woman! thou dost stone my heart,
> And mak'st me call what I intend to do
> A murther, which I thought a sacrifice.[97]

The word "stone" means to strike with stones, not to calcify.
Her protestations of innocence hurt him so that he, although
enough convinced of her guilt to kill her, yet is so persuaded
of her innocence as to call his deed a murder. Before she has
argued with him he has felt that it would be a sacrifice, that
he must kill her "else she'll betray more men." Already
Othello is as confused as he later shows himself to be when

he denies the murder to Emilia. During the entire rest of
the scene beginning with these lines, he is uncertain as to
whether his role is that of executioner or murderer. At the
moment that he kills her he believes himself executioner, but
immediately after that he believes he has been a murderer and
tries to avoid the issue with "Why, how should she be dead?"
"Thou canst not say I did it," to Emilia. The moral in this
play of Shakespeare's is therefore as strongly put as in Heywood's *A Woman Killed With Kindness* and in *Arden of
Feversham*.

Othello is a domestic tragedy in that its plot is based on
adultery, but the variation that Shakespeare uses is of having
the supposed wronged person actually guilty of crime in re-
venge-taking. The repentance comes from unjustified suspicion revealed rather than from extramarital action. This, unjustified suspicion, is really the aspect of adultery of which
Shakespeare writes most often. Similar cases are in *Much Ado
About Nothing, The Winter's Tale, Cymbeline,* and *Othello.*

Bigamy occurs fairly often in the history plays of Shakespeare, but never in his other works, and he often comments
adversely upon it.

Henry VI, betrothed to Margaret by Suffolk acting as
proxy, decides to marry her when he is enchanted by Suffolk's
description. Gloucester, Lord Protector, advises against the
marriage, arguing that if he permits it,

> So should I give consent to flatter sin.
> You know, my lord, your Highness is betroth'd
> Unto another lady of esteem.
> How shall we then dispense with that contract
> And not deface your honour with reproach?[98]

Henry VI, perhaps coincidentally, has an unsuccessful reign,
and Suffolk, at the end of the scene, plans to use the bigamous

marriage with Margaret as a lever with which to control the kingdom:

> Margaret shall now be Queen, and rule the King;
> But I will rule both her, the King, and realm.[99]

Bigamy in this case brings evil in its train, and Suffolk, the person who fosters the action, is depicted unsympathetically.

Edward IV, according to Buckingham, has fathered Edward V illegitimately upon Elizabeth, his third "wife":

> You say that Edward [V] is your brother's [Edward IV's] son.
> So say we too, but not by Edward [V]'s wife;
> For first was he contract to Lady Lucy—
> Your mother lives a witness to his vow—
> And afterward by substitute betroth'd
> To Bona, sister to the King of France.
> These both put off, a poor petitioner,
> A care-craz'd mother to a many sons,
> A beauty-waning and distressed widow . . .
> Seduc'd the pitch and height of his degree
> To base declension and loath'd bigamy.
> By her, in his unlawful bed, he got
> This Edward.[100]

Even rulers, who were in general above the laws of the people, were unsuccessful when they crossed the Church, which forbade such activities. Edward IV dies, apparently aided by Richard of Gloucester, and Edward V is murdered by his uncle, according to Shakespeare. The wages of sin is paid and bigamy is shown to be unprofitable.

In George Wilkins' *The Miseries of Enforced Marriage*, produced in 1607, the problem of bigamy is dealt with in following the true story of Walter Calverly, who was executed in 1605. The play does not include the execution, rather it has a happy ending for the hero. Calverly eventually, in drama, pays for his crime in *The Yorkshire Tragedy* (1606), which seems to be a continuation of Wilkins' play. The unfortunate first bride, Clare, commits suicide in *The Miseries of Enforced Marriage* apparently as partial evidence of the evil effects bigamy can have on all concerned.

William Scarborow, or Walter Calverly, meets and falls in love with Clare Harcop during the first act of Wilkins' play. Immediately they betroth themselves to each other in a *de praesenti* spousal. After the spousal, which may not be made marriage for three years because he is still a ward, Scarborow says to Sir John Harcop, Clare's father, "Your daughter's made my wife, and I your son." This is precisely true, for although the ceremony has been performed without witnesses it is necessarily by that only clandestine *de praesenti*. The two consider themselves contracted indissolubly and Sir John condones the situation. The intent rather than the fact must be considered, and the spousal is valid *de praesenti* except for the element of the elapse of time necessary before marriage.[101]

Before the end of the act, Sir William Scarborow forces his son to marry Katherine, refusing to recognize the betrothal to Clare. William Scarborow objects that such a marriage would make him an adulterer, "My babes being bastards, and a whore my wife."[102] He is nevertheless forced to marry Katherine, and Clare, upon hearing the news, declares herself

> A wretched maid, not fit for any man;
> For being united his with plighted faiths,
> Whoever sues to me commits a sin,
> Besiegeth me, and who shall marry me
> Is like myself, lives in adultery . . .

> Let me live ne'er so honest, rich or poor,
> If I once wed, yet I must live a whore,
> And though that I should vow a single life
> To keep my soul unspotted, yet will [my father]
>   enforce me to a marriage.[103]

She then commits suicide, preferring that to bigamy.

According to Wilkins, then, the ceremony could not be invalidated under any circumstances; and any subsequent marriage by either the injuring or injured person would be bigamous. Clare is not released from her contract by the defection of her spouse, and William Scarborow's marriage to Katherine is bigamous.

Shakespeare's only treatment of a near-bigamous relationship of important characters not in his history plays is in *Romeo and Juliet.* After Juliet has been secretly married to Romeo, her parents force her to a betrothal to Paris, in much the same way that William Scarborow is forced to marry Katherine. Juliet repeatedly states that she would die before she broke her oath to Romeo.[104] Upon the Friar's advice she decides to accept Paris and to pretend to die before the ceremony.

She does not accept Paris verbally at any time: her only statement to her parents is that she will obey her father. At no time is there a spousal in the play between Juliet and Paris. Juliet is incapable of such lying, apparently. Therefore there is no true bigamy in the play, although the impression of it is given the audience.

The problem of adultery is the central one over which the speakers in Fenton's *Monophylo* debate. They believe that a man should love a woman, they find that there is no way of controlling the love, and they also come to the point at which they must decide whether or not it is lawful for a married

woman to grant her favors to a man other than her husband.
The author attempts to equivocate, deciding that marriages
are ordained of God and should be kept inviolate, but that
if a woman does not love her husband they (the author and
the husband) must excuse her unfaithfulness:

> . . . maryage was not ordeyned by man, but erected by the eternall
> deuine pollecie, as the onely mean for conseruation of mankinde
> . . . God commaundes that a woman doe not make hir selfe meete
> for any other, then him to whome the ceremonie of the Church hath
> bounde hir nature, to the ende to enjoy an eternall peace. And yet
> (Madame) if this maryage happen to be one of those in whom is
> such resolute imperfection and contrarietie, as loue cannot be
> brought in, I cannot (in a necessary care for hir worldly felicitie)
> but excuse hir, and approoue the aduice of this Gentleman
> [Monophylo], to bequeath hir selfe to a constant friende: wherein
> though you note me of corrupt counsayle, I haue nature to
> aunswere the cause for me.[105]

Monophylo, who has defined love in the sense of Plato's
Androgyne,[106] and who therefore rests his case upon an element entirely different from the situation of Andreas, feels
that extramarital love, though unavoidable, is "the greatest
wounde that can happen to the heart of man,"[107] and Glaphyro concludes that such love must be avoided: "we must
not suffer to fall into our thoughtes, to bear loue to hir,
whome the lawe hath assigned to another."[108]

The dramatist had to solve the problem of love and marriage, if he chose to deal with it, in the way he believed. Occasionally, as in *Antony and Cleopatra,* Shakespeare's solution is not moral in a Christian sense, although Antony is
shown having a love which has little to do with marriage.
Shakespeare does not advise such love.

The practice of adultery, advocated by *fine amor* under

Andreas' first rule,[109] was not used in the drama of the late sixteenth century, with some few exceptions. The adultery of men and women was seen with horror-stricken eyes. To the sixteenth-century audience Claudius sinned as much as Gertrude, Othello was not correct in believing Desdemona more to blame than Cassio, and Wendoll deserved as much punishment as did Mrs. Frankford.

Chapter VI

CONCLUSION

THE FINAL CHAPTER of this study is to be divided into three sections. In the first pages I shall draw some general conclusions from the material presented in the foregoing chapters. With that as a basis, without pretending to offer a critical panacea, I shall proceed to analyze two Shakespearean plays which have presented some difficulty to critics unaware of the ethical code which I have been herein reconstructing. In the third section I shall draw a general conclusion as to Shakespeare's moral attitudes toward the various phases of courtship as presented by Andreas and other early authors.

I have proved in the course of this paper that there was in the love story a tradition of courtly formalism upon which Shakespeare drew for his dramatic plots. He was not alone among the Elizabethan dramatists in depending upon this material; most of the early writers felt as he. Generally considered, the course of courtship went through five stages: Inception, Development, Betrothal, Ordeal, and Union. Often certain of these stages were truncated and certain others were exaggerated for the purposes of dramatic effectiveness. Each stage, however, had its ritual, each of which I have described.

The Inception of courtship began with the preparation of the two prospective lovers for their first recognition of love. Ordinarily in the sixteenth-century drama that recognition came at the time of the first meeting of the lovers. Before that meeting they had to fulfill dramatic requirements as to birth, nationality, physical and mental ability, and dress and appearance. Since the burden of activity in courtship was placed

upon the lover, the dramatists generally more carefully delineated his traits than those of the beloved. Shakespeare
tends to give equal consideration to women and men, and
many of the women not only are capable of as great a love as
the men but are as carefully portrayed.

The Development in the twelfth century was almost invariably centered upon the lover, who in that period of the
action suffered *hereos,* or love-sickness. In the Elizabethan
drama the illness of the lovers was seldom emphasized. Interest in *hereos* declined, apparently, as interest in marriage increased.

The Inception of the love and its Development were the
two stages most carefully considered by Andreas Capellanus
in his *Art of Love,* and Geoffrey Fenton discusses them at
length in his *Monophylo.* Since the second stage received so
little consideration in the time of Shakespeare although Gascoigne in his *Master F. J.* had considered it so important as
late as 1572, at some time during the interim the courtly love
tradition fostered by Andreas had become less stereotyped and
less idealistic.

The Betrothal was in the medieval society romances and in
the drama which I am considering the crux or central point
of the action. It was often presented upon the sixteenth-century stage, although its presence in these plays is not usually
recognized by modern audiences. For instance, the spousal of
Rosalind and Orlando, early in the fourth act of *As You Like
It,* was not recognized as such by many who saw the 1950
New York production, and there was some stage evidence
that Miss Hepburn did not completely realize the force of the
words she was speaking at that time. It was at this point of
betrothal in a play that the beloved and lover reached an
agreement as to their plans for a future life together. In only

a few instances did the betrothal mean more than a definite promise of future marriage in Shakespeare's work, whether it was a spousal *de praesenti* or *de futuro*. It was to him merely a midpoint and not a culmination. It was to be followed by a fully witnessed religious marriage ceremony.

The Ordeal was the sustaining conflict of dramatic action in the romantic comedies of the Elizabethan dramatists. At the time of the Ordeal some hindrances to the union of the lovers was developed which presented a problem easily solved in the fifth act but which in the heat of the conflict was apparently insoluble. Later dramatists considered the Ordeal a challenge to their ingenuity in finding seemingly insurmountable difficulties which could at the same time be titillating to the audience. Thus one author proposed that his lovers be revealed as brother and sister. The solution, of course in the fifth act, was that they were not really related.

During the Ordeal, too, the lover could suffer from *hereos*. His disease at this time, however, was the result of a separation from his accepted and accepting beloved, and therefore both lovers were susceptible to the disease.

The Union of the sixteenth-century drama was all too often contrived, especially in the romantic works of Shakespeare. Because the Ordeal presented artificial difficulties or obstacles to the lovers, the removal of those difficulties was also obviously contrived. Thus the union of the Duke and Isabella, the inheritance of Orlando, the union of Olivia and Sebastian, seem to be unmotivated or at least inadequately motivated to a modern audience which is willing to accept all manner of improbability in the love story itself so long as the actual marriage seems probable. Occasionally the Union itself was parodied by Shakespeare, as in *As You Like It,* where the ceremony performed for Touchstone by Sir Oliver Martext is interrupted by Jaques.

Courtly love dealt with the artificialities of courtship which preceded the betrothal. It was a formalized concept based on romantic love, and it merely standardized the actions of the lovers and the beloveds. In an attempt to codify these reactions the teachers of *fine amor* fell into the fallacy of proposing the form as a substitute for the feeling of the reaction. This of course gave the lover set phrases, gestures, and attitudes with which to express either a sincere or an insincere love.

The Andrean rules which advocated a morality contrary to Christian ethic were retracted by Andreas himself in the same work in which he set them forth. Those rules which did not run counter to Christian ethic were in general accepted by later writers and their audiences and perpetuated in the bourgeois morality even of the twentieth century. These were utilized by Shakespeare in his love plots.

For the purposes of elaboration and verification of the Shakespearean code herein presented, two plays will be examined rather carefully in the light of the *fine amor* tradition. These, *Measure for Measure* and *Troilus and Cressida*, seem to be unusual in the Shakespeare canon. It is simple to explain that the handkerchief of *Othello* is so important in the play because it is a guerdon, and that the return of Hamlet's gifts by Ophelia is important because the act denotes the breaking of a betrothal. The importance of such details should be obvious from the foregoing examination. But the love of Troilus and Cressida and of the three or four pairs of lovers in *Measure for Measure* follows the details of the cult much less faithfully.

The critical problems of *Measure for Measure* are so many and so diverse[1] that I make no attempt here to analyze them all or to explain the play. My concern is with the aspects of courtship in the work.

Professor W. W. Lawrence attempts to define the functions of the characters from a basis of *All's Well That Ends Well*. The crux of the entire problem is the morality of the "bed-trick," whether or not Isabella is justified in persuading Mariana to go to bed with Angelo. If the bed-trick is immoral, then the play as a whole is immoral, according to critics; and, I suppose, if the bed-trick can be explained as moral, the play is otherwise moral, with the exception of the Lucio and Mrs. Overdone scenes.

There are three distinct love-plots in the play.[2] The first one is presented as a *fait accompli,* the love of Claudio and Juliet. The situation is of a couple who have been betrothed and who have subsequently lived together as man and wife without the formality of a marriage celebrated by the Church. The second one presented is the dissolved spousal of Angelo and Mariana, a couple who are eventually reunited through an intrigue which borders on immorality. The third one presented is the proposed spousal of Duke Vincentio and Isabella, of which the first hint is given in the last scene of the last act. It is to be noted that each love-plot is vitally different from the others, and that the three are in various stages of development. I wish to examine each of these plots from the viewpoint of the rituals of courtship and the type of spousal presented.

The first plot considered here, the last one developed by Shakespeare, is that of Vincentio and Isabella. This courtship is excessively truncated. There is no Inception or Development delineated. The first hint of any love of Vincentio for

Isabella occurs in the last fifty lines of the play. When
Claudio, Isabella's brother, is dramatically revealed as alive,
the Duke casually proposes marriage to Isabella together with
the business of revelation:

> If he be like your brother, for his sake
> Is he pardoned; and, for your lovely sake,
> Give me your hand and say you will be mine,
> He is my brother too. But fitter time for that![3]

The audience, if it sympathizes with either the Duke or Isabella, might well rejoin "Much fitter!" The proposal, part of
a Betrothal, is presented in public by a high-ranking person
to one of much lower rank, practically a Griselda. Professor
Kittredge has no stage-direction in his text following the
Duke's request for Isabella's hand, and it is thus impossible to
tell what he believes of the passage. The player of Isabella's
part, however, should be directed to take the Duke's hand. The
following line, "By this Lord Angelo perceives he's safe,"
implies that there has been some stage action to make Angelo
feel safe from revenge by Isabella. Yet if the Duke had asked
for Isabella's hand and she had refused or had for any reason
not taken it, there could have been no agreement by her to
the Duke's proposal and therefore no reason for Angelo to
be relieved. He has been on trial for two crimes—

> Being criminal in double violation
> Of sacred chastity, and of promise-breach
> Thereon dependent for your brother's life[4]—

and in the same moment he sees a living Claudio and a betrothed Isabella. For

... if a Man, taking a Woman by the hand, do say unto her
(I give thee my Faith that I will take thee to my wife) albeit

the Woman say nothing, yet is the Man bound to Marry her if she will; but the Woman is not to be compelled if she will not, unless it be proved at least by some Sign, that the Woman did consent; as . . . if she being required, did willingly give her hand to receive his promise.[5]

.   .   .   .

. . . albeit the one party use no words at all, but signifie . . . her consent by some Signs, as if the one party say *(I do promise to Marry thee, and if thou be content to Marry me, then . . . give me thy hand);* Whereupon the other party . . . giving hand accordingly, Spousals are thereby Contracted.[6]

If Isabella takes his hand, as apparently she does, then those words of the Duke's constitute a spousal *de futuro,* however abbreviated. Here is no other element of a spousal than the mere words of one person and the sign of another. Yet the sign makes the spousal valid. There is no need for Isabella to speak, but there is need for her to take some action.

The espoused Duke then says, again in a series of statements dealing with other business,

> Dear Isabel,
> I have a motion much imports your good,
> Whereto if you'll a willing ear incline,
> What's mine is yours, and what is yours is mine.[7]

The hint is strong that his "motion" is for marriage.

These are the only speeches in the play which deal with the romance of the Duke and Isabella. There is no Ordeal or Union following.

The Duke has shown no real aspect of a courtly attitude. He has not suffered for love, he does not degrade himself before Isabella, he does not elevate her. He simply proposes to her. The entire situation is wooden, especially since Isabella does not speak again in the play after the first mention

of the Duke's intent. I do not believe that Shakespeare intended that she be tongue-tied, and I would be tempted to
accept Professor J. Dover Wilson's theory of a corrupt text,[8]
if it were necessary. Nevertheless, Isabella has no need to
speak, since silence in this case does give consent.

A second marriage proposed during the final lines, which
Professor Lawrence probably rightly ignored when he said
there are three marriages in the play, is of Lucio and his
whore whom he claims to have gotten with child. The marriage is parallel to that of Bellafront and Matheo in Dekker's
2 *The Honest Whore,* written a year later than *Measure for
Measure.* It is a reminiscence of an Italian law, in force at
this time, which permitted this punishment instead of a
greater one for such crimes as Lucio's.

The second important courtship, that of Claudio and Juliet,
is also very brief. Its general status is discussed by Claudio in
the second scene:

> Thus stands it with me: upon a true contract
> I got possession of Julietta's bed.
> You know the lady. She is fast my wife,
> Save that we do the denunication lack
> Of outward order. This we came not to,
> Only for propagation of a dow'r
> Remaining in the coffer of her friends,
> From whom we thought it meet to hide our love
> Till time had made them for us. But it chances
> The stealth of our most mutual entertainment
> With character too gross is writ on Juliet.[9]

Claudio has been secretly espoused to Juliet without the
knowledge or consent of her friends. It is clear that Juliet has
no living parents, for the dowry is under the control of the
friends. Juliet apparently lives alone, much as Portia, so that

it would be possible for Claudio to live secretly with her. The situation is obviously that Claudio needs the money of the dowry, that the friends are executors of her money and could withhold it if Juliet married against their wishes, and that Juliet at present, being pregnant, is in imminent danger of losing the dowry for good and all as well as losing a husband who is to be killed by Angelo's order. The relationship between Claudio and Juliet as it stands is that of a valid irregular marriage, one binding but not having been celebrated in the Church.

There is no Inception or Development of this plot, either. It begins after the Betrothal with the Ordeal, for Claudio is forcibly separated from his beloved and in imminent danger of dying for his love, or for the consequences of his love. The law which Shakespeare introduces as applying to Claudio is a strange one apparently adopted merely to make the plot. It is carefully explained so that the audience will understand it, which would not be necessary in a well known law.

The next reference of importance to this situation is by the disguised Duke to Juliet in the prison. There he speaks of Juliet's unborn child as "the sin you carry" and asks her to repent it. Juliet acknowledges the child, and therefore the state existing between herself and her husband, to be a sin. This concept might be a part of the author's adherence to the customs of Vienna which he has established for the play, e.g., that the spousal of Claudio and Juliet is not valid by the law which Angelo is enforcing, and that therefore Shakespeare is being consistent. This attitude of the Duke's is reiterated in the last scene when he addresses a single line to Claudio: "She . . . that you wrong'd, look you restore." He feels that Claudio has violated some law or custom in sleeping with Juliet.[10]

What of contemporary England? Swinburne says that even though the spousal is not witnessed, as may well have been Claudio's case, the couple "are very Man and Wife before God." He gives as his reasoning that "proof is not of the Essence of Matrimony." Further, "by the presumption of Law Spousals are translated into Matrimony by a carnal Copulation."[11]

By Swinburne's understanding of English law Claudio and Juliet are married. Shakespeare and the Duke, however, appear to feel that they are not. It is therefore necessary to examine the third romance before a decision can be reached as to precisely what Shakespeare intended.

Angelo, five years before the action of the play, repudiated his contract with Mariana on the grounds, the Duke says, of lack of dowry. Angelo claims, and no one contradicts him, that the dowry was part of the cause of the dissolution, but that he revoked his contract "in chief For that her reputation was disvalued In levity."[12] Schmidt's *Shakespeare-Lexicon* defines this use of "levity" as "lightness, thoughtlessness, inconsiderateness," which, while it may be Angelo's literal meaning here, cannot really be what he is saying. Rather, he is using the word in another Elizabethan sense, that of immorality.

Angelo has been "affianc'd to her by oath" according to the Duke. Mariana obviously has not consented to the dissolution of the spousals. The Duke makes this clear when he discusses the situation with Isabella.[13]

Swinburne understands that in such a case "it is not in the power of either Party alone, without the Consent of the other to renounce or dissolve the Spousals confirmed with an Oath."[14] Canonists, he adds, go even farther, and they declare that neither party can dissolve even an unsworn contract without the consent of the other, unless there is sound reason for such dissolution, such as fornication—with a third party, of course—or leprosy.[15] Angelo claims no such reason, although the Duke says he pretended "in her discoveries of dishonour,"[16] apparently the "levity" mentioned above. Such a pretence would have been unnecessary: it is obviously untrue since Angelo hides his accusation in the cloak of the ambiguous "levity" in the last scene.

Duke Vincentio, too, believes that the contract is still valid. He tells Mariana:

> He is your husband on a precontract.
> To bring you . . . together 'tis no sin,
> Sith that the justice of your title to him
> Doth flourish the deceit.[17]

The words here are unequivocal: Angelo still is Mariana's husband. Mariana herself uses the same tense in the last scene in her explanation: "I am affianc'd this man's wife."[18] I have before explained, but perhaps it bears repeating, that that does not mean that they are married. Shakespeare makes this abundantly clear through the play, and he emphasizes the distinction in the final scene:

Mariana. . . . I will not show my face
         Until my husband bid me.
Duke. What, are you married?
Mariana. No, my lord.
Duke. Are you a maid?
Mariana. No, my lord.
Duke. A widow then?
Mariana. Neither, my lord.[19]

The Duke, after finding her a woman whose betrothal has been confirmed by copulation, although her seducer did not know her, condemns Angelo to "marry her instantly"[20] with the aid of a friar. Swinburne feels that the church ceremony is not necessary, for "Spousals do become Matrimony by carnal knowledge, albeit the Man were constrained, through *fear of death* to know the Woman."[21]

The situation of the Angelo-Mariana courtship appears to be that a "precontract" validated by copulation is binding, but it must be followed by "marriage," a ceremony performed by a member of the clergy. This is Shakespeare's general concept of marriage: a spousal followed by a religious ceremony.

In the same way, the Duke orders Claudio to "marry" Juliet, to whom he has been contracted and with whom he has been living. Again, the marriage is not complete without a church ceremony. But here there is an added concept: living together before marriage is sin. Vincentio says so definitely to Juliet, and she agrees. Since it is not an integral part of the plot that this be considered sin except by Angelo who is to punish the offenders, it is likely that Vincentio and Juliet express a concept which Shakespeare held. There is no definite substantiation of this in his other plays. But Shakespeare does not permit his lovers to sleep together before marriage except in two otherwise explicable plays in which marriage never occurs, *Troilus and Cressida* and *Antony and Cleopatra*.

In brief, according to Shakespeare, if a man contracts to marry a woman in a spousal, whether *de futuro* or *de praesenti,* and follows that contract with copulation as in the case of Angelo and Mariana, Claudio and Juliet, and Lucio and Mistress Kate Keepdown, he must follow the actions with a marriage ceremony.

There is no inconsistency in the play in the courtships: this theory applies to all of Shakespeare's plays. *Measure for Measure* is unusual in that the stages of courtship are almost completely annihilated, and no man suffers *hereos*. Mariana's weeping and suffering are therefore overemphasized to the audience, and the loves of the male characters are understated.

The theses of the play do not at all diverge from Shakespeare's usual concepts except for the pre-marriage physical relations of the characters.

Shakespeare's *Troilus and Cressida* follows the traditional courtly love pattern as delineated earlier in this paper. The play is interesting, however, for the deviations in the actual expression, in the language which Troilus and Cressida and Pandarus use.

This is the story of a faithful lover, a faithless beloved, and a pimp: the unfavorable tradition of these characters Chaucer had tried to stem. Shakespeare's characterization is rather typed, and the plot is precisely, in form, as Chaucer gives it.

The play begins *in medias res*. The Inception is practically omitted, and what little there is is interwoven with the next stage, the Development. In the first scene Troilus is presented as already in love with Cressida. He describes his own condition as that of a lover who is already in the second stage: he cannot control his heart because it does not belong to him, and he suffers from *hereos*.

But Shakespeare immediately makes it clear that he is portraying an enervating courtly love, not an ennobling one. When a man was in love he was expected to fight better, "for it detracts very much from the good character of a man if he is timid in a fight."[22] This is expected even if the love is not yet returned, as is Troilus' case:

. . . to a man not being beloued, and yet continuing in his purpose to possesse hir whome he pursueth, a most proper and fitte way were, (in my experience) to stande vpon encrease of merites, and by his readie seruices, to declare the vehement nature of his loue to his mistresse.[23]

Troilus feels no such ennoblement. He has found himself, as a result of his love for Cressida,

> . . . weaker than a woman's tear,
> Tamer than sleep, fonder than ignorance,
> Less valiant than the virgin in the night,
> And skilless as unpractis'd infancy.[24]

He has not, so far in the course of the Development, bene-fited from his love. He thinks of his beloved constantly:

> And when fair Cressid comes into my thoughts—
> So, traitor? 'when she comes'? When is she thence?[25]

but the thought does not help him, does not strengthen him. Here is a man whose love-sickness is repugnant to a modern audience and apparently to Shakespeare.

It is not surprising, then, that Troilus should describe his beloved in negatives. In poetry the concrete word carries the imagery, and the negative does not destroy the image. A good poet avoids the common use of negatives unless he wishes to convey a double image, as Milton in his description of hell-fire. In this case, Troilus thinks of Cressida in one way, and Shakespeare intends the audience to think of her in another:

> . . . I tell thee I am *mad*
> In Cressid's love. Thou answer'st "She is fair"!
> Pour'st in the *open ulcer* of my heart
> Her eyes, her hair, her cheek, her gait, her voice;
> Handlest in thy discourse, O, that her hand,
> In whose comparison all whites are *ink*
> Writing their own reproach, to whose soft seizure
> The cygnet's down is *harsh* and spirit of sense
> *Hard as the palm of ploughman!*[26]

The imagery of the words is ugly. The impression given is not only that Cressida's hands are white, which is intended by Troilus, but also that they are inky; that they are harsh and hard to the touch. And all this description of an unlovely Cressida is introduced by the phrase which might have come from Thersites in describing love, "the open ulcer of my heart." Love wounds, according to the tradition, but it should not fester, and ideally the wound, being invisible, should have no such description concretely stating that love does no good but is an undesirable disease.

Pandarus helps this unlovely imagery by the same use of the negative when he cries of her, "I care not an she were a blackamoor!" Cressida is not a blackamoor. She is blonde. She is considered beautiful, although it is significant that the best description of Cressida as beautiful comes from herself at various points in the play.[27]

Troilus ends the scene by drawing a comparison, again unconsciously, between his love and the love of Paris for Helen.

> Let Paris bleed! 'Tis but a scar to scorn;
> Paris is gor'd with Menelaus' horn![28]

This time-honoured reference to cuckolding points out clearly the ugliness of courtly love. Paris, so in love with Helen, is not to be honoured for that love. Rather he is to be mocked and censured in obscenities. There are only two beloveds in the play, Helen and Cressida. The one must take her coloring from the other as Beatrice becomes more womanly for the presence of Hero. Helen, whose face to Marlowe was beautiful enough to launch a thousand ships, is, to Shakespeare, merely a whore for Paris. What, then, must Cressida be to Troilus?

The qualifications of the lovers needed for the Inception

are mentioned during the Development. From this it appears
that Troilus is at the most twenty-two years old. Pandarus
describes him as "the prince of chivalry," but Cressida is not
interested in such description, for she hushes him: "Peace,
for shame, peace!" when he apparently says it too loudly.
When Pandarus expatiates in detail on Troilus' character as
an ideal lover it is again in the familiar negative: "Is not
birth, beauty, good shape, discourse, manhood, learning,
gentleness, virtue, youth, liberality, and such-like, the spice
and salt that season a man?" He does not say that Troilus has
those traits, he merely implies it. There are many evidences of
his equivocation without lying in the play.[29]

Such an ideal person as Pandarus describes, Cressida immediately describes as "a minc'd man," thereby destroying
any concept that she will love Troilus for such qualities. It is
thus obvious that the Inception, which is here worked in with
the Development, is unnecessary to Shakespeare except to degrade the cause of love. Cressida is not described as to age,
breeding, intelligence, or marital status. She is merely the
unbated and dangerously sharp foil upon which Troilus' thus-
wounded heart has developed an open ulcer. Troilus is un-
beautifully sick. Pandarus is a pimp. The three are revealed
in the first two scenes of the play as an unlovely crew.

The conclusion of the Development and the Betrothal are
scarcely motivated. Cressida, at the end of Act I, scene ii, acknowledges that she will accept a token from Troilus, even
though she has determined that she will be difficult of
achievement:

> That she belov'd knows naught that knows not this:
> Men prize the thing ungain'd more than it is.[30]

Here, too, she echoes the Andrean rule: "The easy attainment of love makes it of little value; difficulty of attainment makes it prized."[31] But she makes it an important part of the woman's attitude the while. Andreas advocated the policy to enhance the lady's value in the eyes of the man. If the lover had difficulty in achieving the lady she was more valuable. But it was expected that the woman would be difficult not in order to excite the man but merely because she prized her virtue, or, better, her reputation for virtue. Cressida declares in so many words that she values her honor more than her chastity, and any act, "Myn honour sauf," would be within her canon.

She simplifies Troilus' problems, however, by offering to accept a token from him. Shakespeare does not tell what it is, but its meaning, the right of copulation, is implicit.

Before Troilus and Cressida meet for the spousal, he and Hector debate the question of love.[32] Troilus and Paris argue for the traditional courtly love, Hector argues for a licit and sincere love. Hector begins by denying Cressida's words last quoted above:

> . . . value dwells not in particular will:
> It holds his estimate and dignity
> As well wherein 'tis precious of itself
> As in the prizer.[33]

Cressida does not value her chastity as anything more than a commodity to be used to link Troilus to her in concupiscence. Hector asserts that such chastity is of little value either to the lover or to the beloved. He adds, in a hit against courtly love in general, " 'Tis mad idolatry To make the service greater than the god."[34] Troilus' love, as fostered by Cressida and Pandarus, is intensified by his inability to achieve her. This exaltation of the form without the content is abominable to Hector, who later moralizes:

>   . . . Now
> What nearer debt in all humanity
> Than wife is to the husband? If this law
> Of nature be corrupted through affection . . .
> There is a law in each well-ord'red nation
> To curb those raging appetites that are
> Most disobedient and refractory . . .
>   Thus to persist
> In doing wrong extenuates not wrong,
> But makes it much more heavy.[35]

Troilus answers that the Trojans' keeping of Helen ennobles them:

>   . . . But, worthy Hector,
> She is a theme of honour and renown,
> A spur to valiant and magnanimous deeds,
> Whose present courage may beat down our foes,
> And fame in time to come canonize us.[36]

This is not what Troilus expresses as his affection for Cressida in the first scene of the play, and therefore his speech is made to appear more an argument than a belief. If the Troilus who declares he cannot fight because of his love for Cressida immediately goes out to fight when Aeneas calls him, thus contradicting himself, the same Troilus again contradicts himself here. He has already shown the audience how little love really ennobles him. The argument he adduces here is specious. Later in the play he again shows his true attitude.

With this thorough preparation—Hector's solid moral arguments and Troilus' insincere contrary ones—Shakespeare is almost ready for a betrothal. But not quite. For he uses the second scene of the third act to contrast the love of Paris and Helen with that of Troilus and Cressida. Paris is not

ennobled in his love, for he says that those afield fighting
are "Hector, Deiphobus, Helenus, Antenor, and all the
gallantry of Troy. I would fain have arm'd today, but my
Nell would not have it so." His beloved, far from inciting
him to honor, keeps him from it. And Pandarus has just
previously epitomized the attitude when he said: "Is this the
generation of love—hot blood, hot thoughts, and hot deeds?
Why, they are vipers! Is love a generation of vipers?"[37]

Pandarus has here used a phrase from the Christian Bible,
one which Jesus uses and which therefore sounds strange
coming from a pre-Christian Trojan, but stranger coming
from a pimp. Perhaps in the Elizabethan age the context
would be more strikingly evident to an audience than it would
today. The passage in *Matthew* most likely to have been in
Shakespeare's mind is the speech to the scribes and Pharisees:

> . . . ye are like unto whited sepulchres, which indeed appear
> beautiful outward, but are within full of dead men's bones, and of
> all uncleanness. Even so ye also outwardly appear righteous unto
> men, but within ye are full of hypocrisy and iniquity. . . . Ye
> serpents, ye generation of vipers, how can ye escape the damnation
> of hell?[38]

This is a description of Helen, of Cressida, and of the love
for which they stand.

So when the next scene opens with Troilus before the
door of Cressida's house the mood has been set, and Troilus
does nothing to destroy it. Professor Tillyard feels that "to
turn Troilus into an adept at lechery is to wreck one of
Shakespeare's masterpieces of characterization and to go flat
against what his poetry is telling us."[39] And to prove it he
quotes the first lines of this scene as great poetry showing a
great love. But Professor Tillyard uses only the first three

lines of a continuous speech, and he strangely omits the succeeding ones, which are a part of the same effect:

> . . . I stalk about her door
> Like a strange soul upon the Stygian banks
> Staying for waftage. O, be thou my Charon,
> And give me a swift transportance to those fields
> Where I may wallow in the lily beds
> Propos'd for the deserver![40]

Had Troilus been an exalted lover he could have chosen a
better verb than "wallow" to describe his desire. Shakespeare
uses the word on only one other occasion, and there bitterly
when Bolingbroke speaks of a series of impossibles beginning "O, who can . . ." and concluding:

> . . . wallow naked in December snow
> By thinking on fantastic summer's heat?[41]

Here the word connotes rolling one's body[42] and thus refers
to bodily sensations. There is no character ennoblement in
such imagery, it suggests instead abandonment to sensuality.

Before the entrance of Cressida, Troilus describes his
lovesickness:

> . . . a passion doth embrace my bosom.
> My heart beats thicker than a feverous pulse,
> And all my powers do their bestowing lose,
> Like vassalage at unawares encount'ring
> The eye of majesty,[43]

and upon her entrance he loses his ability to speak.[44] Such a
description of his condition is again not beautiful. Troilus
suffers from a passion which enervates him.

The ritual of the spousal is followed in the succeeding

passage. The consent of the lovers is given by a kiss at the beginning, upon which Pandarus remarks

What, billing again? Here's "In witness whereof the parties interchangeably."[45]

This is followed by Cressida's shameful rather than modest declaration of love. Pandarus *in loco parentis* gives Cressida to Troilus:

Cressida. Well, uncle, what folly I commit I dedicate to you.
Pandarus. I thank you for that. If my lord get a boy of you, you'll give him me. Be true to my lord. If he flinch, chide me for it.
Troilus. You know now your hostages—your uncle's word and my firm faith.[46]

Pandarus acts, too, as witness to the oaths which the lovers exchange,[47] the irony of which should be obvious to the audience:

Troilus. True swains in love shall in the world to come
      Approve their truth by Troilus. When their rhymes . . .
      Want similes . . .
      "As true as Troilus" shall crown up the verse
      And scanctify the numbers.[48]
Cressida. If I be false, or swerve a hair from truth,
      When time is old and hath forgot itself . . .
      . . . yet let memory
      From false to false, among false maids in love,
      Upraid my falsehood![49]

This ceremony is followed by the traditional handclasp:

Pandarus. Go to, a bargain made! Seal it, seal it; I'll be the witness. Here I hold your hand; here my cousin's.[50]

and by the blessing:

Pandarus. Say "Amen."
Troilus. Amen.
Cressida. Amen.
Pandarus. Amen.[51]

To assure the audience that this is not a legal spousal in the way of marriage, Pandarus immediately adds the epithalamium:

Whereupon I will show you a chamber with a bed, which, because it shall not speak of your pretty encounters, press it to death. Away!
　　And Cupid grant all tongue-tied maidens here
　　Bed, chamber, Pandar to provide this gear![52]

Certainly this is a parody of the ceremony, as O. J. Campbell has pointed out.[53] But I feel it is a parody of a real marriage ceremony and not of a courtly love spousal. It would be unusual to mock that which is mock in itself. This is a true courtly spousal, with ironic overtones, which perhaps even almost coincidentally is parallel to a serious romantic spousal.

Of the nine aspects of a spousal mentioned in the preceding chapter, this ceremony includes all but the dowry. There is no stage direction for a kiss at the conclusion of the oath, either, but one precedes the ceremony and might well come too in its proper place in a staging of the play.

This, then, is a close imitation of the spousal which was used to unite a couple in an unbreakable oath, and which should lead, according to Shakespeare, to a marriage ceremony. Its object here is twofold. In the first place it emphasizes the defection of Cressida when she later goes to Diomedes, because in no other Shakespearean play does a character break a spousal successfully. Beatrice and Benedick of *Much Ado About Nothing* may have been betrothed;

Angelo has certainly cancelled his spousal oath with Mariana, in *Measure for Measure*. But they are eventually reunited.

In the second place, the spousal here is a mockery of true romantic love which leads to marriage. Here, despite the form, the words are again in the negative as they were in the first scene, and they connote the obscene rather than the beautiful of the match. Cressida, who might well have been made to say that she will be true, as Troilus declares, uses the contrary supposition that she will be false. Of course that makes for dramatic irony, but it also makes for a tone of incongruity in such a ceremony.

The fallacy of Hamill Kenny's article[54] attempting to prove that this is a *sponsalia de praesenti* has been pointed out by Campbell, whose refutation is, however, perhaps too opposite a statement when he declares that "some such phrase as 'I take you for my husband' "[55] is necessary to a troth-plight. The *sponsalia de praesenti* of *The Duchess of Malfi* does not use this or any similar phrase in the ceremony uniting the Duchess and Antonio. This in *Troilus and Cressida* is not a troth or a spousal *de praesenti*, it is a courtly love betrothal, or a mock of a spousal or marriage ceremony. It is part of Shakespeare's moral that the two be considered identical: that a courtly betrothal is merely a parody of a true spousal. When Kenny attempts to pass on the morality of the situation he exceeds the bounds of impartial criticism and verges to a dangerous value judgement based on twentieth-century morality.

From this point in the play the action declines into the Ordeal the following morning after Troilus and Cressida have succeeded once more in degrading their relationship by their and Pandarus' lascivious remarks concerning the preceding night. The best method for analysis of this passage, which is an *aubade,* is to parallel the situations of Troilus and Cressida and Romeo and Juliet, each couple in a similar situation:

Troilus. O Cressida! but that the busy day
Wak'd by the lark hath rous'd the ribald crows,
And dreaming night will hide our joys no longer,
I would not from thee.
Cressida. Night hath been too brief.
Troilus. Beshrew the witch!
With venomous wights she stays
As tediously as hell, but flies the grasps of love
With wings more momentary-swift than thought.
You will catch cold, and curse me.[56]

Romeo. It was the lark, the herald of the morn;
No nightingale. Look, love, what envious streaks
Do lace the severing clouds in yonder East.
Night's candles are burnt out, and jocund day
Stands tiptoe on the misty mountain tops.[57]

Night, which is considered beautiful by Shakespeare's sympathetic characters, becomes ugly to those who use it for ugly purposes. Macbeth and Lady Macbeth describe night as evil, Romeo and Juliet find it beautiful. It seems to take the coloring of the mood and character of the describer. So to Troilus night is evil, and therefore he himself has been committing some evil. That is a point which Shakespeare seems consistently to emphasize in his plays.

Troilus, almost immediately after this searched for by Aeneas in Cressida's house, violates the adjuration to secrecy of the courtly love code by appearing when demanded. But there has obviously been no more than a slight attempt at secrecy before, for Aeneas knows where to find Troilus when he needs him.

Upon the separation of the lovers, reported by Aeneas, Troilus and Cressida exchange gifts. Troilus gives her a sleeve, and she gives him a glove.[58] The gifts which had been vaguely mentioned previously are not identified. But the glove and sleeve are mentioned in the fifth act, and the sleeve itself is as symbolic of Cressida's love as the ring Portia gives Bassanio and the handkerchief Othello gives Desdemona are of theirs.

The Ordeal proper begins with the actual separation. Even before Cressida leaves, Troilus suffers from

> . . . a kind of godly jealousy,
> Which I beseech you call a virtuous sin,[59]

and which she tacitly accepts as not only normal but probable. The Ordeal continues with the witnessing by Troilus of the promise of seduction of Cressida by Diomedes. This scene so tortures Troilus that he goes temporarily mad at the sight, as the courtly lover should react to the knowledge or belief of his beloved's perfidy.

> This she? No, this is Diomed's Cressida!
> If beauty have a soul, this is not she;
> If souls guide vows, if vows be sanctimonies,
> If sanctimony be the gods' delight,
> If there be rule in unity itself—
> This is not she. O madness of discourse,
> That cause sets up with and against itself!
> Bifold authority! where reason can revolt
> Without perdition, and loss assume all reason
> Without revolt: this is, and is not, Cressid![60]

There were many other examples of such lovers in literature besides Yvain and Tristram.

The last stage, ordinarily the Union, is in this case the recovery of Troilus from the love of Cressida, evidenced by his destroying her letter, although he first reads it.[61] In this passage he is sane again and searching for his honor, but definitely not for Cressida's return. So he says

> . . . Proud Diomed, believe
> I come to lose my arm or win my sleeve,[62]

although he recognizes that Cressida

> My love with words and errors still . . . feeds,
> But edifies another with her deeds.[63]

From this he proceeds immediately to combat with Diomedes, to whom he ignominiously loses his horse. Diomedes feels that with the token defeat of Troilus he has earned the right to Cressida:

> Present the fair steed to my lady Cressid.
> Fellow, commend my service to her beauty;
> Tell her I have chastis'd the amorous Troyan
> And am her knight by proof.[64]

Troilus is then revolted from the entire affair. His honor has been damaged first by losing Cressida to Diomedes and then by his defeat in battle by him. He therefore turns against all memory of Cressida, and even reviles Pandarus, as he does not in Chaucer's version.

> Hence, broker, lackey! Ignomy and shame
> Pursue thy life and live aye with thy name![65]

Thersites comments on the Greek and military concepts of the play; Pandarus comments on the Trojan and love parts of it.[66] Perhaps Thersites is, as Professor Tillyard claims, a licensed fool and thus a privileged person.[67] Then he cannot injure the reputations of the Greeks. Perhaps Pandarus is an impotent fool too, when considered alone. But the chorus of the two is sufficient to destroy any greatness of the play's theme and to make it one of the dark comedies, a comedy of a mock-spousal and therefore of a mock-love. Mock-love, according to Shakespeare in the play, is to be despised.

In the two plays which I have analyzed in this chapter it is apparent that Shakespeare, far from having turned in revulsion from love and from romance, has merely restated his constantly-recurring theme in another form, this time in negatives. Such earlier plays as *The Two Gentlemen of Verona,* which presents the conflict of love and honor, permitting the hero, Valentine, temporarily to decide in favor of honor, but forcing him willy-nilly to settle for love at the conclusion of the work; and the romantic *Twelfth Night* and *As You Like It,* which present the humorous inversion of courtship by the woman; are merely parts of the same cloth Shakespeare is weaving in the dark comedies. Love, says Shakespeare, is a sincere affection between two people of opposite sexes which leads to matrimony. He does not consider whether his ideas come from Plato or from Castiglione or Fenton or Andreas. But he does feel that there is, if not a ritualistic aspect to its development, at least a constant set of factors which will tend to bring about the ending of marriage which he envisions from the time of the first meeting of the lovers. Many of his similarities, such as love at first sight between the characters, may be explained as exigencies used to speed the action of the play. Others, such as parental opposition, are deliberately introduced to slow the culmination of the play.

But in almost every instance the actions of the lovers in Shakespeare are strikingly similar to the actions of the lovers in Dekker and Webster and Kyd, as well as to the lovers of past centuries in the romances.

This study began with the belief that there is to be found a consistent traditional pattern and morality in Shakespeare's treatment of the amorous relationships of man and woman, and investigation has borne out that belief. Consciously or not, Shakespeare has accepted the pattern of the medieval romances for his romantic plots. This pattern of Inception, Development, Betrothal, Ordeal, and Union Shakespeare occasionally uses simply by assigning one aspect to each of his five acts, as in *As You Like It* and *Romeo and Juliet.* More occasionally, he emphasizes some phase, truncating others, and in general he finds the last three stages more useful to his dramatic method than the first two.

Within these stages are the more specific details of a still more complicated pattern, that of the relationships of the lovers in a traditional interaction of minutely-prescribed behavior. These minutiae of ritual have been designated courtly love or *fine amor* when their emphasis is upon form without content and when the desired culmination is not marriage.

Shakespeare's courtships almost invariably end in marriage or death or both, and the lovers with whom he sympathizes intend marriage from the Inception. Although they are traditional in many of their actions, it would be wise not to accuse Shakespeare of an adherence to the code of courtly love: he appears to follow the code when it really follows human probability. Shakespeare found himself in difficulties, therefore, when he tried to handle the story of Troilus and Cressida, for he took the material of a formalized courtly pattern which Chaucer himself had trouble justifying dramatically, and he satirized it so that his characters occasionally got out of hand and became types rather than the individuals he so invariably delineated. Shakespeare did not take kindly to formalized activity, and he could not accept a tradition which ran deliberately counter to Christian morality.

Therefore, when courtly love diverges from the conservative middle-class morality of the Elizabethan age Shakespeare rejects it. His men and women love not for an age but for all time. They are faithful even though presumed faithless, they do not alter their loves even after death or presumed death of the beloved. A man and woman in Shakespeare marry once and once only. If they should appear to slide from moral strictness, Shakespeare tends to withdraw his sympathy, as in *Antony and Cleopatra* or *All's Well That Ends Well*.

I have added nothing to the stature of Shakespeare: I could not hope to do so. If I have helped, in the course of this book, in the understanding of some of the plays by showing the complete process of courtship in Shakespeare as he intended it and as his contemporary audience understood it, I have succeeded in my purpose.

NOTES

NOTES TO I: FINE AMOR

1. Tatlock, *The Mind and Art of Chaucer*, p. 39.

2. Andreas Capellanus, *The Art of Courtly Love*, p. 21.

3. *Ibid.*, pp. 100, 163, 137. (The page citations in the notes follow consecutive order within each paragraph.)

4. *Ibid.*, pp. 122, 167.   5. *Ibid.*, pp. 100, 136 ff., 171.

6. This is modeled on the outline given by Barrow in *The Medieval Society Romances*, p. 9.

7. Andreas Capellanus, pp. 32, 39, 184.

8. *Ibid.*, pp. 150, 149.

9. *Ibid.*, pp. 49, 85, 87.   10. *Ibid.*, p. 185.

11. *Ibid.*, pp. 85, 35, 65, 34, 113, 60.

12. *Ibid.*, pp. 57, 64, 174.   13. *Ibid.*, pp. 152, 155, 157, 85.

14. *Ibid.*, pp. 144, 155, 59, 31, 156, 170, 33, 191, 30, 154, 169, 152, 82 (Rule XI).

15. Kilgour, *The Decline of Chivalry*, pp. xi-xix.

16. Lowes, "The Lovers Maladye of Hereos," *Modern Philology*, XI, No. 4, 18 ff.

17. Andreas Capellanus, pp. 185-86.   18. *Ibid.*, cf. p. 158.

19. *Ibid.*, p. 36. Here, loss of speech in the presence of the beloved is reproved. It seems to be praiseworthy, however, on p. 45.

20. Chrétien de Troyes, *Arthurian Romances*, pp. 129-30.

21. *Ibid.*, p. 141.

22. Andreas Capellanus, pp. 34, 81, 82, 86, 156, 173, 175.

23. *Ibid.*, p. 165.   24. *Ibid.*, p. 173.

25. *Ibid.*, pp. 174-75.   26. *Ibid.*, p. 145.

27. *Ibid.*, p. 176.   28. *Ibid.*, p. 184 (Rule IV).

29. *Ibid.*, pp. 152, 159.   30. *Ibid.*, p. 68.

31. *Ibid.*, p. 157.

32. See, for instance, Chaucer's *Troilus and Criseyde* and Shakespeare's *Romeo and Juliet,* as well as Chrétien's *Yvain.*

33. Chrétien de Troyes, p. 127.   34. *Ibid.,* p. 126.

35. *Ibid.,* p. 127.   36. *Ibid.,* p. 129.   37. *Ibid.*

38. *Ibid.,* pp. 130, 143, 144, 139.

39. *Ibid.,* pp. 147, 146, 144.   40. *Ibid.,* pp. 139, 140.

41. *Ibid.,* p. 121.   42. Ephesians, V, 3-16.

43. Chrétien de Troyes, p. 160.

44. Andreas Capellanus, pp. 184, 167.

45. Chrétien de Troyes, p. 178.

46. Mott, *The System of Courtly Love, Studied as an Introduction to the "Vita Nuova" of Dante,* p. 47.

47. Andreas Capellanus, p. 15. Compare Mott, pp. 47 and 49: "It is true that in one point Chrétien . . . departs from the courtly conception. In that code love was declared incompatible with marriage . . . in *Yvain* he proceeds to present the most refined courtly love with all its subtleties, as existing between husband and wife. . . . The other conventions are almost all to be found fully developed."

48. "No sooner had [Owain] beheld [the Countess of the Fountain], than he became inflamed with her love, so that it took entire possession of him." Guest (trans.), *The Mabinogion,* p. 161.

49. Chrétien de Troyes, p. 197.   50. *Ibid.*   51. *Ibid.*

52. *Ibid.,* p. 196.   53. *Ibid.,* p. 202.   54. *Ibid.,* p. 200.

55. *Ibid.,* p. 205.   56. *Ibid.*

57. *Ibid.,* p. 206. I have inserted the names of the speakers. Mott, p. 50, quotes this passage in the same connection.

58. Chrétien de Troyes, p. 206.   59. *Ibid.*

60. *Ibid.,* p. 208.   61. *Ibid.*   62. Barrow, p. 17.

63. Chrétien de Troyes, p. 216.   64. *Ibid.,* p. 212.

65. *Ibid.,* p. 216.   66. *Ibid.*

67. Andreas Capellanus, p. 186.

68. Chrétien de Troyes, p. 268.   69. *Ibid.,* pp. 268-69.

70. Mott, p. 49, on other evidence, reaches a similar conclusion.

71. Mott, p. 47.   72. Tatlock, p. 39.   73. *Ibid.,* p. 46.

74. *The Canterbury Tales,* IV, 1421, in Chaucer, *The Complete Works of Geoffrey Chaucer.*

75. *Troilus and Criseyde,* Book III, lines 169-72.

76. Tatlock, p. 40.

77. *Troilus and Criseyde,* Book I, lines 477-81.

78. *Ibid.,* Book III, lines 1802-6.

79. *Ibid.,* Book II, lines 638-44.

80. *Ibid.,* Book II, lines 659-65.

81. Bennet, *Chaucer and the Fifteenth Century,* p. 55.

82. *Troilus and Criseyde,* Book II, lines 673-79.

83. John Strong Perry Tatlock, in a lecture at the University of California, 1942. Since the statement is taken from my notes, the quotation may not be precisely accurate. The idea, however, is Dr. Tatlock's.

84. *The Canterbury Tales,* I, 1359-75.

85. *Troilus and Criseyde,* Book I, lines 484-87.

86. *Ibid.,* Book I, lines 358-60.

87. *Ibid.,* Book III, line 1090.

88. *Ibid.,* Book III, line 1685.

89. *Ibid.,* Book I, lines 459-60.

90. *Ibid.,* Book I, lines 488-91.

91. *Ibid.,* Book I, line 278.

92. *Ibid.,* Book I, lines 498-99.

93. *Ibid.,* Book I, lines 436-41.

94. *Ibid.,* Book III, line 1092.

95. *Ibid.,* Book IV, lines 370-71.

96. *Ibid.,* Book I, lines 358, 547, 806; Book II, line 1305; Book IV, lines 220, 947; Book V, line 471.

97. *Ibid.,* Book V, line 715.

98. *Ibid.,* Book V, lines 708-12.

99. Andreas Capellanus, p. 165.

100. *Troilus and Criseyde,* Book I, lines 988-94.

101. *Ibid.,* Book V, lines 1737-43.

102. Christine de Pisan, *The Book of the Duke of True Lovers*, pp. 49-50.

103. *Troilus and Criseyde*, Book III, lines 1366-69.

104. *Ibid.*, Book III, lines 1370-72.

105. *Ibid.*, Book V, lines 1040-41.

106. *Ibid.*, Book V, lines 1660-63.   107. *Ibid.*

108. *Ibid.*, Book III, line 885.

109. *Ibid.*, Book V, line 1013.

110. *Ibid.*, Book V, lines 1037-43.

111. Andreas Capellanus, p. 176.

112. *Troilus and Criseyde*, Book III, lines 1208-29.

113. *Ibid.*, Book III, lines 965-66.

114. *Ibid.*, Book III, line 1368. This was mentioned on p. 36 *supra*.

115. For a true spousal described by Chaucer, see that of the marquis and Griselde in "The Clerk's Tale," IV, 344 ff.

116. Tatlock, p. 42, reached a somewhat similar conclusion. In dealing with Chaucer, I have no true idea how many concepts are mine, how many Dr. Tatlock's.

117. Gascoigne, *The Complete Works of George Gascoigne*, I, 383-453. The date (1573) is of the first edition. The Italianization of the work occurred in the second edition, of 1576. I have consulted both in this edition of Cunliffe. All succeeding Gascoigne references are to Vol. I.

118. *Ibid.*, p. 453.   119. *Ibid.*, pp. 428-29.

120. *Ibid.*, p. 387. Annie Oakley, in *Annie Get Your Gun*, puts her head awkwardly to one side, hangs her mouth open, and gazes unblinkingly at her beloved, Frank, when she first sees him. This is the identical tradition.

121. *Ibid.*, p. 396.   122. *Ibid.*, pp. 401, 405.

123. *Ibid.*, pp. 390, 406.   124. *Ibid.*, p. 412.

125. Prouty, *George Gascoigne, Elizabethan Courtier, Soldier, and Poet*, p. 209.

126. Gascoigne, p. 413.   127. *Ibid.*, p. 401.

128. *Ibid.*, p. 417.   129. Prouty, p. 209.

130. Andreas Capellanus, p. 153.

131. Fenton, *Monophylo,* Vol. I, fol. 53r.

132. *Ibid.,* Vol. II, fol. 4r.   133. Gascoigne, p. 419.

134. *Ibid.*   135. *Ibid.,* p. 420.   136. *Ibid.,* p. 427.

137. *Ibid.,* p. 433.   138. *Ibid.,* p. 497.

139. *Ibid.,* p. 435.   140. *Ibid.,* pp. 437, 453.

141. *Ibid.,* p. 434.

142. *Ibid.,* pp. 426 (she at the same time gives him a pillow-case, which seems to be a unique instance of such a gift between lovers in the romances), 392.

143. *Ibid.,* p. 433.   144. Prouty, p. 209.

145. Gascoigne, p. 453.

NOTES TO II: INCEPTION: THE FIRST MEETING

1. Dates, authorship, and performance of plays as given in this book are according to Harbage, *Annals of English Drama, 975-1700.*

2. Adams, *English Domestic or Homiletic Tragedy, 1575-1642,* p. 159.

3. I, i, 1759-66.

4. III, iii, 263-67, in Shakespeare, *The Complete Works of Shakespeare.* All Shakespeare quotations in this paper are from this edition.

5. Quoted in Powell, *English Domestic Relations, 1487-1653.*

6. Quoted in Andreas Capellanus, *The Art of Courtly Love,* p. 32n.

7. *A Short History of Marriage,* p. 145.

8. I have used the 2d ed., London, 1686.

9. IX, 2 (p. 47).   10. *Ibid.*

11. II, i, in Horne, *Nero and Other Plays,* p. 118.

12. Lines 131-36.

13. V. ii. 13-17, in Brooke, *Shakespeare Apocrypha.*

14. I, ii, 41-55.   15. V, i, 252.   16. V, iii, 8.

17. *Ibid.*, V, iii, 75.   18. IV, i, 6; V, iii, 31.

19. *Ibid.*, I, ii, 1.   20. I, i, 55.   21. I, ii, 256.

22. Page 201.   23. *Ibid.*, p. 5.

24. *Romeo and Juliet*, I, iii, 69-73.   25. *Ibid.*, I, iii, 15-18.

26. Quoted in Powell.

27. Fenton, *Monophylo,* Vol. I, fol. 21r.

28. Andreas Capellanus, p. 54.

29. Freeman, *The History of the Norman Conquest of England*, V, 482.

30. Kelso, *The Doctrine of the English Gentleman of the Sixteenth Century,* pp. 85-86.

31. Andreas Capellanus, pp. 45, 47, 49, 54, 85, 87, 143, 149-50, 161, 181, and 185 (Rule XI).

32. Fenton, Vol. II, fol. 13r.   33. *Ibid.*, Vol. I, fol. 20v.

34. *Ibid.*, Vol. I, fol. 17r.   35. III, i, 145-49, in Brooke.

36. Cf. Andreas Capellanus, p. 185 (Rule XI): "It is unseemly to love one whom one would be ashamed to marry."

37. *Ibid.*, p. 141.

38. Moseley, *The Bourgeois Consciousness of Thomas Dekker,* considers the awareness of class differences in the plays of Dekker. For a discussion of classes in Elizabethan England see Wright, *Middle Class Culture in Elizabethan England.*

39. Dekker, *Dramatic Works of Thomas Dekker,* I, 11.

40. *Ibid.*, p. 9.   41. *Ibid.*, p. 58.

42. That love is considered now even more powerful than it was in the sixteenth century can be seen in the British production of *Stairway to Heaven.* Its thesis is that the love of a man for a woman is stronger than the law of God.

43. *The Merry Wives of Windsor*, III, iv, 4-6.

44. I, iv, 8-12.   45. *Ibid.*, I, iv, 57-59.

46. Dekker, I, 76.   47. Andreas Capellanus, p. 45.

48. *Ibid.*, p. 142.

49. Lyly, *Euphues, The Anatomy of Wit*, p. 151.

50. *Hamlet*, III, i, 159-61.

51. I, ii, 124.   52. III, ii, 153-55.

53. V, ii, 180 ff., in Webster, *The Works of John Webster,* Vol. II.

54. *The Love-Game Comedy,* pp. 199-200. Wrestling, as verse-writing, was a gentlemanly accomplishment.

55. *Hamlet,* I, iii, 19-21.   56. I, iii, 162-65.

57. *Othello,* I, ii, 21-24.   58. Andreas Capellanus, p. 87.

59. Quoted in Anderson, *Elizabethan Psychology and Shakespeare's Plays.*

60. Anderson, p. 119.   61. Fenton, Vol. I, fol. 56r.

62. *Romeo and Juliet,* II, ii, 13 and 71-72.

63. *A Midsummer Night's Dream,* I, i, 183; II, ii, 120-22.

64. I, iii, in Ford, *The Works of John Ford,* I, 124.

65. *Romeo and Juliet,* I, i, 219-20.   66. I, ii, 440-41.

67. *As You Like It,* III, v, 16-27.

68. Castiglione, *The Book of the Courtier,* p. 59.

69. II, i, 25-26, in Brooke.

70. *A Midsummer Night's Dream,* I, i, 183-85.

71. Jonson, *The Best Works of Ben Jonson,* I, 280.

72. IV, iii, 105-7, in Middleton, *The Works of Thomas Middleton,* Vol. III.

73. IV, iv, 136-40.

74. *The Duchess of Malfi,* I, i, 194-98, in Webster, Vol. II.

75. I, i, in Middleton, VI, 8-9.   76. V, iii, 65-71.

77. *Much Ado About Nothing,* III, ii, 60-62.

78. I, ii, 268-69.   79. *Ibid.,* I, iii, 1-3.

80. *Pericles,* II, ii, 56-57.   81. Andreas Capellanus, p. 113.

82. Andreas has the same idea. *Ibid.,* p. 34.

83. Pearson, *Elizabethan Love Conventions,* has a valuable outline of Castiglione's conventions on pp. 326-27.

84. Book II, chap. iii, p. 125.   85. III, i, in Dekker, I, 340.

86. I, ii, 49-55.   87. IV, iii, 5-8, in Middleton, Vol. III.

88. *The Two Gentlemen of Verona,* II, i, 76-84.

89. *Hamlet,* II, i, 78-80.

90. *The Two Gentlemen of Verona,* II, i, 76-84.

91. Moseley, p. 8.

92. *Old Fortunatus,* in Dekker, I, 130. See Cyril Tourneur, *The Atheist's Tragedy* (1609), in Tourneur, *Works in The Best Works of Webster and Tourneur,* pp. 260-61. Castabella expresses the same preference for a soldier.

93. V, ii, 180-83, in Webster, Vol. II.

94. *Henry V,* V, ii, 149-75.   95. Kelso, p. 15.

96. *Pericles,* II, v, 55-58.

97. *The Atheist's Tragedy,* I, iv, in Tourneur, pp. 260-61.

98. Kelso, p. 93.   99. *Othello,* I, iii, 167-68.

100. *Hamlet,* III, i, 159-62.   101. Kelso, p. 76.

102. Fenton, Vol. I, fol. 56r.

103. *Romeo and Juliet,* II, v, 56-58.

104. *1 The Honest Whore,* in Dekker, II, 39.

105. *Much Ado About Nothing,* II, i, 394-95.

106. I, i, in Ford, I, 115.

107. Kelso makes the social equality of the knight and gentle-man much of her thesis.

108. *A Woman Killed With Kindness,* I, i, in Heywood, *Best Works of Thomas Heywood,* p. 6.

109. *The Duchess of Malfi,* I, i, 194-214, in Webster, Vol. II.

110. *Pericles,* V, i, 121-23. See also *Measure for Measure,* III, i, 184 ff.; and *The Tempest,* I, ii, 457. Duncan's comment in Mac-beth, I, iv, 11-12, that "There's no art To find the mind's construc-tion in the face" is a remark of disillusionment made after he had mistakenly trusted Cawdor. But he had believed as Pericles above until he was proved wrong.

111. *The Winter's Tale,* IV, iv, 156-59.

112. *Romeo and Juliet,* I, v, 54-55, 136-37.

113. II, i, 285-91.   114. *Measure for Measure,* II, ii, 177 ff.

115. *The Taming of the Shrew,* I, i, 155-61.

116. *As You Like It* I, ii, 265-66.   117. *Ibid.,* I, ii, 257.

118. *Ibid.,* I, ii, 268-69. V. also *1 Henry VI,* V, iii, 60 ff.; *As You Like It,* V, ii, 32 ff.; *The Tempest,* I, ii, 440-41 and III, i, 64-66.

119. Dekker, II, 35.
120. Marlowe, *Hero and Leander*, fol. B2r.
121. II, i, in Marston, *The Plays of John Marston*, II, 91.
122. I, i, 35-42.   123. *Mucedorus*, IV, i, 28-34, in Brooke.
124. *1 Henry VI*, V, v, 1-4.

NOTES TO III: DEVELOPMENT: THE LOVERS APART

1. Fenton, *Monophylo*, Vol. I, fol. 22v.
2. Coulton, *Chaucer and his England*, chap. V, has a discussion of the problem.
3. Goodfriend, *If You Were Born in Russia*, pp. 65, 106-107.
4. Fenton, Vol. I, fol. 36r.
5. Andreas Capellanus, *The Art of Courtly Love*, p. 122.
6. Castiglione, *The Book of the Courtier*, p. 321.
7. Haydn, *The Counter-Renaissance*, p. 327.
8. Andreas Capellanus, p. 167.
9. See the quotation from *Monophylo* on p. 88 *supra*.
10. Castiglione, p. 319.
11. Plato, *Phaedrus*, etc., p. 34.
12. Cumont, *The Oriental Religions in Roman Paganism*, pp. 137-38.
13. Fenton, Vol. I, fol. 23r. See Burton, *The Anatomy of Melancholy*, pp. 701-708. Burton castigates the practice as lustful.
14. Fenton, Vol. I, fol. 40r.
15. Stevenson, *The Love-Game Comedy*, p. 98. Many medieval romances ended in marriage.
16. Moseley, *The Bourgeois Consciousness of Thomas Dekker*, pp. 118 ff. Downer, *The British Drama*, pp. 99 ff.
17. "A new love drives away the old." Andreas Capellanus, p. 185.
18. "A true lover is constantly and without intermission possessed by the thought of his beloved." *Ibid.*, p. 186.

19. *Othello*, I, iii, 306.   20. Andreas Capellanus, p. 144.

21. *Othello*, IV, ii, 200-202.

22. This would imply merely a common source in tradition. Shakespeare had undoubtedly never read Andreas Capellanus.

23. Burton, pp. 149-50.   24. Fenton, Vol. I, fol. 2r.

25. *The Poetaster*, in Jonson, *Best Works of Ben Jonson*, I, 346.

26. *A Midsummer Night's Dream*, III, ii, 318-20. See also *The Tempest*, III, i, 64-66.

27. *The Winter's Tale*, I, ii, 110-11.

28. *As You Like It*, I, iii, 12-17.

29. *The Duchess of Malifi*, I, i, 514-16, in Webster, *The Works of John Webster*, Vol. II.

30. Burton, pp. 664 ff.

31. Andreas Capellanus, p. 186 (Rule XXX).

32. Fenton, Vol. I, fol. 27v.

33. See Lawrence, *Shakespeare's Problem Comedies*, p. 62.

34. "No one can be bound by a double love." Andreas Capellanus, p. 184.

35. Dekker, *The Dramatic Works of Thomas Dekker*, Vol. II.

36. *The Raigne of K. Edward the Third*, II, ii, 32-37, in Brooke, *Shakespeare Apocrypha*.

37. III, v, 83.   38. *Romeo and Juliet*, I, i, 244.

39. Thomas of Britain, *The Romance of Tristram and Ysolt*, chaps. XXX-XXXI.

40. See Burton, pp. 737-38, for a discussion of love for ugly women.

41. Fenton, Vol. I, fol. 56v.   42. *Ibid.*, Vol. I, fol. 17v.

43. *Mucedorus*, I, iii, 21-22, in Brooke.

44. *The Poetaster*, in Jonson, I, 346.

45. *The Merry Devil of Edmonton*, II, iii, 35, in Brooke.

46. *A Woman Killed With Kindness*, II, iii, in Heywood, *The Best Works of Thomas Heywood*, p. 22.

47. *All Fools*, I, i, 30 ff., in Chapman, *The Best Works of George Chapman*.

48. *The Changeling*, I, i, 158-59, in Middleton, *The Works of Thomas Middleton*, Vol. VI.

49. *'Tis Pity She's a Whore*, I, ii, in Ford, *The Works of John Ford*, I, 121-22.

50. *Ibid.*, I, iii, p. 122.

51. *The Two Gentlemen of Verona*, II, iv, 144-47.

52. *The Taming of the Shrew*, I, i, 181.

53. *Romeo and Juliet*, I, v, 105.   54. *Ibid.*, I, v, 95-96.

55. See p. 100 *supra*.   56. *Romeo and Juliet*, II, ii, 113-14.

57. *A Midsummer Night's Dream*, I, i, 106-10.

58. *As You Like It*, III, ii, 377-81.

59. *All's Well That Ends Well*, I, i, 108-9; I, iii, 210-13.

60. *The Tempest*, I, ii, 417-19, 421-22.

61. D'Urfé, *L'Astrée*, Part II, Book ix, p. 389.

62. *Romeo and Juliet*, II, iii, 69-78, 87-88.

63. *Ibid.*, III, iii, 83.   64. *Ibid.*, I, i, 219-21.

65. *Old Fortunatus*, in Dekker, I, 130.

66. *As You Like It*, V, ii, 89.

67. *The Poetaster*, in Jonson, I, 289.

68. Burton, pp. 714-15, finds this weeping false in women.

69. *Romeo and Juliet*, III, iii, 84-87.   70. *Ibid.*, III, v, 70.

71. *Much Ado About Nothing*, II, iii, 152-55.

72. *As You Like It*, IV, i, 221-23.

73. *All's Well That Ends Well*, I, iii, 122-24.

74. I, iii, p. 126.

75. Andreas Capellanus, p. 185 (Rule XIII).

76. Burton, p. 337.   77. *Romeo and Juliet*, I, i, 130-40.

78. Fenton, Vol. I, fol. 2v.   79. II, i, 21.

80. *The Poetaster*, IV, vi, in Jonson, I, 345.

81. *The Witch of Edmonton*, III, i, in Dekker, IV, 381.

82. Burton, pp. 336 ff.

83. *'Tis Pity She's a Whore*, II, vi, in Ford, I, 153.

84. Burton, p. 337, so describes the melancholic. They "will diet themselves, feed, and live alone."

85. *The Two Gentlemen of Verona*, II, iv, 131.

86. *Ibid.*, II, i, 25.   87. *Ibid.*, II, i, 30-34.

88. *Ibid.*, II, iv, 141-43.   89. *Hamlet*, II, ii, 147-51.

90. *Ibid*, V, i, 294-300.

91. *Old Fortunatus*, in Dekker, I, 129.

92. See Burton, p. 326, for application of leanness to melancholy persons in general.

93. *'Tis Pity She's a Whore*, I, iii, in Ford, I, 125.

94. *2 The Honest Whore*, in Dekker, II, 157. See also *The Merry Devil of Edmonton*, I, iii, 91-98, in Brooke.

95. *The Two Gentlemen of Verona*, II, iv, 133-35.

96. *Much Ado About Nothing*, II, iii, 136-39.

97. *Ibid.*, II, iii, 18-19.

98. *2 The Honest Whore*, in Dekker, II, 157-58.

99. Fenton, Vol. I, fol. 20v.

100. Burton, p. 342, writes of melancholics who *"dream of graves still, and dead men, and think themselves bewitched or dead."*

101. *Romeo and Juliet*, V, i, 1-11.

102. *A Midsummer Night's Dream*, I, i, 152-55.

103. *Ibid.*, II, ii, 147-50.

104. *Troilus and Cressida*, V, iii, 6.

105. *Othello*, III, iii, 416-26.

106. *The Two Gentlemen of Verona*, IV, iv, 86.

107. See Burton, pp. 723-24.

108. *The Raigne of K. Edward the Third*, II, i, 6-10, in Brooke.

109. *Romeo and Juliet*, II, v, 72-73.   110. *Ibid.*, III, ii, 14.

111. *As You Like It*, III, iv, 55-57.

112. *A Midsummer Night's Dream*, III, ii, 96-97.

113. *Romeo and Juliet*, III, v, 57-59.

114. *All's Well That Ends Well*, I, iii, 173-79.

115. *The Family of Love*, IV, iii, 5-8, in Middleton, Vol. III.

116. *Much Ado About Nothing*, I, i, 250.

117. *Romeo and Juliet*, III, iii, 65-69.

118. *Much Ado About Nothing*, II, iii, 153.

119. *Troilus and Cressida*, IV, ii, 113.

120. *King Lear*, III, i, 7.

121. *King John*, III, iv, 43-48.

122. Fenton, Vol. I, fol. 6v.

123. *Romeo and Juliet*, I, i, 197-201.

124. *As You Like It*, III, ii, 420-24.

125. Marston, *Jack Drum's Entertainment*, fol. F2v, H4v.

126. *1 The Honest Whore*, in Dekker, II, 82.   127. *Ibid.*

128. *A Mad World, My Masters* (1608), Act IV, in Dodsley, *A Select Collection of Old Plays*, V, 339.

129. *Hamlet*, II, ii, 146-50.   130. *Ibid.*, II, ii, 207-8.

131. *Ibid.*, II, ii, 630-32.   132. Burton, p. 122.

133. *Ibid.*, pp. 327-38.

134. *The Two Gentlemen of Verona*, II, i, 17-20.

135. *Love's Labour's Lost*, IV, iii, 133-36. See also *The Family of Love*, I, ii, 1-5, in Middleton, Vol. III.

136. *The Family of Love*, II, iv, 106-27, in Middleton, Vol. III.

137. *Ibid.*, II, iv, 140-58.   138. *Hamlet*, III, iv, 142-44.

139. Fenton, Vol. II, fol. 4v.   140. Burton, p. 763.

141. Fenton, Vol. I, fol. 33r.

142. *Mucedorus*, III, i, 58-60 in Brooke.

143. Marston, *Jack Drum's Entertainment*, fol. E4v, Flr.

144. *All's Well That Ends Well*, I, i, 93-103.

145. *The Winter's Tale*, III, ii, 95-96.

146. *A Midsummer Night's Dream*, II, i, 243-44.

147. *Ibid.*, II, ii, 155-56.

148. *As You Like It*, IV, i, 95-108.

149. Burton, pp. 765-96, finds numerous other cures. I do not find in the literature of the age that such cures were sympathetically considered efficacious, although they were occasionally recommended as such by misunderstanding parents.

150. Fenton, Vol. I, fol. 2r.

151. Marston, *Jack Drum's Entertainment*.

152. *The Changeling*, IV, iii, in Middleton, VI, 90.

153. *'Tis Pity She's a Whore*, I, iii, in Ford, I, 124.

154. *Much Ado About Nothing*, V, iv, 94-97.

NOTES TO IV: THE LOVERS TOGETHER

1. *Romeo and Juliet*, II, ii, 85-89.

2. Andreas Capellanus, *The Art of Courtly Love*, p. 185 (Rule XIV).

3. *Romeo and Juliet*, II, ii, 95-101. See, for the same concept, Prospero's remark when Ferdinand and Miranda fall in love: "But this swift business I must uneasy make, lest too light winning Make the prize light" (*The Tempest*, I, ii, 450-52). See also Olivia's reaction to Viola in *Twelfth Night*, I, v, in which she at least slantingly speaks of her love at the first meeting.

4. II, ii, 143-46.   5. *As You Like It*, I, ii, 268-69.

6. Andreas Capellanus, p. 165.

7. II, i, 45-48, in Kyd, *The Works of Thomas Kyd*.

8. *The Duchess of Malfi*, I, i, 391-92, in Webster, *The Works of John Webster*, Vol. II.

9. *The Taming of the Shrew*, I, i, 160-63.

10. *Romeo and Juliet*, III, v, 241-43.

11. V, i, in Jonson, *The Best Works of Ben Jonson*, I, 253.

12. II, ii, in Ford, *The Works of John Ford*, I, 139.

13. II, iv, 198-209.   14. II, i, 141-46.

15. *Ibid.*, I, i, 100 ff.   16. *Ibid.*, IV, iv.

17. *Ibid.*, I, ii, 1-2.   18. *Ibid.*, II, vii, 1-5.

19. *Ibid.*, I, ii, 34 ff.   20. I, ii.   21. II, i, 309-12.

22. II, i, 342-44.

23. Dekker, *Dramatic Works of Thomas Dekker*, II, 128.

24. *Ibid.*, p. 129.

25. Dodsley, *A Select Collection of Old Plays*, V, 283-358.

26. *Ibid.*, p. 293.   27. I, ii, *et seq.*   28. IV, ii.

29. II, iv.   30. III, i.

31. Powell, *English Domestic Relations, 1487-1653*, p. 19.

32. Swinburne, *A Treatise of Spousals*, I, i, Bv.

33. *Ibid.*, II, 4 (pp. 6-7).

34. *The Two Gentlemen of Verona*, IV, ii, 120-26.

35. *Ibid.*, IV, iv, 123-25.

36. *Much Ado About Nothing,* II, iii, 271-73.

37. I, iii, 41-43, in Kyd.

38. *Ibid.,* I, iii, 48-49. See *The Duchess of Malfi,* III, iii, 30-36, in Webster, Vol. II. Count Malateste is mocked for his lack of courage in battle by the comment that he would defend his scarf-guerdon by running away.

39. III, ii, 170-71.

40. *The Two Gentlemen of Verona,* IV, ii, 5-6.

41. I, v, 42-46.   42. V, ii, 137-42.

43. *Ibid.,* V, ii, 66-83.   44. *Ibid.,* V, ii, 90-92.

45. Andreas Capellanus, p. 185 (Rule XIII).

46. *Troilus and Cressida,* V, ii, 93-94.

47. *Ibid.,* V, ii, 95-96.

48. Haughton, *Englishmen for my Money,* lines 74-78.

49. I, iv, 100-3, in Kyd.

50. *Love's Labour's Lost,* V, ii, 47-50.   51. Page 143 *supra.*

52. *The Two Gentlemen of Verona,* II, i, 1-5.

53. *Much Ado About Nothing,* III, iv, 62.

54. Dekker, Vol. I, pp. 35-36.

55. III, i, in Chapman, *Best Works of George Chapman,* p. 86.

56. Haughton, lines 71-73.   57. Dekker, II, 127.

58. I, ii, 257-58.

59. IV, i, in Heywood, *Best Works of Thomas Heywood,* p. 299.

60. III, iii, 436.   61. I, ii, 211 ff., in Webster, Vol. I.

62. Dekker, II, 130.   63. I, ii, 211-15, in Webster, Vol. I.

64. III, ii, 66-67, in Middleton, *The Works of Thomas Middleton,* Vol. III.

65. Matthew Flowerdale, in the anonymous *The London Prodigal* (1604), in Brooke, *Shakespeare Apocrypha,* accepts money from Luce, but he is an early Restoration libertine whose plot is for money, not love.

66. Laurentia, one of the three daughters in Haughton's *Englishmen for my Money,* receives a gift of money from her beloved. The heroine of the secondary plot in Heywood's *A Woman Killed*

With Kindness receives money from her beloved, but not in the same way.

67. Letters and poems are often given as gifts. See *Love's Labour's Lost*, V, ii, 53-54; *A Midsummer Night's Dream*, I, i, 28-29; Haughton's *Englishmen for my Money*, lines 68-70; *Hamlet*, II, ii, 108-25; *All's Well That Ends Well*, III, vi, 121-23; *A Woman Killed With Kindness*, IV, ii, in Heywood, p. 46; *2 The Honest Whore*, in Dekker, II, 172.

68. II, i, 132-39.   69. II, i, 150-59.   70. II, i, 171-74.

71. *Much Ado About Nothing*, V, iv, 88-90.

72. *Ibid.*, II, iii, 132-34.   73. *Ibid.*, II, iii, 147-49.

74. *Hamlet*, II, ii, 109-24.   75. III, ii, 93-100.

76. *Ibid.*, III, ii, 174-75.   77. *1 Henry VI*, V, iii, 65-66.

78. V, iv, 85-90.   79. I, iv, 79-81, in Ford, Vol. I.

80. *Ibid.*, V, iii, 22-26.   81. *Romeo and Juliet*, II, ii, 34-36.

82. *Ibid.*, II, ii, 49-51.   83. *Ibid.*, II, ii, 116-28.

84. *The Tempest*, III, i.

85. *The Two Gentlemen of Verona*, II, iv, 178-81.

86. *The Merchant of Venice*, III, ii, 140 ff.

87. *Othello*, III, iv, 63-65.

88. *The Two Gentlemen of Verona*, II, iv, 179-83.

89. IV, iv, 49-51.   90. *Ibid.*, IV, iv, 371-74.

91. *Twelfth Night*, IV, iii, 22-28.

92. *All's Well That Ends Well*, IV, iii, 17-22.

93. *As You Like It*, I, ii, 268-69.

94. *Much Ado About Nothing*, II, i, 321-23.

95. I, i, 8-11, in Kyd.

96. "When one lover dies, a widowhood of two years is required of the survivor." Andreas Capellanus, p. 185 (Rule VII).

97. I, iii, in Heywood, p. 26.

98. II, i, 76-79, in Webster, Vol. II.

99. IV, iii, in Ford, I, 181.

100. *As You Like It*, V, ii, 36-45.

101. Fenton, *Monophylo*, Vol. I, fol. 50r.

102. *As You Like It*, V, ii, 89-99.

103. *The Tempest*, III, i, 83-86.

104. *Ibid.*, III, i, 64-66. 105. Fenton, Vol. I, fol. 50r.

106. II, i, 72-73, in Brooke.

107. *The Two Gentlemen of Verona*, II, iv, 1-8.

108. *All's Well That Ends Well*, I, iii, 164-65.

109. Fenton, Vol. I, fols. 33r, 34v.

110. II, iv, 229, in Middleton, Vol. III.

111. *Ibid.*, III, iii, 11. 112. *Romeo and Juliet*, III, v, 43.

113. *Ibid.*, IV, i, 18. 114. *Ibid.*, V, iii, 91.

115. *Ibid.*, II, ii, 50. 116. Swinburne, IV, 3 (p. 14).

NOTES TO V: SPOUSALS

1. Swinburne, *A Treatise of Spousals*, II, i (p. 5). Compare Schmidt, *Shakespeare-Lexicon*, II, 1105: "*Spousal*, marriage, nuptials. . . ."

2. Westermarck, *A Short History of Marriage*, p. 142.

3. Alleman, *Matrimonial Law and the Materials of Restoration Comedy*, pp. 8-9.

4. Swinburne, fol. A3r. 5. *Ibid.*, II, 4 (pp. 6-7).

6. *King John*, II, i, 521-26. 7. III, ii, 170-71.

8. *King John*, II, i, 527-30. 9. *Ibid.*, II, i, 531-33.

10. *Richard III*, I, ii.

11. Swinburne, *A Briefe Treatise of Testaments and Last Wills*, pp. 334-35.

12. Swinburne, *A Treatise of Spousals*, XI, 19 (p. 87).

13. V, i, 155-59, in Brooke, *Shakespeare Apocrypha*.

14. *The Taming of the Shrew*, II, i, 321-22.

15. I, i, 549-57, in Webster, *The Works of John Webster*, Vol. II.

16. II, i, 318-23.

17. Powell, *English Domestic Relations, 1487-1653*, p. 18.

18. V, i, 159-60.

19. IV, v, 111, in Dodsley, *A Select Collection of Old Plays,* Vol. V.

20. *King John,* II, i, 531-33.

21. *1 Henry VI,* V, iii, 160-62.

22. D1, in Marston, *Jack Drum's Entertainment.*

23. II, i, 533-35.

24. *The Merchant of Venice,* III, ii, 186-88.

25. *Much Ado About Nothing,* II, i, 313-15.

26. II, ii, in Horne, *Nero and Other Plays,* p. 150.

27. *The Merchant of Venice,* III, ii, 170-71.

28. "The public spousal was performed either at the bride's house or at the church porch, but in either case the priest was recognized as the official witness." Powell, p. 19.

29. V, i, 162.   30. D1, in Marston.

31. Swinburne, *A Treatise of Spousals,* XV, 8 (p. 211).

32. Powell, p. 19.   33. IV, iv, 76.   34. I, ii, 201.

35. I, i, 33.   36. III, ii, 171.   37. II, ii, 5 ff.; V, i, 162.

38. IV, ii, 39 ff.

39. Swinburne, *A Treatise of Spousals,* XVII, 26 (p. 229).

40. *Ibid.,* III, 1, 4-6 (pp. 8, 10-11).   41. V, iii, 127.

42. V, ii, 266-72.   43. *The Tempest,* III, i, 86-90.

44. *Romeo and Juliet,* II, ii.   45. *1 Henry VI,* V, iii.

46. II, i.

47. *The Duchess of Malfi,* I, i, in Webster, Vol. II. See pp. 170-72 *supra* for a discussion of competent witnesses.

48. Swinburne, *A Treatise of Spousals,* XV, 3 (pp. 205-6).

49. *Twelfth Night,* II, ii, 23-24.

50. *Romeo and Juliet,* II, ii, 107-8, 116-18.

51. *The Tempest,* III, i, 68-73.

52. Quoted in Sisson, *Lost Plays of Shakespeare's Age,* p. 28.

53. *The Duchess of Malfi,* I, i, 544-568, in Webster, Vol. II.

54. Underhill, "Law," in Raleigh, *Shakespeare's England,* I, 407.

55. Powell, p. 16.

56. Pollock and Maitland, *The History of English Law Before the Time of Edward I*, II, 368-69.

57. Swinburne, *A Treatise of Spousals*, XIV, 2 (p. 194). See p. 171 *supra*.

58. IV, ii, in Heywood, *Best Works of Thomas Heywood*, p. 304.

59. Quoted in Powell, p. 40.   60. Quoted in Powell, p. 41.

61. Swinburne, *A Treatise of Spousals*, XI, 6 (p. 79); XI, 7 (p. 81).

62. *Ibid.*, XVI, 2 (pp. 213, 216); XI, 6 (p. 79).

63. *Ibid.*, XI, 6 (p. 81). This discussion has been a necessary antecedent to my analysis of *Measure for Measure* in chapter VI.

64. I, ii, 126-33, in Middleton, *The Works of Thomas Middleton*, Vol. III.

65. *Ibid.*, V, ii.

66. Swinburne, *A Treatise of Spousals*, XVI, 6 (p. 218).

67. Lines 1842-59, in Haughton, *Englishmen for my Money*.

68. *Ibid.*, lines 2288-90.   69. *Ibid.*, lines 2573-80.

70. Westermarck, pp. 142-43.

71. I, ii, in Tourneur, *Best Plays of Webster and Tourneur*, p. 252.

72. *Ibid.*

73. Swinburne, *A Treatise of Spousals*, XVII, 9 (p. 223).

74. *The Atheist's Tragedy*, III, i, in Tourneur, p. 291.

75. IV, iv, 49-51.   76. IV, iv, 499-503.

77. V, i, 203-5.

78. In Dekker, *Dramatic Works of Thomas Dekker*, II, 87.

79. *Ibid.*, p. 88.   80. *Ibid.*, p. 89.

81. II, i, in Heywood, p. 183.

82. Swinburne, *A Treatise of Spousals*, XIV, 2 (p. 194).

83. "By the Civil Law, whosoever having contracted Spousals *de futuro*, doth, without just Cauce, refuse to deduce the same Spousals into Matrimony, doth not only lose the token (which is commonly a Ring) given to the other Party in pledge, and earnest of the Contract, together with all other gifts whatsoever simply

bestowed in hope of future Marriage; but is bound to make two-fold Restitution of the tokens and pledges received in Confirmation of the said Contract. . . ." *Ibid.,* XVIII, 7 (p. 237).

84. Pollock and Maitland, Vol. II, pp. 368-69.

85. Wilson, *What Happens in "Hamlet,"* pp. 292-94.

86. *Hamlet,* I, ii, 156-57.   87. *Ibid.,* IV, i, 6-8.

88. *Ibid.,* III, iv, 180-86.   89. *Ibid.,* III, iv, 197-99.

90. There is contradiction in the play. We do not *know* whether the queen has committed adultery or murder or neither or both. Wilson offers good evidence for adultery, however, and for the purposes of the present argument I accept his conclusion.

91. Wilson, pp. 292-94.   92. IV, i, 46-51.

93. *A Woman Killed with Kindness,* IV, vi, in Heywood, p. 56.

94. V, v, 14-18, in Brooke.   95. *Ibid.,* V, v, 34.

96. *Othello,* V, ii, 16-17.   97. *Ibid.,* V, ii, 63-65.

98. *1 Henry VI,* V, v, 25-29.   99. *Ibid.,* V, v, 107-8.

100. *Richard III,* III, vii, 177-91.

101. Wilkins, *The Miseries of Enforced Marriage,* in Dodsley, V, 13-15.

102. *Ibid.,* p. 20.   103. *Ibid.,* p. 32.

104. III, v, 244; IV, i, 53-54; IV, i, 77-78; IV, iii, 22-23.

105. Fenton, *Monophylo,* Vol. I, fol. 18v.

106. *Ibid.,* Vol. I, fols. 34r-36r.

107. *Ibid.,* Vol. I, fol. 31r.   108. *Ibid.,* Vol. I, fol. 20r.

109. "Marriage is no real excuse for not loving." Andreas Capellanus, *The Art of Courtly Love,* p. 184.

NOTES TO VI: CONCLUSION

1. For a good resume of the difficulties see Campbell, *Shakespeare's Satire,* pp. 121 ff.

2. The courtship of Lucio and Mistress Kate Keepdown is useful as a parallel to the other couples, but since none of its action occurs on the stage I shall not consider it a love-plot.

3. *Measure for Measure*, V, i, 495-98.

4. *Ibid.*, V, i, 409-11.

5. Swinburne, *A Treatise of Spousals*, X, 20 (p. 70).

6. *Ibid.*, X, 20 (p. 69).

7. *Measure for Measure*, V, i, 540-43.

8. *Measure for Measure*, ed. Wilson and Quiller-Couch, pp. xxxi-xxxiii. All other references to *Measure for Measure* in this chapter are to the Kittredge edition.

9. *Measure for Measure*, I, ii, 149-59.

10. *Ibid.*, II, iii, 19; V, i, 531.

11. Swinburne, XI, 19 (p. 87); XVI, 6 (p. 218).

12. *Measure for Measure*, V, i, 220-22.

13. *Ibid.*, III, i, 222; III, i.

14. Swinburne, XVI, 4 (p. 216).

15. *Ibid.*, XVI, 4 (p. 217).

16. *Measure for Measure*, III, i, 235-36.

17. *Ibid.*, IV, i, 72-75.   18. *Ibid.*, V, i, 227.

19. *Ibid.*, V, i, 169-76.   20. *Ibid.*, V, i, 382.

21. Swinburne, XVII, 19 (p. 226).

22. Andreas Capellanus, *The Art of Courtly Love*, p. 152.

23. Fenton, *Monophylo*, Vol. II, fol. 13v.

24. *Troilus and Cressida*, I, i, 9-12.

25. *Ibid.*, I, i, 30-31.   26. *Ibid.*, I, i, 51-59. Italics added.

27. *Ibid.*, I, i, 79-80, IV, ii, 113-15.   28. *Ibid.*, I, i, 114-15.

29. *Ibid.*, I, ii, 255-56, 249, 250, 275-78.

30. *Ibid.*, I, ii, 314-15.

31. Andreas Capellanus, p. 185 (Rule XIV).

32. *Troilus and Cressida*, II, ii.   33. *Ibid.*, II, ii, 53-56.

34. *Ibid.*, II, ii, 56-57.   35. *Ibid.*, II, ii, 174-88.

36. *Ibid.*, II, ii, 198-202.   37. *Ibid.*, III, i, 147-50, 143-45.

38. *Matthew*, XXIII, 27, 28, 33.

39. Tillyard, *Shakespeare's Problem Plays*, p. 50.

40. *Troilus and Cressida*, III, ii, 9-14.

41. *Richard II*, I, iii, 294, 298-99.

42. Schmidt, *Shakespeare-Lexicon*, II, 1330.

43. *Troilus and Cressida*, III, ii, 37-41.

44. *Ibid.*, III, ii, 46-47.   45. *Ibid.*, III, ii, 60-62.

46. *Ibid.*, III, ii, 110-16.   47. *Ibid.*, III, ii, 205.

48. *Ibid.*, III, ii, 180-90.   49. *Ibid.*, III, ii, 191-98.

50. *Ibid.*, III, ii, 204-6.   51. *Ibid.*, III, ii, 212-15.

52. *Ibid.*, III, ii, 215-20.

53. Campbell, *Comicall Satyre and Shakespeare's "Troilus and Cressida,"* p. 209.

54. Kenny, "Shakespeare's Cressida," *Anglia*, LXI, pp. 163-76.

55. Campbell, p. 209.

56. *Troilus and Cressida*, IV, ii, 8-14.

57. *Romeo and Juliet*, III, v, 6-10.

58. *Troilus and Cressida*, IV, iv, 72-73.

59. *Ibid.*, IV, iv, 82-83.

60. *Ibid.*, V, ii, 137-46.   61. *Ibid.*, V, iii, 100-112.

62. *Ibid.*, V, iii, 95-96.   63. *Ibid.*, V, iii, 111-12.

64. *Ibid.*, V, v, 2-5.   65. *Ibid.*, V, x, 33-34.

66. Campbell, *Shakespeare's Satire*, p. 117.

67. Tillyard, p. 37.

BIBLIOGRAPHY

Adams, Henry. Mont-San-Michel and Chartres. Cambridge, Mass., 1933.

Adams, Henry H. English Domestic or Homiletic Tragedy, 1575-1642. New York, 1943.

Alleman, Gilbert Spencer. Matrimonial Law and the Materials of Restoration Comedy. Wallingford, Pa., 1942.

Anderson, Ruth L. Elizabethan Psychology and Shakespeare's Plays. Iowa City, 1927.

Andreas Capellanus. The Art of Courtly Love, trans. John Jay Parry. New York, 1941.

Barrow, Sarah F. The Medieval Society Romances. New York, 1924.

Baskin, Jane Feild. "The Courtly Ideal in Shakespeare." Unpublished Ph.D. dissertation, University of California at Berkeley, 1928.

Bastiaenen, Johannes Adam. The Moral Tone of Jacobean and Caroline Drama. Amsterdam, 1930.

Bennet, Henry S. Chaucer and the Fifteenth Century. Oxford, 1947.

Brooke, C. F. Tucker. The Shakespeare Apocrypha. Oxford, 1918.

Burton, Robert. The Anatomy of Melancholy, trans. Floyd Dell and Paul Jordan-Smith. New York, 1948.

Campbell, Oscar James. Comicall Satyre and Shakespeare's "Troilus and Cressida." San Marino, Calif., 1938.

——— Shakespeare's Satire. New York, 1943.

Castiglione, Baldassare. The Book of the Courtier, trans. Sir Thomas Hoby. London, 1948.

Chambers, Edmund K. English Literature at the Close of the Middle Ages. Oxford, 1947.

Chapman, George. The Best Works of George Chapman, ed. William Lyon Phelps. London, 1895. Mermaid Series.

Chaucer, Geoffrey, The Complete Works of Geoffrey Chaucer, ed.

Fred N. Robinson. Cambridge, Mass., 1933. I have used this text invariably in quoting Chaucer in this study.

Chrétien de Troyes. Arthurian Romances, trans. W. W. Comfort. London, 1935.

Christine de Pisan. Book of the Duke of True Lovers, trans. Laurence Binyon and Eric R. D. MacLagan. London, 1909.

Coulton, G. G. Chaucer and his England. London, 1937.

Crane, Thomas Frederick. Italian Social Customs of the Sixteenth Century. New Haven, 1920.

Cross, Tom Peete, and William Albert Nitze. Lancelot and Guenevere: A Study in the Origins of Courtly Love. Chicago, 1930.

Cumont, Franz. The Oriental Religions in Roman Paganism. Chicago, 1911.

Dekker, Thomas. Dramatic Works of Thomas Dekker. 4 vols. London, 1873.

Denomy, Alex. J. "Andreas Capellanus: Discovered or Re-discovered," Medieval Studies, VIII (1946), 300-301.

—— "The De Amore of Andreas Capellanus and the Condemnation of 1277," Medieval Studies, VIII (1946), 107-49.

—— "An Enquiry into the Origins of Courtly Love," Medieval Studies, VI (1944), 175-260.

Dodd, W. G. Courtly Love in Chaucer and Gower. Boston, 1913.

Dodsley, Robert, ed. A Select Collection of Old Plays. 12 vols. London, 1825.

Downer, Alan S. The British Drama, A Handbook and Brief Chronicle. New York, 1950.

D'Urfé, Honoré. L'Astrée. Lyon, France, 1926.

Elyot, Sir Thomas, The Governour. London, n.d.

Ewing, S. Blaine. Burtonian Melancholy in the Plays of John Ford. Princeton, 1940.

Farnham, Willard. Shakespeare's Tragic Frontier, Berkeley, Calif., 1950.

Fenton, Geoffrey. Monophylo . . . A Philosophicall Discourse and Diuision of Loue. London, 1572. I have used a microfilm of the copy in the Folger Library.

Ford, John. The Works of John Ford, ed. the Reverend Alexander Dyce. 3 vols. London, 1869.

Freeburg, V. O. Disguise Plots in Elizabethan Drama. New York, 1930.

Freeman, Edward A. The History of the Norman Conquest of England. 5 vols. Oxford. 1869-79.

Gascoigne, George. The Complete Works of George Gascoigne, ed. John W. Cunliffe. 2 vols. Cambridge, England, 1907-10.

Goodfriend, Arthur. If You Were Born in Russia. New York, 1950.

Gordon, George. "Shakespearean Comedy" and Other Studies. Oxford, 1944.

Guest, Lady Charlotte, trans. The Mabinogion. London, n.d.

Harbage, Alfred. Annals of English Drama, 975-1700. Philadelphia, 1944.

—— As They Liked It. New York, 1947.

Haughton, William. Englishmen for my Money, or A Woman Will Have Her Will, ed. Albert C. Baugh. Philadelphia, 1917.

Haydn, Hiram. The Counter-Renaissance. New York, 1950.

Herford, C. H. "Shakespeare's Treatment of Love and Marriage" and Other Essays. Oxford, 1921.

Heywood, Thomas. The Best Works of Thomas Heywood, ed. A. Wilson Verity. London, n.d. Mermaid Series.

—— II If You Know Not Me, You Know Nobody. Oxford, 1934. Malone Society Reprints.

Horne, Herbert P., Havelock Ellis, Arthur Symons, and A. Wilson Verity, eds. Nero and Other Plays. London, n.d. Mermaid Series.

Howard, George E. A History of Matrimonial Institutions. 3 vols. Chicago, 1912.

Jonson, Ben. The Best Works of Ben Jonson, ed. Brinsley Nicholson and C. H. Herford. 3 vols. London, n.d. Mermaid Series.

Kelly, Amy. "Eleanor of Aquitaine and Her Courts of Love," Speculum XII (1937), 3-19.

Kelly, Amy. Eleanor of Aquitaine and the Four Kings. Cambridge, Mass., 1950.

Kelso, Ruth. The Doctrine of the English Gentleman in the Sixteenth Century. Urbana, Ill., 1929.

Kenny, Hamill. "Shakespeare's Cressida," Anglia, LXI (1937), 163-76.

Kilgour, Raymond Lincoln. The Decline of Chivalry. Cambridge, Mass., 1937.

Kirby, Thomas Austin. Chaucer's "Troilus": A Study in Courtly Love, University, La., 1940.

Kyd, Thomas. The Works of Thomas Kyd, ed. Frederick S. Boas. Oxford, 1901.

Lawrence, William Witherle. Shakespeare's Problem Comedies. New York, 1931.

Lewis, Clive Staples. The Allegory of Love. London, 1948.

Lowes, John Livingston. "The Lovers Maladye of Hereos," Modern Philology, XI (1914), No. 4, 18 ff.

Lyly, John. Euphues, the Anatomy of Wit, ed. Edward Arber. London, 1868.

Lynch, Kathleen M. Social Mode of Restoration Comedy. New York, 1926.

Marie de France. French Medieval Romances, trans. Eugene Mason, London, 1924.

Marlowe, Christopher. Hero and Leander. London, 1924. The Haslewood Reprints. No. 2.

—— The Works of Christopher Marlowe, ed. A. H. Bullen. 3 vols. Boston, 1885.

Marston, John. Jack Drum's Entertainment. London, n.d. Old English Drama, Students' Facsimile Edition. Vol. 63.

—— The Plays of John Marston, ed. H. Harvey Wood. 3 vols. Edinburgh, 1938.

Middleton, Thomas. The Works of Thomas Middleton, ed. A. H. Bullen. 8 vols. Boston, 1885.

Moseley, Edwin Maurice. "The Bourgeois Consciousness of

Thomas Dekker." Unpublished Ph.D. dissertation, Syracuse (New York) University, 1947.

Mott, Lewis Freeman. The System of Courtly Love, Studied as an Introduction to the "Vita Nuova" of Dante. Leipsig, 1924.

Pearson, Lu Emily. Elizabethan Love Conventions. Berkeley, Calif., 1933.

Plato. Phaedrus, etc., trans. Lane Cooper. New York, 1938.

Pollock, Frederick, and Frederick William Maitland, History of English Law before the Time of Edward I. 2d ed. 2 vols. Cambridge, England, 1898.

Powell, Chilton Latham. English Domestic Relations, 1487-1653. New York, 1917.

Prayer Book of Queen Elizabeth, The. Charles J. Thynne, ed. London, 1912.

Prouty, Charles T. Gascoigne. Elizabethan Courtier, Soldier, and Poet, New York, 1942.

Raleigh, Sir Walter, ed. Shakespeare's England. 2 vols. Oxford, 1916.

Salomon, Louis Bernard. The Rebellious Lover in English Poetry. Philadelphia, 1931.

Schmidt, Alexander. Shakespeare-Lexicon. 2 vols. Berlin and London, 1886.

Shakespeare, William. The Complete Works of William Shakespeare, ed. George Lyman Kittredge. Boston, 1936.

—— Measure for Measure, ed. J. Dover Wilson and Sir Arthur Quiller-Couch. Cambridge, England, 1922.

Silverstein, Theodore. "Andreas, Plato, and the Arabs: Remarks on Some Recent Accounts of Courtly Love," *Modern Philology*, XLVII (1949), No. 2, 117-26.

Sisson, C. J. Lost Plays of Shakespeare's Age. Cambridge, England, 1936.

Stevenson, David L. The Love-Game Comedy, New York, 1946.

Stoll, Elmer Edgar. Shakespeare's Young Lovers. New York, 1937.

Swinburne, Henry. A Briefe Treatise of Testaments and Last Wills. London, 1640.

Swinburne, Henry. A Treatise of Spousals; or, Matrimonial Contracts. London, 1686.

Tatlock, John Strong Perry. The Mind and Art of Chaucer. Syracuse, N. Y., 1950.

Thomas of Britain. The Romance of Tristram and Ysolt, trans.
Roger Sherman Loomis. New York, 1951.

Tillyard, E. M. W. Shakespeare's Problem Plays. Toronto, 1949.

Tourneur, Cyril. Works in The Best Works of Webster and Tourneur, ed. John A. Symonds. London, n.d.

Trevelyan, George M. Illustrated English Social History. Vol. I.
London, 1949.

Webster, John. The Works of John Webster, ed. F. L. Lucas. 4
vols. London, 1927.

West, Constance Birt. Courtoisie in Anglo-Norman Literature.
Oxford, 1938.

Westermarck, Edvard. A Short History of Marriage. London,
1926.

White, Edward J. Commentaries on the Law in Shakespeare. St.
Louis, Mo., 1911.

Wilson, J. Dover. What Happens in "Hamlet." London, 1936.

Wright, Louis B. Middle Class Culture in Elizabethan England.
Chapel Hill, N. C., 1935.

INDEX